DARKNESS NOW VISIBLE

In the fall of 2016 those promoting patriarchal ideals saw their champion Donald Trump elected president of the United States and showed us how powerful patriarchy still is in American society and culture. *Darkness Now Visible: Patriarchy's Resurgence and Feminist Resistance* explains how patriarchy and its embrace of misogyny, racism, xenophobia, homophobia, and violence are starkly visible and must be recognized and resisted. Carol Gilligan and David Richards offer a bold and original thesis: that gender is the linchpin that holds in place the structures of oppression through codes of masculinity and femininity that subvert the capacity to resist injustice. Feminism is not an issue of women only, or a battle of women vs. men – it is the key ethical movement of our age.

Carol Gilligan is University Professor of Applied Psychology and the Humanities at New York University. She is the author of *In a Different Voice: Psychological Theory and Women's Development* (1982), *The Birth of Pleasure: A New Map of Love* (2003), and *Joining the Resistance* (2011). She is coauthor of *Meeting at the Crossroads: Women's Psychology and Girls' Development* (1992) with Lyn Mikel Brown, and *The Deepening Darkness: Patriarchy, Resistance, and Democracy's Future* (2008) with David A. J. Richards. In 1996 she was named by *Time* magazine as one of the twenty-five most influential Americans. She was the Patricia Albjerg Graham Professor of Gender Studies at Harvard University.

David A. J. Richards is Edwin D. Webb Professor of Law at New York University School of Law. He is the author of twenty books, including *The Deepening Darkness: Patriarchy, Resistance, and Democracy's Future* (with Carol Gilligan, 2008), *Fundamentalism in American Religion and Law: Obama's Challenge to Patriarchy's Threat to Democracy* (2010), *The Rise of Gay Rights and the Fall of the British Empire* (2013), and *Why Love Leads to Justice: Love across the Boundaries* (2016).

Darkness Now Visible

Patriarchy's Resurgence and Feminist Resistance

Carol Gilligan

New York University

David A. J. Richards

New York University

CAMBRIDGE
UNIVERSITY PRESS

CAMBRIDGE
UNIVERSITY PRESS

University Printing House, Cambridge CB2 8BS, United Kingdom

One Liberty Plaza, 20th Floor, New York, NY 10006, USA

477 Williamstown Road, Port Melbourne, VIC 3207, Australia

314–321, 3rd Floor, Plot 3, Splendor Forum, Jasola District Centre, New Delhi – 110025, India

79 Anson Road, #06–04/06, Singapore 079906

Cambridge University Press is part of the University of Cambridge.

It furthers the University's mission by disseminating knowledge in the pursuit of education, learning, and research at the highest international levels of excellence.

www.cambridge.org
Information on this title: www.cambridge.org/9781108470650
DOI: 10.1017/9781108686228

First published 2018

Printed in the United States of America by Sheridan Books, Inc.

A catalogue record for this publication is available from the British Library.

ISBN 978-1-108-47065-0 Hardback

Yet again, for our lovers, Jim Gilligan and Donald Levy, the most loving of men

The ideal subject of totalitarian rule is not the convinced Nazi or the convinced Communist, but people for whom the distinction between fact and fiction (*i.e.*, the reality of experience) and the distinction between true and false (*i.e.*, the standards of thought) no longer exist.

Hannah Arendt, *The Origins of Totalitarianism*, p. 474

Contents

Acknowledgments		*page* ix
Introduction		1
1	Patriarchy Comes Out of Hiding	9
2	Infidelity and Silence	17
	Infidelity	19
	Silence	27
3	Why Didn't We See It?	34
4	Why Now?	49
	Anger, Violence, and the Shaming of Manhood	49
	The Resurgence of Patriarchy	54
	Trump's Appeal	59
	How Trump's Politics Muted Resistance	60
	Women of Liberia Mass Action for Peace and Women Wage Peace (Israel/Palestine)	66
5	The Endgame of Patriarchy?	70
6	Maps of Resistance	77
7	The Power and Invisibility of Gender	80
8	Democracy's Future	95
	Hawthorne and Melville: *The Scarlet Letter* and *Moby Dick* as Prophetic Novels	95
	August Wilson on Nonviolence and Violence	106
	Feminism through the Lens of Patriarchy	110
	Freeing Democracy from Patriarchy	113
9	Why Feminism and Why Now?	115

Notes   130
Bibliography   147
Index   156

Acknowledgments

We are grateful to the students in our Resisting Injustice seminar who in the fall of 2016 and 2017 discussed with us and helped to refine many of the ideas in this book. We owe a particular debt of gratitude to those students from the 2016 seminar whose writing for the seminar directly informed our thinking about betrayal and self-silencing. In granting us permission to quote from their work, some requested that we change their names and remove identifying details. Thus we must thank our 2016 students collectively while acknowledging by name the members of our seminar in 2017: Nelson Adams, Yasmin Amin-Reimer, Dipona Bandy, Christine Braithwaite, Mariela Cisneros, Micah Desaire, Xuan Gong, Ciara Grubbs, Ana Koff, Lauren Kratovyak, William Lee, Paul Leroux, Joanna Loomis, Gabriel Malone-O'Meally, Andrew Marnell, Evan McCants-Goldman, Elizabeth McLean, Kashira Patterson, Chelsea Plyer, Madz Reeve, Astrid Rayes, Benjamin Scrimshaw, Hannah Stern, Lillian Wu, and Caleb Younger.

Our work on this book was inspired by conversations with Jim Gilligan and most particularly by his insights about shame and guilt and their relation to manhood and to violence. His reading of *Moby Dick* in the seminar on Retributivism that David and he taught in the fall of 2017 was invaluable to our analysis of Melville and Hawthorne. We are also indebted to Naomi Snider for her insights into patriarchy and its relation to the psychology of loss, which she and Carol have now developed in their coauthored book, *Why Does Patriarchy Persist?* (in press). David also wishes to thank Phillip Blumberg and Donald Levy for conversations bearing on central themes of this book.

Our deepest gratitude to John Berger, our editor at Cambridge University Press, for his encouragement and support for our collaborative work. From the outset, when we first proposed the idea to him in the fall of 2016, his enthusiasm gave us the confidence we needed to develop our thoughts following Trump's election into a sustained argument and ultimately a thesis.

This book was researched and written in part during leaves and summers supported by generous research grants from the New York University School of Law Filomen S'Agostino and Max E. Greenberg Faculty Research Fund. We are grateful as well for the support of our dean, Trevor Morrison, and for the assistance of Lavinia Barbu in preparing the book for publication.

Introduction

We conceived and wrote *The Deepening Darkness*[1] during the years when George W. Bush was president. Our title flagged a threat we saw playing out in our midst: a patriarchal psychology and politics were jeopardizing democracy's future. Our intention was to name the threat, to expose its roots in our personal and cultural histories, and to highlight a potential for resistance grounded not in ideology but in what can be thought of as the better angels of our nature – capacities integral to our humanity. Ironically, in the name of morality, patriarchy was dimming our ethical intelligence. With global warming accelerating and inequality deepening, a misguided war in Iraq had been joined by renewed efforts to restrict access to birth control and to ban same-sex marriage. A visitor arriving from another galaxy might well have concluded that people on earth had lost their minds.

Yet in 2008 when *The Deepening Darkness* was published, our title no longer seemed so apt. Barack Obama had been elected president; a black family (Barack and Michelle, the girls and grandma) were living in the White House, and our president, a man of immense grace and wise beyond his years, reached across many lines of division. Having been raised by a nontraditional mother and her parents, having worked as a community organizer and married a woman clearly his equal, he exemplified a manhood whose core impulses were democratic rather than patriarchal. Despite the setbacks under George W. Bush, with the election of Obama the moral arc of the universe seemed truly to be bending toward justice.

And then in 2016, we were taken aback. Suddenly our book appeared prophetic. No longer hiding in democracy, patriarchy was all too visible. The adjective "patriarchal" appeared on the op-ed pages of the *New York Times* along with the analogy comparing the fate of American democracy under Trump to the shift from republic to empire in Rome under Augustus. Our claim that patriarchy had been hiding in democracy was

1

echoed by Paul Krugman's observation that in the Rome of Augustus, the move to empire had been concealed by the retention of republican forms.[2] Our 2008 argument was all too contemporary.

Despite all predictions to the contrary, an unapologetically patriarchal voice had triumphed, first in the Republican primary and then in the election. Openly undemocratic in its misogyny, racism, xenophobia, homophobia, and contempt for the rule of law ("If I don't like the results of the election, I might not accept them"), this voice found resonance among a large enough segment of the population to secure an electoral college victory and hence the presidency for Donald J. Trump. To the disbelief of many onlookers including prominent Republicans, neither mocking the disabled nor insulting veterans, neither boasting of grabbing pussies nor inciting his supporters to violence (Should Hillary win, Trump told them, you can take your guns and assassinate her), had barred him from becoming the president. If anything, they seemed to have accelerated his ascension. "Lock her up," he said of his opponent, "Such a nasty woman." Faced with disagreement, he found it sufficient to dismiss any truths he found inconvenient by saying simply, "I do not believe it." Here was the patriarch unvarnished, naked in his claim to authority, presenting himself as the arbiter of truth and morality, his manhood invested in being rougher and tougher, bigger and better, superior rather than inferior, a winner not a loser.

To put it baldly, we have to talk about gender. Irrelevant to democracy, it is essential to patriarchy. The gender binary that divides human capabilities into either "masculine" or "feminine" and the gender hierarchy that elevates the masculine, are the DNA: the building blocks of a patriarchal order. It is important to emphasize from the outset that in bringing gender to the forefront of our analysis, we in no way intend to discount or diminish the importance of race and class, sexuality, religion or any other of the grounds that have been used to rationalize the division of humans into the superior and the inferior, the touchables and the untouchables. Quite the contrary. In saying that we have to talk about gender, we in no way mean that we do not have to talk about race, class, caste, and sexuality. Rather, our point is that without talking about gender we cannot explain how the human capacities that otherwise would lead us to recognize oppression and to resist injustice come to be muted or repressed, thus opening the way to the various intersections of race, class, and gender, fueling homophobia and religious intolerance, and, to speak more generally, impeding our capacity to recognize our common humanity and our desire to love and to live democratically.

To put it simply, the reconsideration that has been spreading through the human sciences since the 1970s has as its core the recognition that as humans we are inherently relational and responsive beings, born with a voice – the ability to communicate our experience – and with the desire to engage responsively with others, that is, to live not alone but in a relationship. Empathy and cooperation are part of our evolutionary history, key to our survival as a species. Thus rather than asking how do we come to gain the capacity for empathy so that we pick up and respond to the feelings of others, how do we learn to take the point of view of the other and overcome the pursuit of self-interest, we are prompted instead to ask, how do we lose these basic human capacities. How do we come not to know or to care about what others are experiencing, how do we lose our desire and our ability to love?

With this reframing of human development, it became obvious that to establish and maintain hierarchy, it is necessary to interrupt or more precisely to stunt and to shame the human capacities that would otherwise stand in the way: that is, our capacity for empathy, mind-reading, and cooperation, which are the components of mutual understanding. Gender enters into our argument about patriarchy because it is in the name of and for the sake of becoming or being recognized as a "real" man or a "good" woman that our relational abilities come to be compromised or rendered ineffective. In *Descartes's Error*, Damasio, the neuroscientist, shows that the splitting of reason from emotion, long seen as the *sine qua non* of rationality, is in fact a manifestation of brain injury or trauma.[3] What Damasio doesn't say is that the splitting of reason from emotion and the elevation of mind over body also are manifestations of the gender binary and hierarchy of patriarchy, that privilege the masculine (reason and mind) over the feminine (emotion and body). When we say we have to talk about gender, what we mean is that we need to see the role that gender divisions play in undercutting or injuring the human capacities that otherwise would lead us to resist injustice, whether it takes the form of racism, sexism, religious intolerance, homophobia, or what have you. Put starkly, patriarchy with its codes of masculine honor and feminine goodness dims our ethical intelligence. In this light, we were struck by how readily, even in what from a gender perspective was the potentially historic 2016 election, gender dropped out of the conversation – at least with respect to the way in which we are accustomed to talking about gender (as an issue of women).

In the United States, codes of white patriarchy – scripts of masculinity and femininity keyed to the privileging of whites over people of color – have played a particularly vicious role in enforcing the racism of American society. The historian W. E. B. Du Bois writing about double-consciousness,[4] the artists Richard Wright[5] and James Baldwin in recounting their experiences as black men in America,[6] the courageous journalist Ida B. Wells who exposed the lie behind Southern lynchings,[7] the activist Sojourner Truth,[8] the writer Harriet Jacobs,[9] were all pioneers in illuminating the intersections of racism and patriarchy, which have since become more widely recognized, in the fiction and non-fiction of Toni Morrison,[10] in Audre Lorde's *Sister Outsider*,[11] Robin Coste Lewis's *Voyage of the Sable Venus*,[12] and in Michelle Cliff's *The Land of Look Behind* and *Free Enterprise: A Novel of Mary Ellen Pleasant*.[13] The black community in America may have been less surprised by the election of Trump, and more skeptical about the future of democracy in the US, given our history of racism and patriarchy. To reiterate a key point, in putting gender forward as a linchpin that holds structures of oppression in place, our intention is not to discount the effects of racism or social class but to show how constructions of manhood and of womanhood can function to subvert the capacity to resist injustice in its many and intersectional forms.

Two observations:

In the weeks leading up to November 2016, following the release of the pussygate tape, both the *New York Times* and the *New Yorker* ran headlines announcing that women's votes would take down Trump. The gender gap in the forthcoming election, we were told, would be the largest ever recorded. The story then disappeared without a trace.

As it turned out, the gender gap in 2016 was no larger than it had been in 2012. Again there was a twelve point spread in both directions with more women voting Democrat and more men voting Republican. Again, women's votes split with single women and women of color voting overwhelmingly Democrat whereas married white women voted Republican by a slight majority. In contrast to African Americans, who had voted en masse for Barack Obama, women as a group did not show the same support for Hillary Clinton.

Second, in the run-up to the 2008 election, in response to the controversy over his association with the Reverend Wright, Obama made an extraordinary speech about race, urging Americans to understand the animosity toward one another felt by both blacks and whites and then to transcend racial divisions. At no point, either in 2008 or 2016, did Clinton make a comparable speech about gender. What's more, whether such a speech could be effective is not immediately obvious.

Along with many Americans, we were shocked on the morning of November 9 to discover that Donald Trump was to be our next president. Despite having written about the ongoing tensions between democracy and patriarchy, we were not prepared for the resonance his unequivocally patriarchal voice had found in many of our country's men and women.

Gender was the proverbial elephant in the room. It seemed at times as though everything could be spoken about except the threat that patriarchal gender codes pose to democracy. Looking more closely into what was in fact said and not said, we found ourselves wondering whether the reluctance to talk about gender in this way stemmed in part from the fact that the gender dynamic playing out in the election was not the one we are accustomed to seeing. Hillary Clinton did in fact win the popular vote by close to 3 million, although in the rush now to blame her, this is quickly overlooked or forgotten. Along with the fact that Hillary was the one who had said unequivocally that women's rights are human rights and human rights are women's rights, and that from the very beginning, she had been tireless in her support for women and children. Still, it was Trump who played a gender hand brilliantly by appealing to a shamed American manhood. It's tempting here to compare him to Hitler, who came to power on the campaign promise "to undo the shame of Versailles." Trump's promise was to undo the shame of white American men whose claim to superiority had been shaken. His campaign slogan "Make America great again," was a thinly veiled pledge to restore the patriarchal order. He was the one who would take on the enemy and rescue white patriarchy from political correctness.

Most striking to us, however, because it was this that we did not anticipate or see, was the realization that Trump, whether inadvertently or intentionally, had shifted the framework. Rather than looking through a democratic lens and seeing gender as one among many issues (the others being race, class, sexuality, etc.) that raise concerns about equal voice and respect, for Trump, gender was the lens through which he viewed the world. The gender binary and hierarchy shaped his perception and judgment. Little Marco didn't measure up as a man, crooked Hillary was not a good woman. Seen through a democratic framework, these were insults, manifestations of disrespect. When the lens was patriarchy, they were simply statements of fact. Marco Rubio wasn't big enough to be the president; Hillary wasn't good enough. It was just how things are. As anyone could see, Jeb Bush was low in energy and, however unfortunate (sad, was Trump's word), some women are not as attractive as others.

The shift in the framework was not politically correct because as Americans we aspire to be a democratic nation. The surprise was that it turned out to be politically effective. Perhaps it was the shift in the framework that made it impossible for those of us who continued to view things through a democratic lens to see what was happening. Perhaps this is why for many Americans what was going on felt so disorienting and confusing. But for a significant number of Americans, the patriarchal lens was instantly clarifying. In their minds, finally someone had the courage to see and to say what was happening.

To make our approach transparent, two things need to be stressed at the outset:

1. Feminism is not an issue of women only or a battle of women vs. men. Feminism is one of the great liberation movements of human history; it is the movement to free democracy from patriarchy.
2. In freeing democracy from the grip of patriarchy, feminism is in the interests of everyone, men included, because the structures of patriarchy, the gender binary, and hierarchy, disrupt human nature. For example, when reason is gendered masculine and emotion feminine, it becomes challenging for men to reflect on what they are feeling without feeling that their masculinity is on the line. Or for a woman to see herself as a woman and also as a rational being. In the gendered universe of patriarchy, humans are under pressure to become half-human in the name of becoming real men or good women. Just as the gender hierarchy that privileges some men over other men and all men over women is antithetical to democratic ideals and values, so the gender binary that splits intelligence (masculine) from emotion (feminine) and the self (masculine) from relationships (feminine), constrains our humanity. In the name of morality then, for the sake of establishing or preserving masculine honor and feminine goodness, patriarchy both undermines democracy and subverts moral character.

In this book, we argue that Trump's election shows us how powerful patriarchy still is in American society and culture and also what happens when a patriarchal framework takes over – when patriarchy became the lens. Then, rather than seeing gender as an issue that along with race and class is potentially problematic from a democratic standpoint, given the value on equal voice and respect for persons, gender shapes our way of seeing. The displacement of a democratic by a patriarchal framework in the 2016 election has not only been profoundly disorienting and destabilizing. The shift in frame has contributed to the breakdown of public discourse because we literally cannot agree on what we are seeing. Reality itself becomes contested or, as Hannah Arendt put it, both the reality of experience and the standards of thought no longer exist.

Many observers have commented on the rising level of anger along with the pervasiveness of violence. In *Violence: Reflections on a National Epidemic*,[14] James Gilligan draws our attention to the emotion of shame as the proximal cause of violence, the necessary although not sufficient cause of violent behavior. More precisely, he focuses our attention on how the shaming of manhood leads to violence – how in some instances it makes violence inescapable because for some men violence is the only way of undoing shame and restoring honor. Overpowering another is a way in which one can assert or reclaim one's superiority.

Taking his argument further, James Gilligan identifies patriarchy as a shame culture, preoccupied with issues of honor and status and highly sensitive and reactive to insult. From a democratic standpoint, the resistance movements of the 1960s and 1970s were constitutional advances; in their recognition of civil rights, women's rights, gay and lesbian and transgender rights, they were advancing democracy. Seen through a patriarchal lens, they were insults to American manhood by challenging the position of straight white men who saw themselves as rightfully superior. A hierarchy that had been assumed (white over black, men over women, straight over gay) was being contested on constitutional grounds, and the use of force (think of the response to the civil rights demonstrators) became necessary to hold the old order in place.

It was Virginia Woolf who made the analogy explicit. Patriarchy is to private life as fascism is to public life. In her brilliantly conceived essay *Three Guineas*, written on the eve of World War II, she observes that "the public and private worlds are inseparably connected; that the tyrannies and servilities of the one are the tyrannies and servilities of the other."[15] Woolf's insights into the intricate links between patriarchy and fascism were not seen by either Hannah Arendt or George Orwell, brilliant though their analyses of fascism otherwise are. Yet evidence of the gender binary and hierarchy was right before their eyes. As they are now once again in plain sight. All of the elements of the gender binary that orchestrate fascist politics have been invoked by Trump: strength vs. weakness, winners vs. losers, us vs. them, along with the appeal to America First, the rage at any perceived insult or humiliation, the scapegoating, the lies, the pseudo-science, the demand for absolute loyalty, the absence of doubt, the bullying, the misogyny, and the evocation of a glorified past: "Make America great again."

Are we now witnessing the endgame that we predicted in 2008? Is the Trump election and presidency a final confrontation in the long struggle between democratic ideals and values and patriarchal privilege and power? And if so, what maps do we have for the resistance? What guidelines can we offer for ensuring democracy's future?

As patriarchy comes out of hiding and its repression of dissent becomes more hysterical, we can see more clearly the psychological fragility in its construction of both manhood and womanhood. These markers of identity rest on a psychological fault-line: the gender binary and hierarchy. Increasingly, the gendered division between reason (masculine) and emotion (feminine) and the elevation of mind over body and the self over relationships, once viewed as signaling the achievement of rationality and personal autonomy, have been recognized instead as manifestations of injury or trauma. As resistance becomes more urgent, more politically and ethically essential, we can draw on advances in the human sciences to provide us with a map, showing a way out of our current impasse.

In exposing the darkness now visible in our midst, we argue that feminism is the key ethical movement of our age. Understood as the movement to free democracy from patriarchy, feminism alone pinpoints and resists the gender binary and hierarchy that cripple love and impair our capacity to engage in the communication and the relationships that are vital for democratic citizenship.

1 Patriarchy Comes Out of Hiding

The research for our 2008 book led us to a radical thesis: Because patriarchy rests on a gender binary and hierarchy, it subverts basic human capacities. By forcing a division between what is perceived as masculine (for example, intelligence) and what is considered to be feminine (emotional responsiveness), it compromises our ability to think about what we are feeling and to bring empathy and compassion along with logic to bear in solving human problems. Thus patriarchy can render us careless, with others and ourselves, and tone deaf to injustice. It's not that gender trumps race or class. Rather, it's because looking through a patriarchal lens leads us to split reason (masculine) from emotion (feminine) and to abstract mind and self (masculine) from bodies and relationships (feminine), and this gendered way of seeing and speaking then compromises our ethical intelligence. It impedes our ability to recognize and resist the injustices of race and class, sexuality and religion, as well as of gender. As the latest research in neuroscience shows, when we split thought from emotion and mind from body, we lose our capacity to register our own experience and to pick up what others are experiencing. Losing touch with the voice of experience, we can become captive to the voice of false authority.

Democracy rests on a premise of equal voice as the condition for free and open conversation or debate. It also rests on the presumption of a voice that speaks from experience. For democracy to be truly a government of, by and for the people, everyone's voice becomes vital. Hence the need, as Hannah Arendt argues in *The Human Condition*,[1] for a public arena where everyone can come and speak. Arendt warns that the notion of representation where one person becomes a stand in for another carries with it the implication that some lives are in fact dispensable.[2] To Arendt and others, voice is the irreplaceable foundation of democratic politics.

In earlier work, one of us (Richards) introduced the concept of moral slavery to draw attention to the structural injustice that occurs when the

voices of those who would most reasonably challenge the unjust demands
of authority are repressed or dismissed – a dismissal rationalized as in
the nature of things (for example, women by their very nature lack the
capacity to think rationally or judge objectively).[3] One of us (Gilligan)
has written about moral injury to explain how our capacity to care
becomes shattered.[4] Patriarchy and democracy are incompatible on psychological as well as political grounds. It is not only that patriarchy as a
hierarchy based on gender and privileging fathers is at odds with the
premise of equal voice and equality on which democracy is founded;
it is also because the gender binary and hierarchy disrupt the human
capacities that are requisite for living with integrity in relationship with
others – that is, for living democratically and functioning as a citizen in
a democratic polity.

We have defined patriarchy as:

> an anthropological term denoting families or societies ruled by
> fathers. It sets up a hierarchy – a rule of priests – in which the priest,
> the *hieros*, is a father, *pater*. As an order of living it elevates some men
> over other men and all men over women; within the family, it separ-
> ates fathers from sons (the men from the boys) and places both women
> and children under a father's authority.[5]

Patriarchy, thus understood, has existed in human civilizations as long as
we have had written records, including the rule of absolute priest-kings-
gods in Egypt, Babylonia, and Imperial China, as well as many other
civilizations. These civilizations were, of course, politically absolutist.
In our 2008 book, we focused on the more hidden role that patriarchy
played in more secular ancient democracies (Athens) and republics
(Rome), as revealed, for example, by the gender assumptions that carry
the argument in Aeschylus's *Oresteia*.

The *Oresteia*, the oldest trilogy in the canon of theater, celebrates the
founding of Athenian democracy. Aeschylus argues for the superiority of
the Athenian democracy over autocracies like the rule of kings in Argos
and Sparta and Persia because only democracy with its jury system can
end the cycle of retributive violence or blood vengeance. In the final play
of the trilogy, Athena, a motherless daughter born from the head of Zeus,
casts the deciding vote in favor of acquitting Orestes for the crime of
killing his mother (who had killed her husband, who had sacrificed their
daughter). She makes her argument for acquittal on normative grounds:
killing a mother is bad but not so bad as killing a father and a king.
Because she has no mother, Athena's judgment is considered impartial,
unlike the Furies who are pursuing Orestes. In the end, Athena persuades
the Furies to give up their anger over the murder of Klytemnestra

(Orestes's mother) and the sacrifice of Iphigenia (Orestes's sister) as the price for their admission into the new city of Athens. The Furies, the women who are furious on behalf of women, thus become the Eumenides, the kindly minded, the good women of Athens.

The *Oresteia* – the story of Orestes – links the founding of democracy with the reinstatement of patriarchy. It gives precedence to fathers over mothers, men over women, and silences women's anger as the condition of their inclusion. The argument for democracy is thus at the outset deeply flawed along gendered lines. The normative claim that killing a father is worse than killing a mother is not justified but deemed self-evident because it is stated by Apollo, the god of reason. Athenian rationality thus embodies the mind-set of a patriarchal god. Athena enforces the patriarchal gender binary and hierarchy that elevate reason (masculine) over emotion (feminine) and force the suppression of women's anger in the name of rationality and kindness.

Furthermore, the play's alleged solution to the cycle of violence does not solve it at all: violence against women is overlooked (Agamemnon's sacrifice of his daughter Iphigenia, and Klytemnestra's killing of Cassandra, Agamemnon's concubine), and, the violence of men (the Trojan War and Orestes's killing of his mother) is accepted as in the nature of things. What's more, as Athena states:

> ... Let our wars
> rage on abroad, with all their force, to satisfy
> our powerful lust for fame. But as for the bird
> that fights at home – my curse on civil war.[6]

Athenian democracy is celebrated not because it has solved the problem of violence (which it has not) but because it has redirected that violence from civil war to imperialistic wars. Athens was, of course, an imperialistic state, whose wars, as its greatest historian Thucydides tells us, were often unjust in their ends and means, sometimes including what we would call genocide.[7] These wars end in the sheer stupidity of the Peloponnesian War, which Athens lost, leading, in time, to the end of the democracy.

We began our 2008 book with a discussion of the *Oresteia* because its argument illuminates how, at the very inception of democracy, its claims to equality were subverted by the forces of patriarchy that were very much alive in Athenian culture. Patriarchy hides in the *Oresteia* in the way the play's superficially plausible rationality at crucial points darkens Athenian political intelligence. Its celebrated aim   ending the cycle of blood vengeance – in fact is contingent on the suppression of women's voices and women are divided into the bad and the good, as the Furies become the kindly minded, good women of Athens, praised, as Pericles put it, for "to be least talked about by men."[8] In addition the destructive force of imperialistic wars, which is to say most of the wars in human history, is unleashed and celebrated in the name of power and fame.

The vaunted rationality of Athenian argument – alleged to distinguish the Athenians from barbarian autocracies – hides within it and crucially turns on the gender binary and hierarchy, which darken and indeed subvert Athenian democratic political intelligence. Our insight here rests on our feminism – not a feminism that itself buys into the gender binary by pitting women against men, or that reverses the hierarchy by elevating women over men. Seen in this light, the opposite of patriarchy is not matriarchy as many would claim, but democracy which is founded not on hierarchy (men over women or women over men) but on equality. Closely examined, the gender binary and hierarchy impede the human capacity to love and to live democratically in ways that affect women and men differently. But across all genders, patriarchy, by inflicting moral injury, seeds the ground for moral slavery. Feminism with its ethic of care then becomes the key to liberation, because as the movement to free democracy from patriarchy it acts both to prevent the moral injury inflicted by patriarchy and to release us from moral slavery.

In our polarized political culture, feminism is commonly regarded as only for women and at the expense of men, an understanding very much at the root of Clinton's defeat and Trump's victory. But given the recognition that patriarchy, with its gender binary and hierarchy, harms men as well as women because it harms everyone, the question becomes why was it so easy to divide men from women, and also women from women, as the election of 2016 showed?

When patriarchy came out of hiding in the run-up to the 2016 election, we were suddenly besieged with "fake news" and "alternate facts." As if it were no longer possible to tell what is true and what is not, what is real and what is only said to be happening. For example, is climate change real or a hoax? Is the crime rate rising or falling? The voice of experience was displaced by the voices of warring authorities, a cacophony of voices with seemingly no way of choosing among them. Hence the resort of some journalists to being "even-handed." Hence the dangers of false equivalency. Hence the race becoming a contest between winners and losers, and hence Trump's victory, to the extent that he did in fact win.

It was like watching a sleight of hand. The pussygate tapes were visually displaced by the row of Bill Clinton's accusers at the second debate. Watching the gender card played by Trump, we saw it brilliantly played from a patriarchal standpoint in that he succeeded in shaming Hillary and branding her as untrustworthy, "crooked Hillary," when according to Jill Abramson's tally, she was the candidate who lied the least.[9] Trump's politics were "wolf whistle politics," invoking misogyny and appealing to male honor and superiority (America First) as his central strategy.[10]

There is a political psychology that explains how this happened. Following Trump's election, two classic texts, both dealing with totalitarianism, became best sellers – Hannah Arendt's *The Origins of Totalitarianism*,[11] and George Orwell's *1984*.[12] Arendt's great book identifies fascism in Germany under Hitler and Stalinism in the Soviet Union as forms of totalitarianism. As such, they draw their power in part from their assault on the psyche. Orwell's novel explores how individuality both of thought and feeling is crushed through Big Brother's domination of the psyche. In our concern with how the politics of the 2016 election could have led to a widespread loss of the sense of reality and truth, we along with others have been drawn to these examples. Our epigraph, which we took from Hannah Arendt's *Origins*, should resonate widely with Americans in 2017:

> The ideal subject of totalitarian rule is not the convinced Nazi or the convinced Communist, but people for whom the distinction between fact and fiction (i.e., the reality of experience) and the distinction between true and false (i.e., the standards of thought) no longer exist.[13]

The analogy to fascist politics, which after all took power in Germany democratically, seems to many now particularly apt, and we ourselves will pursue the analogy. But neither Arendt nor Orwell saw what Virginia Woolf had laid out so clearly.

The links between fascism and patriarchy are center stage in Woolf's late essay, *Three Guineas*.[14] Her beloved nephew, Julian Bell, had been killed in the Spanish Civil War in 1937, the year Neville Chamberlain became prime minister of Great Britain. What Woolf came to see in the rise of fascism in Spain, Germany, and Italy was something Winston Churchill had also seen, leading him to call for resistance before it was too late: namely, that the violence of fascism was rooted in humiliated manhood. Woolf carries Churchill's insight one step further to expose the patriarchal roots of fascist violence and to explore the potential for resistance on the part of the daughters of educated (read patriarchal) men.

What makes the analysis of *Three Guineas* so astonishing is not only Woolf's path-breaking insights into the patriarchal roots of fascism but also her larger call for a resistance in which women join with men. At issue, she argued, were what Josephine Butler called "the great principles of Justice and Equality and Liberty." Addressing men, Woolf counters their disparagement of feminism by identifying feminists as the "advance guard" of their fight against fascism and for democracy:

> The words are the same as yours; the claim is the same as yours. The daughters of educated men who were called, to their resentment, "feminists" were in fact the advance guard of your own movement. They were fighting the same enemy that you are fighting and for the same reason. They were fighting the tyranny of the patriarchal state as you are fighting the tyranny of the Fascist state.[15]

The same moral and political values justify resistance to patriarchy and to fascism: namely, "the democratic ideals of equal opportunity for all."[16] Woolf clearly sees and also states the injustice of what we have called moral slavery, the common roots of anti-Semitism, racism, and sexism.[17]

Woolf frames her argument by focusing on "the daughters of educated men"[18] whom she sees as having the potential to be at once inside and outside the structures of patriarchy. Consequently they have the possibility for an independence men do not have, caught up as educated men are in the great processions of British professional and public life.[19] The four teachers of women – poverty, chastity, derision, and freedom from unreal loyalties – also give the daughters of educated men an advantage by rendering them more impervious to patriarchy's seductions and threats. Even the injustice done to women in the area of sexuality can be used to advantage by women as part of their unpaid-for education: "how great a part chastity, bodily chastity, has played in the unpaid education of our sex," Woolf suggests, adding that, "[i]t should not be difficult to transmute the old ideal of bodily chastity into the new ideal of mental chastity – to hold that if it was wrong to sell the body for money it is much more wrong to sell the mind for money, since the mind, people say, is nobler than the body".[20] For this reason, she calls upon women to pledge "not to commit adultery of the brain because it is much more serious than the other."[21]

Woolf anchors her call for women's resistance in a recognition of women's different position within a patriarchal order. It is because women are "[d]ifferent ... as facts have proved, both in sex and in education," that "our help can come, if help we can, to protect liberty, to prevent war."[22] Women's distinctive strengths can flourish as grounds for resistance if women through access to education gain the power of an independent opinion and then through entry into the professions, gain the means to support that opinion with an independent income. Then, as Woolf would have it, armed with the power of an independent opinion supported by an independent income, the daughters of educated men can use their different position as at once inside and outside of patriarchy to form an "Outsiders' Society."

The Society of Outsiders has the same ends as your society – freedom, equality, peace; but it seeks to achieve them by the means that a different sex, a different tradition, a different education, and the different values which result from those differences have placed within our reach.[23]

Thus women can best help men prevent war "not by repeating your words and following your methods but by finding new words and creating new methods."[24] In doing so, women will refuse the function Woolf had earlier observed them playing in patriarchy, a function to which men had become addicted:

Women have served all these centuries as looking-glasses possessing the magic and delicious power of reflecting the figure of men at twice its natural size. Without that power probably the earth would still be swamp and jungle. The glories of all our wars would be unknown.[25]

In *Three Guineas*, Woolf seeks to break the hypnotic spell of a patriarchally rooted male narcissism – the wounded honor or shame that fueled the mass appeal of Hitler and Mussolini.[26] What makes her argument path-breaking is the way she connects the forms of public and private violence and the importance she accords to this linking of public and private worlds. As she writes, "the public and private worlds are inseparably connected . . . the tyrannies and servilities of the one are the tyrannies and servilities of the other. . ."[27] To examine these connections critically, she urges that "it is time for us to raise the veil of St. Paul and to attempt, face to face, a rough and clumsy analysis" of how the Christian tradition has treated women.[28] Finally, in recognizing how far women have come in resistance to patriarchy, she observes how aggressively patriarchy has responded to women's resistance.

Woolf saw what neither Arendt nor Orwell could see, namely, the psychological link between fascism and patriarchy. Our approach both in *The Deepening Darkness* and here builds on Woolf's insight, an insight still not widely appreciated nor for the most part recognized. Even now, *Three Guineas* is not a best seller. In contrast to Arendt's *Origins* and Orwell's *1984*, it is not near the top of Amazon's list. Totalitarianism and fascism can be discussed, must be discussed many now would assert, but once again we are struck by the reluctance to talk about gender.

Building on research in developmental psychology and neuroscience, we have underscored the role trauma plays in the initiation into patriarchy of both men and women.[29] It is through a loss of voice and of memory that patriarchy becomes mistaken for nature. In this book we deepen our argument by drawing on what we have learned from papers written by students in our seminar on resisting injustice in the fall of 2016 following Trump's election.

The 2016 election shocked our students as much as it did us and many others. It led roughly a third, almost equally divided between men and women, to write about what they had come to recognize as their own implication in what had happened. Without a conscious thought and in spite of themselves, they had complied with patriarchal demands. Their papers, which read like confessions, were written as statements of fact. This is what happened.

For the men, the confessions were of infidelity: they had been unfaithful to themselves in renouncing what they loved. For the women, the confessions were of silence; they had not spoken honestly; they had acted as if they did not know what they knew. The students wrote either of something they had once loved and then abandoned or of something they knew but did not say or act on. They recognized the ways in which patriarchal codes and scripts of manhood and womanhood had damaged their ability to love and to speak. And they pointed to ways in which their initiations into patriarchy had injured their ethical sensibilities.

Reading our students' papers at the end of the fall term of 2016, we found ourselves asking: Had we witnessed this same dynamic playing out on a mass scale in the presidential election?

2 Infidelity and Silence

Perhaps, as many have asserted, it was a failure to listen that explains the surprise at the outcome of the 2016 election. Not all Americans were surprised, but there was general recognition of a failure to listen along with a tendency to disparage rather than engage with those with whom one disagrees. Our experience with students, however, led us to suspect that the experience of surprise may also reflect a reluctance to confront the part that patriarchy has played in our own lives – a reluctance, that is, to confront our own complicity.

For more than ten years now we have been teaching a seminar on resisting injustice – a popular elective at NYU School of Law that attracts a diverse group of students. In the fall of 2016, the election hung over our classroom, for the most part a silent guest. Our discussions of gender were heightened by the realization that for the first time in American history, a woman had been nominated by a major political party and was a serious candidate for the presidency. Yet for several of our women students, who did not flinch from speaking about Obama as black, the word "women" was contentious; some found it personally offensive. In the week we read *Lysistrata*[1] and *Three Guineas* and asked the students to consider in their reflection papers whether women's voices are key to preventing or stopping war, these women were outraged by our question. The term women was "too binary" they told us; what about queer and transgender people? Furthermore, *Lysistrata* was offensive because women's sexuality should not be the grounds for their resistance. The affect was high in these sessions and carried over into debates about feminism and criticisms of Hillary Clinton, but aside from the contention over the word women, our discussions in class, although lively and engaging, were not notably different from what they had been in previous years. As in the past, the readings on psychological development had stirred memories and led students to reflect on their own experiences, often in a new and to them revealing light.

Men in the class had experienced a shock of recognition in reading Judy Chu's *When Boys Become Boys*,[2] recalling how they too around the age of five had begun to shield those aspects of themselves that would have led them to be perceived as not a real boy and called girly or gay. Many found a strong resonance in the voices of the adolescent boys in Niobe Way's *Deep Secrets*,[3] where they describe the intimacy and closeness of their friendships with other boys and yet, as Way's research shows, by the end of high school most no longer have a best friend. Over the four years of high school, many boys come to renounce their desire for emotional closeness with other boys and in the name of becoming a man, to keep their secrets to themselves.

Taken together, Chu and Way's studies illuminate a process of initiation that begins with boys around the ages of four and five and then picks up again in adolescence. Their research shows the costs to boys of a masculinity defined in opposition to and as the opposite of anything perceived as "feminine." For example, to establish their masculinity, the four- and five-year-old boys in Chu's study had formed "The Mean Team" – a team created by the boys and for the boys to prove that they were in fact boys, not girls. Because girls were perceived by them as being good and nice, the main activity of The Mean Team was, in the words of one of the boys, "to bother people." In her studies of adolescent boys' friendships, Niobe Way documented how in "learning how to be more of a man," over 75 percent of the boys, across a range of ethnicity and class, by the end of high school no longer had a best friend, meaning a friend to whom they could tell their deep secrets.

Women in the class had similarly been struck by the resonance they found in the voices of the girls who took part in the Harvard Project studies of girls' development. In particular, many had responded to the frank and fearless voices of girls on the cusp of adolescence – voices that sounded to them at once familiar and surprising. They recalled the pressures they had faced to silence an honest voice for the sake of having relationships, and like Neeti, one of the participants in the studies – a top student and school leader – they had buried deep inside themselves "the voice that stands up for what I believe in." Like many of the girls in the Harvard Project studies, the women in our seminar were aware of the costs of saying what they really thought and felt, especially when what they had seen and heard was said not to be happening.[4]

Still, nothing prepared us for the final papers we received in the fall of 2016 from a third of our students (four men and five women). The searing honesty and the starkness of their confrontation with their own implication in perpetuating patriarchal codes of manhood and womanhood, were unlike anything we had read in previous years. The only explanation we found plausible was the 2016 election. It was as though the election had startled them into the awareness of a betrayal that previously they had not been conscious of or seen in this light. It was not simply that these students were aware of having been initiated into a culture of manhood or womanhood that had forced them, in the case of men, to shield what were considered "feminine" qualities, or for the women to tone themselves down. The confessions were of a self-betrayal. In the course of their initiation into the codes and scripts of patriarchal manhood or womanhood, these students wrote of having been unfaithful to or having silenced themselves.

INFIDELITY

With the publication in 2014 of Judy Chu's *When Boys Become Boys* and in 2011 of Niobe Way's *Deep Secrets*, we now have the testimony of boys' voices to show how what previously had been seen as steps in a developmental progression leading toward rationality and autonomy are more accurately viewed as responses to an initiation that is wounding to boys and leaves a scar. The four- and five-year-olds in Chu's study and the adolescents in Way's research had in the course of becoming one of the boys or learning how to be more of a man been unfaithful in the sense that they had turned away from or renounced what they had loved. One of us (Gilligan), both in her foreword to Chu's book[5] and in her paper on moral injury,[6] had written about Donald Moss, the psychoanalyst who in the epilogue to his book *Thirteen Ways of Looking at a Man*,[7] recalls his experience of initiation when he was in the first grade in precisely these terms: he had been unfaithful to what he loved.

In previous years, our students had read about Moss both in the foreword to Chu's book and in the paper on moral injury. But it was only in 2016 that two of the men in the seminar identified themselves directly with Moss. I was Donald Moss, one wrote in recalling how he too had been unfaithful to and betrayed what he loved. Why? – that was the aching question. Why had they done what they had done? And hovering over that question, was the implicit query: had they colluded in this way with the forces that had led to the election of Trump?

On reflection, what distinguished the final papers written by our students following Trump's election was that in the spirit of Virginia Woolf, they were connecting private and public worlds. There was no guise to their confessions of acquiescence to the demands of patriarchal masculinity. They had internalized "without a conscious thought," as Adam, a third-year law student wrote, "an ancient framework of patriarchy and manhood" that was older than the *Oresteia*. That was the force acting on him that led him to go against his impulse which was not to betray but to keep his "true bond" with Ollie, his friend since childhood, even after he learned that Ollie was gay. Had someone told him he would succumb to patriarchy, Adam wrote, he would have laughed in their face. And yet, the effects were unmistakable. His paper was a confession of what had happened but it was joined with an astute observation: the force acting on him was real but intangible: "The culprit was a ghost."

Jonathan Shay, a psychiatrist working with Vietnam veterans who were suffering from severe and chronic post-traumatic stress disorders, had coined the term "moral injury" to describe the shattering of trust that follows a betrayal of what's right, in a high stakes situation, where the betrayal is sanctioned by someone in a position of legitimate authority.[8] That is, when the betrayal of what's right is culturally sanctioned. As Shay discovered, the veterans were suffering not from a disorder but from an injury; not from a failure of character but from a betrayal of what's right that had "ruin[ed] good character." This distinction was crucial not only for understanding the cause of the injury but also how to approach treatment; "healing from trauma depends on communization of the trauma." Telling the story to someone who will listen and can be trusted to bring the story into the community. Therapy alone was not sufficient; the community itself had to be healed because it had legitimized the betrayal.

Hearing Jonathan Shay speak about his concept of moral injury, one of us (Gilligan) was struck by the realization that what he was describing – a betrayal of what's right in a high stakes situation where the betrayal is sanctioned by someone in a position of legitimate authority – also applied in the context of what passes for the everyday. Her research on development and that of her colleagues had provided strong evidence that children experienced the betrayal of relationship as a betrayal of what's right. When this betrayal is sanctioned in the name of growing up or standing on your own two feet and becoming a man – not needing someone to be there for you – or in the name of being good and becoming a selfless woman, someone who is there for others but not really present herself, the stakes are high. Masculinity or femininity is on the line, with all the psychological ramifications and social consequences of not being seen as a real man or good woman. When parents or teachers or others held up to children as authorities or community leaders sanction this betrayal as necessary or good or in the nature of things, then children's ability to trust those on whom of necessity they rely is shattered. In the research on development, children responded to this initiation with signs of resistance and to the betrayal with signs of psychological distress. It wasn't the extremity of moral injury that Shay had encountered in his work with combat veterans, but the pattern he described was the same.

"I often felt like Donald Moss," Adam, a third-year law student wrote in his final paper for the seminar on resisting injustice. He had asked if as his final project for the class, he could compose a song to Ollie – the best friend whom he had betrayed, explaining that in turning his back on Ollie once he knew that Ollie was gay, he had also turned away from his love of music. In composing and performing the song, which he recorded for us, he would be publicly acknowledging both betrayals. In his paper, he offered his analysis of what had happened. Like the psychoanalyst Donald Moss, Adam felt that he had been "unfaithful" in betraying what he had loved and he remembers the betrayal as part of his initiation into manhood.

The initiation Moss remembers took place in first grade. He was the age of the boys in Chu's study. As one of us (Gilligan) recounts, drawing on Moss's epilogue to his book *Thirteen Ways of Looking at a Man:*[9]

> Every week [in first grade] the children learned a new song and were told that at the end of the year, they would each have a chance to lead the class in singing their favorite, which they were to keep a secret. For Moss, the choice was clear: "The only song I loved was the lullaby, 'When at night I go to sleep [Fourteen angels watch do keep]' from *Hansel and Gretel.*" Every night he would sing it to himself, and like the song said, the angels came, saving him from his night terrors and enabling him to fall asleep. It "was, and would always be, the most beautiful song I had ever heard."
>
> The first graders had learned the song in early autumn, and in late spring, when Moss's turn came, he stood in front of the class. The teacher asked what song he had chosen. Moss recalls:
>
> "I began to tell her: 'it's the lullaby...' But immediately, out of the corner of my eye, I saw the reaction of the boys in the front row. Their faces were lighting up in shock ... I knew, knew in a way that was immediate, clear and certain, that what I was about to do, the song I was about to choose, the declaration that I was about to make, represented an enormous, irrevocable error ... what the boys were teaching me was that *I was to know now, and to always have known*, that 'When at night I go to sleep' could not be my favorite song, that a lullaby had no place here, that something else was called for. In a flash, in an act of gratitude, not to my angels but to my boys, I changed my selection, I smiled at the teacher, and told her I was just kidding, told her I would now lead the class in singing the 'Marines' Hymn': 'From the Halls of Montezuma to the shores of Tripoli...'" (italics added).[10]

"I was to know now and to always have known" – meaning, he was to erase from his memory what he had once known. To not know what he had loved (the lullaby) meant that he had to rewrite history. What followed – what happened as a result of this lesson in manhood – was that something he had learned (what could and could not be his favorite song) became not something learned but something he had always known. Something – culture, a culture of manhood – would then come to seem like nature.

As Carol reflected, Moss remembers the initiation that Judy Chu observed, remembers it as involving an act of "treachery:" he had been "unfaithful" to his angels: he had betrayed them, had "renounced them in public and continued to do so for many years." The "Marines' Hymn" could be the song of the Mean Team formed by the boys Chu studied. Across several decades and despite all the progress that had been made, the initiation was remarkably unchanged.

> Writing from the vantage point of middle age, Moss says that his book "can be thought of as an extended effort to unpack that moment in front of the class and indirectly, to apologize to the angels for my treachery." He had been "unfaithful" to them, had "renounced them in public and continued to do so for many years." The residue was a melancholia, tied to the boy's awareness that, [in Moss's words]:
>
> "What he is 'really' doing in that fateful turning outward is simultaneously preserving and betraying his original love of angels, affirming and denying his new love of boys; after all, now he and the boys are joined together in looking elsewhere for the angels they might have all once had."[11]

The haunting conclusion to Moss's recollections lies in his realization that in spite of his treachery, the angels "are still here."

Reflecting on his experience of initiation, Adam refers to the "Love Laws" – taking the phrase from Arundhati Roy's novel *The God of Small Things* that we had read and discussed in the seminar.[12] The Love Laws, in Roy's depiction, are the laws that lay down "who should be loved, and how. And how much."[13] In the seminar, we had discussed the function of laws regulating love as a mainstay of a patriarchal order, given the power of love to upset hierarchy. Adam writes:

> At this point, it was clear to me that my decision to stop calling Ollie my best friend back in the tenth grade was far more prophetic than it was accurate at the time I said it. I had achieved exactly what I had set out to achieve. I had distanced myself from my best friend at a time when boys aren't supposed to have best friends anymore, and certainly not best friends who might be breaking the love laws. And yet, I had an overwhelming sense of sadness. I remembered the conversation I had had with my brother so many years before. I could hear myself say to him, "How cool is it that out of everyone [on the soccer team], we get to be best friends with Ollie?" And all I could think was, well, congratulations, you're not anymore.

Across a span of many years, including years that witnessed substantial changes in people's attitudes toward gender (the anti-war movement in the era of Vietnam, the women's movement and the gay rights movement), Adam's infidelity is hauntingly similar to the unfaithfulness Moss described. In drawing out the parallel, Adam says in effect that in doing what he felt he was supposed to do, he had been unfaithful to his gut sense of what was right.

> Looking back on my childhood, I realize how often I felt like Donald Moss in front of his first grade class, trying not to embarrass himself by admitting to liking the lullaby from Hansel and Gretel that helped him to fall asleep at night ... I find myself pondering on how often I chose to follow my gut, rather than do what I felt like I was supposed to do. I never felt this more than when I considered my relationship with Ollie. I loved and cared deeply for him. Ours was a brotherly love, familial rather than sexual, but it created a true bond that I did not want to break. And yet, I acted in opposition to that impulse.

More precisely, he felt he needed to separate his mind from his emotions. He hadn't thought of himself as acted on by forces that, in light of the seminar readings, he now recognized as predating the *Oresteia*. He hadn't seen himself as having been initiated into "a framework of patriarchy and manhood," and describing that framework – because we don't see the framework when we're inside it – he compares it to a ghost:

> It was as if something was telling me that I needed to separate my mind and my emotions, but I wasn't aware of what exactly it was, and I wasn't going to rock the boat to find out what would happen if I didn't. In fact, I'm sure that I would have either rolled my eyes or laughed out loud if somebody had told me that the forces acting on me were forces predating Aeschylus's 458 BCE trilogy, the Oresteia. In fact. I was being initiated into a framework of patriarchy and manhood without so much as a conscious thought about it. This is the problem with patriarchy. Its force, while massive, is non-tangible, and its effects are both indirect and pervasive. Better said, the culprit is a ghost, and even if it were something articulable, its effects are so far-reaching that it would be implausible to believe that such affects could share a singular root cause.

In retrospect, Adam recognizes that "this unseen initiation was, in effect, a form of moral injury. An injury that I believe led me to desert a friend who was threatening to break the love laws."

We had written about the Love Laws. The concept wasn't new to our students. But it was only in the fall of 2016, following Trump's election, that several men in the class wrote so directly about how they had betrayed what they loved in taking on as their own a framework of patriarchy and manhood that was at once intangible and massive, forceful and far-reaching in its effects.

Another law student in our seminar in the fall of 2016, a man whom we shall call Steve, wrote about his struggle to resist his hard-driving father. He connected his relationship with his father and the manhood he represented with renouncing what he loved. Like Adam, Steve compared himself to Donald Moss. In his desire to be with other boys and also with girls, he had been unfaithful to his love of music. He too was trying to make sense of what otherwise seemed inexplicable. He was aware of a force that was acting on him. This force had led to a split up with the woman who was the most loving person he knew, along with his mother. The woman he split up from was, he writes, the only person he had fallen in love with.

> When I was 18 I fell in love for the first and only time in my life. She had the most beautiful blue eyes and a personality that would light up a room. She loved to talk to strangers and her laugh was contagious. Most importantly though, she had so much love to give. She was the only person other than my mother who gave me so much unconditional love and I soaked it up. To this day I believe we were split up by patriarchal terms.

It was, Steve says, "patriarchal terms" that had split them up – he and the woman he loved. What made him especially bitter was his parents had voted for Trump. The specter of Trump's election hung over Steve's depiction of his initiation into his college fraternity, which he describes as "a night of torture" at the end of which they were "literally covered in blood." Steve is clear as to what this brotherhood was about: they were "indoctrinated by nothing but pain-inducing patriarchal norms."

> Our initiation, the last day of pledge-ship, consisted of a night of torture. We were first stripped down to our underwear and forced into a small bath of ice, where we sat for an hour. We were then herded into a room full of sand, spread evenly over a brick tile floor. In that room, we were told that on "the count of three" we must all drop to our knees at the same time, so that only one loud thump could be heard in the room. We were told to remove our legs from under us so that our knees hit the ground, buckling without any support. After hitting the ground, we were forced to spin in a circle so that the tops of our bare feet would drag across on the floor. My friends who were ridiculed the most for being "unfit" as a pledge brother were harassed the most during this event, as older brothers would jump in and grind their feet amongst the brick and sand while they spun. The older brothers were yelling things like "faggot" and "pussy" as, time and time again, we fell to the

floor. The master of the fraternity would yell, "'As one! You're not dropping as one!" This of course was a ploy. Regardless of how well we dropped, we were destined to drop thirty times.

By the end of this nightmare, each one of us was covered in blood, and perfect rings of blood surrounded each one of us where our feet had been spinning.

Finally, all of us lined up outside on the driveway, sitting "Indian style" in six rows. At 3:00 a.m. in the morning, it was twenty degrees outside. We were individually doused with water to ensure our discomfort. There was nothing to keep us warm but a fire at the front of the first row. Different older brothers would get up and make speeches; usually involving a story about a time they had an unusual and objectifying sexual experience. Our backs twisted and ached only to be momentarily relieved as the head master yelled "switch!" in which case the front row quickly scurried to the back of the formation to allow the fire to warm the next closest row. As we sat there, objects were thrown at our heads like ice or empty beer cans. Finally as the sun rose, the nightmare was over. We were all officially "brothers" in a fraternity, indoctrinated by nothing but pain inducing patriarchal norms.

The undisguised misogyny and homophobia summoned to create this band of brothers echo Trump election campaign. The concern with male aggression – being a man, not a faggot or a loser – had animated Steve's college experience. "My college experience was built around an activity [football] where male aggression and athletic ability were celebrated above all else. When football began on Saturday, everything else stopped. If you did not like football you were a 'fag' or a 'loser'." What Steve came to see was the frailty of the male ego and the costs exacted by these patriarchal rites of passage. He saw the effects in his pledge brothers and college roommates, many of whom were arrested or ended up in rehab or depressed, and also in himself.

I began to feel rightfully depressed. My friends placed an importance on money and women over everything else. The fraternity served as a breeding ground for the fragile male ego. Not many of us were actually happy, all seeking acceptance we did not find in others. Out of nineteen pledge brothers, or guys who were in my class in the fraternity, sixteen were arrested, and some of them twice. After all, that was the only way we were going to be able to meet hot girls ... Women were treated like objects. We abused drugs. Four of my pledge brothers ended up in Rehab. For the first few years at college, I did not grow as a person in this environment, rather I shrank. Of my six roommates Junior year, three admittedly suffered from depression.

The manhood he saw in his father, in Trump, in his fraternity brothers, was part of a cultural environment that he describes as a nightmare, an environment in which men, including himself, did not grow but shrank as persons. As Steve came to see it, becoming a man in these terms meant sacrificing love and becoming less than human.

Another student, who had attended an Ivy League university, told a similar story. He had joined a fraternity in which the brothers also had bonded over a manhood proven by objectifying women and the dehumanizing of gays. In the initiation, the first prize was the "yellow jersey" (YJ), awarded to the young man who had achieved the most stunning sexist adventures with women – "[t]he brother with the craziest story of how he hooked up with a woman, what he did to her, or even how he disrespected her in a way that would make us laugh the most"; the YJ – yellow jersey – was worn on campus by the winner of this contest.

The student was so repelled by this that he resigned from his fraternity. Yet in the light of Trump's victory, he felt compelled to revisit this experience as a way of making sense of Trump's election. Although his family was Egyptian and its culture patriarchal, growing up in America he had experienced firsthand at one of its top universities, the culture of toxic manhood that had elected the president.

For gay men, the struggle with patriarchy is inescapable because being gay they are, in patriarchal terms, not men. We've always had gay men in our seminar. In fact, it was only when we took the word "gender" out of the name of the seminar and called it simply Resisting Injustice, that straight men were more drawn to enroll. In the past, our gay and lesbian students explored the implications that many knew firsthand of choosing love and resisting patriarchy. One of us (Richards) has written about how love that crosses the boundaries (of gender, sexuality, race, class, or of marriage) can free a voice of ethical resistance and also free creativity.[14] The gay man whose paper riveted us in the fall of 2016 had struggled to acknowledge his sexuality and to reveal it to his Roman Catholic parents. He wrote a searing depiction of the initiation that had led him to be unfaithful to his love and of the honesty he had to come to within himself and in his relationships in his efforts truly to break free. As he wrote, "I decided that it was crazy for me to continue living a lie."

In the wake of Trump's election, four men in our seminar on resisting injustice thus confessed to what in their eyes had been acts of infidelity – acts where they had betrayed themselves in betraying what they loved. In the course of their initiation into the manhood of American patriarchy, they had dissociated themselves from parts of themselves, disavowing love as the price they paid for establishing their manhood. In the terms set by the gender binary and hierarchy, manhood is readily exposed to shaming. Any action or feeling that is perceived as being like a woman or gay, brands one as not a man but a pussy or a faggot; anything that spells weakness rather than strength, inferiority rather than superiority, becomes an insult to masculinity. Defined in these terms, manhood becomes a tinderbox, and violence as a means of asserting dominance and thus proving superiority, holds the power to undo shame and restore honor.

Seeing this framing of manhood so starkly displayed in the public arena, hearing it glorified by Trump and witnessing his electoral triumph, several of the men in our seminar had sought in their final papers to explore on the basis of their own experience as men in America, the question that beset many Americans: How could this have happened? And what would it take to resist a force that "while massive, is non-tangible," a force whose effects are "both indirect and pervasive." It struck us that it was humbling for our otherwise successful law students to recognize what they were up against, and to reflect on what it meant to them to be fighting, in Adam's words, a ghost.

Our students have long recognized the problem of men's violence. What some of the men saw so piercingly in the wake of Trump's election was how their initiation into a framework of patriarchy and manhood had led them to betray love. A formless threat had led them to be unfaithful to what they knew to be their real convictions and feelings, and thus to wrong themselves. In their betrayals of love, they saw a betrayal of what's right, culturally sanctioned and socially enforced. In confronting themselves as white men, because in our otherwise diverse seminar, the men whose papers we cited including the Egyptian would be considered white, they were also explicating for us the racist forces that drove Trump's victory. Although they had not voted for Trump, they knew the psychology at work firsthand on the basis of their own experience. With the darkness of patriarchy now visible, it was easier to see its costs to themselves.

SILENCE

In their final papers for the seminar on resisting injustice in the wake of Trump's election, five of the women in the seminar wrote about their silence. Their papers also read as confessions as they sought to understand and come to terms with what on the face of it seemed inexplicable. These outspoken women, law students and Ph.D. students, had by their own admission not spoken from conviction. They had silenced what they knew deep down to be true. They had muted the voice of their own experience.

It wasn't the first time that women in our seminar had written about self-silencing. It was not the first year our students had read the findings of the Harvard Project on Women's Psychology and discovered a resonance in the voices of girls that surprised them. Because they had been girls and listening to girls' voices was a reminder of some of the times when they had been outspoken, when speaking had not been fraught.

It was of particular interest to law students that the research that prompted *In a Different Voice*[15] had been conducted in the immediate aftermath of the US Supreme Court decision in *Roe* v. *Wade*.[16] The Court's ruling, which has remained in contention, directly countered the injunction to women in patriarchy, that to be good, a woman must be selfless: responsive to the needs and concerns of others and seemingly without a voice or desires of her own. The fragility of patriarchal womanhood is exposed by this construction of goodness because in fact, as humans, women have a voice. In a different way from men then, patriarchy forces women in the name of morality to conceal their humanity.

This of course was the charge brought against Hillary Clinton. To many, she seemed less than human and also not a good woman. There was no way for her to win. But following what for many Americans, including the millions upon millions who had voted for her, was the shock of her loss, some of the women in our seminar began to examine the extent to which they too had been caught within the very same framework, trapped within the terms of the gender binary and hierarchy.

All four of the men whom we asked gave us permission to quote from their papers; two asked us not to use their names. Adam, who consented to use of his name, had suggested that we speak of him as a student in the seminar because that would more accurately characterize how he had come to the insights he came to. Of the five women we approached, four gave us permission; the fifth said that although she had broken her silence in writing for us, she was not prepared to go public with a voice that previously she had kept to herself.

Mattie, one of the women who gave us permission to use her name and quote from her paper, writes about a dream in which she is babysitting or tutoring a girl of thirteen – a girl of mixed race who seems not to have any parents. Mattie begins:

> I'm supposed to be babysitting: or maybe tutoring this girl. She's probably 13 or so. I don't think she has any parents. I'm on Fort Hamilton army base. She's mixed race. We are in a room with nothing in it. Just white walls. There is a door cut into the wall I'm sitting against that leads to an office. In the office sits the lady who hired me for this job. She is severe, blonde, older. The dream skips to my original interview. The woman asks: "Is it in your nature to follow the rules?" I think, "That question seems a little strange, but then again we are on an army base." I answer, "Yes, it is in my nature. Only by following rules do you have room for flexibility." The dream skips back

to the girl and me. She is asking me questions about my family. After some time she takes her hair down. She runs her fingers back and forth over her scalp, teasing up her hair until it engulfs her entire body, leaving only her face visible. I say to her, "With your hair like that you look like such a child!" "I do not!?" But she did, and I suggest we have a photo shoot to prove it. I set up cameras, lights, and music. We begin to play and laugh. I take pictures of her as she changes costumes and poses. And then the music stops. "I thought you said you could follow the rules and now look at what you're doing!" The woman from the interview has reappeared. She is screaming. I yell back, "You cannot keep this girl locked up. Kids need to have fun!" I am summarily fired, gather my things, and leave.

I exit through a crowded kitchen. It is filled with women. I desperately try to find someone to feed the child I just left, to give her the food that I have prepared, but there is no one willing. And then I see him, the teacher who in many ways disrupted my own girlhood, just as the woman had disrupted the young girl's by ending our play. I follow him outside, but lose him in the crowd. I wait near the entrance of the building, straining my eyes for his face. And then I spot him. We are separated by a fence. He is in a wheelchair. I run along the fence, searching for a gate, an opening of some kind, and then suddenly we are face to face. Somehow I know that I am the cause of his paralysis. My betrayal of our secret literally broke his back. But I am not ashamed. I am not apologetic. I tell a joke and the dream ends.

In analyzing her dream, Mattie, who is white, identifies with the mixed-race thirteen-year-old girl whom she sees as "future-potential," "a shadow self," a "self that is less understood, but eager to understand," a wild and playful thirteen-year-old, locked up by a blond (white) woman who screams at the girl, ending her play and forcing Mattie to leave her. In the second part of the dream, Mattie sees the teacher who had "disrupted my own girlhood" by sexually abusing her. He's in a wheelchair and in the dream Mattie knows that she was the cause of his paralysis: "My betrayal of our secret literally broke his back." But "I am not ashamed. I am not apologetic." She ends by telling a joke.

In her dream, Mattie captures and confronts the challenge posed by the initiation that marks the transition from girl to woman:

> It is a struggle women are all too familiar with: the question of how to transition from girl to woman while preserving the inner voice. How do we feed that inner child, the child who knows how to play and question, while living in the world run by both women and men who seek to stamp it out? We all have a shadow self, but who casts the shadow?

Her dream also reflects what many found surprising in the 2016 election: the collusion of white women in perpetuating patriarchy. Speaking of the teacher who appears in the dream, she explains that he was by no means the only man who betrayed her. This thought then leads her to Trump and to the question of where power lies and how to resist:

> Other men would also betray me. When a teacher sexually assaults me, I add it to the pile. When a judge tells me I should consider wearing a skirt in court, I add it as well. When Trump opens his mouth, I add those words to the stack. When I hear his words in the mouths of my old high school classmates, I see the pile grow taller, and its shadow longer. I want to go back to my room under the water, to escape. I want to feel power in my solitude. But maybe that's wrong. Maybe the power of the [white-walled] room was not in escape or solitude, but in unity, the unity between sisters, singing together.

Like the other women whose papers stood out for their insights into the sexist and racist culture that elected Trump, Mattie writes of the forces that shut a girl up – the girl who knows how to play and question. She sees that power lies not in escape or solitude but in unity, in the voices of mixed-race sisters singing together, but she is also aware of how women as well as men are invested in keeping this from happening. The girl in the dream is not fed; no one is willing to give her the food that Mattie has prepared for her. The blond woman in the office forces Mattie to leave the wild-haired girl, and then in the next segment of the dream, the teacher appears – the teacher who sexually abused her in high school. Without apology or shame, without remorse, Mattie realizes in the dream, that it was her betrayal of this secret that had broken his back. The dream ends with Mattie telling a joke and thus perhaps with the question: can this be taken seriously?

A student we shall call Jasmin wrote of her experience with her father, an African American man, who, while serving in the army in Europe, had met and married her mother, a European woman. "I learned very early on who was in charge of my house. We all knew we had to walk on egg shells, my mom included. Make a wrong move and you could be hit. I just remember my childhood being a cycle of fear and hopelessness."

Because her mother "has lost her voice both literally and figuratively," Jasmin's resistance had consisted in becoming her voice and defending her. Yet when she and her mother visited Europe she saw in her mother a very different person. Funny and full of life, like the girl, the shadow self in Mattie's dream. "My mom was a different person. She was confident and carefree and for the first time in my life I saw her as truly being happy. She was funny and full of life, and it was during this time I realized how beautiful she was."

Although bi-racial, Jasmin could pass as white. "What are you?" her friends would ask her. She had witnessed her father's humiliation when a policeman yelled at him and she had bridled at her mother's use of a racist epithet to characterize black patients at the hospital where she worked as a nurse. Reading the incident in *Dreams from My Father*[17] where Barack Obama recalls his white grandmother responding with a racist epithet to a black panhandler, Jasmin saw the analogy. Like Obama, she too had made it a point to identify as black: "I cannot just turn a blind eye to the injustices I've witnessed within my community or disassociate myself just because I have the ability to 'pass.'"

In addition to refusing to pass as white, Jasmin had set out to dismantle the structures of patriarchy in her relationships with men. Her intention was so fierce that she had hit her boyfriend when he didn't listen to her. This incident led her to recognize that it was equality not dominance she was seeking in her determination that she be listened to. She had, she realized, "over-asserted my voice," in that in her insistence that others listen to her, she had not listened to them.

For Camille, a Cuban-American woman, her desire to listen to others had led her to interview each member of her large Cuban family. She then decided to write in each of their voices. By taking on this challenge, she found herself coming to a new understanding of the complex dynamics of race, gender, and sexuality.

For Jackie, a Dominican-American woman, the challenge was to listen to herself.

Jackie had been raped by one of her classmates at the elite college they attended. She writes, "[a]lthough it was accepted that I was raped, I was expected to 'get over it,' to not make waves, to not ruin Tom's life. These social mantras worked when I was most vulnerable in the aftermath of the rape, yet, with Tom's admission, I could no longer not know what I knew." She had written a long email to Tom explaining how the rape had affected her. He had responded by email with remorse, but not with the personal apology she had expected. She was haunted by "the silence that came after ... a betrayal of everything I had ever believed in. I felt like I was drowning, the feeling of helplessness and the lack of ability to speak my truth."

Jackie had come to see women's silence – a silence enforced in the name of womanhood – as "integral to propping up the patriarchy." She also saw women's silence as a consequence of an initiation that presents women with a catch-22.

> Young women are initiated into a culture where they find themselves in a Catch-22: they can't say how they really feel because if they did, they would threaten their relationships, yet a relationship that is not

honest is not a real relationship. As I watch my younger sister grow up, I already see her articulating the social pressures of staying silent, of being agreeable, of "locking feelings inside.". . .

I feel a sense of powerlessness in watching this cycle continue, in having to fight to break it.

I have seen this silence mirrored in our class, women across a spectrum of identities, all silent about the ways we can relate to one another. Most importantly, the silence is not merely silence, but antagonistic to the idea that there is a common shared experience between women. The investment in keeping women apart, separate from one another, has social utility for patriarchy. It is dangerous to the maintenance of patriarchal structures and norms for women to bond over their shared experience because then they rise up to question, to confront, to challenge, and to change.

The silence among women that Jackie saw mirrored in our class, the antagonism to the idea that there are commonalities among women, that as women women share certain experiences, became in Jackie's eyes a strategy, whether deliberate or seemingly in the very nature of things, to thwart the danger women would pose to patriarchy should they bond over their shared experiences. In the absence of women "singing together," as Mattie envisioned it, if women don't rise up to question, confront, and challenge the injustices of patriarchy, if women don't act in concert to change things, then, Jackie writes:

> acts of everyday sexism, are so normalized, that people fail to discuss them as the tools of oppression that they are. For instance, Trump's commentary on "grab her by the pussy," could easily be dismissed as "locker room talk." My cousins, all women, were surprised that I was so upset by pussygate. They accepted that men talked like that and defended the right to say it. Yet, at the same time my cousins were defending Trump, across the country women were breaking their silence. Trump's comment had hit a nerve; they were remembering comments and actions that did not treat them as equal human beings. They remembered when the fact that they were women meant that men were entitled to their bodies. It was a consciousness raising moment.

Both Jackie and Mattie connect the silences of women with Trump's election. How was it that women – any woman, although in fact it was almost exclusively white married women – voted for Trump after he had boasted about grabbing them by the pussies? In the fall of 2016, women in our seminar on resisting injustice were grappling with the question of how in a democracy where women have the vote and women constitute a majority, Trump had been elected? What was impeding the ability of women to recognize and resist injustice?

Jackie turned her attention to the silence she had observed in our class discussions: "There was something heartbreaking about our class this semester, something that I continue to grapple with."

> The oppression Olympics between race, class, and gender is a mechanism of silence. Theories such as intersectionality, which try to explain the multiple oppressions a black women might find herself under, ... caught between gendered oppression and social pressure to not betray her race – are meant to liberate and break the silence. Yet because our culture rests on the silence of women, these theories are often used to further silence; having to choose between different identities, at different times, only maintains silence because ultimately it is the gendered identity that often becomes invisible.

In the end, Jackie comes to our question. Writing about intersectionality, she asks, why among the various identities that intersect is it the gendered identity that often becomes invisible?

We are reminded of Tolstoy who mid-way through *Anna Karenina*, writing about Anna's husband Karenin, recognizes that there is a crude, powerful, and ultimately mysterious force that shapes people's lives in a way that on the face of it is perplexing because it turns what seems natural and good (love and tender compassion) into something perceived as bad and improper.[18] For our women students, it seems the reverse was true. The force at work is one that turns something bad (shutting up a child, raping a woman) into something that is somehow acceptable, or at least should not be spoken about. Asking in their papers what it would take to break the back of the patriarchy, they answer: women speaking in concert with one another, drawing on their shared experiences and ending what had previously been their collusion with men in keeping the abuses of patriarchy secret. Mattie's dream image captures it starkly: she had paralyzed the man who had sexually abused her by betraying what had been "our secret," that is, by making his secret no longer her secret.

Our seminar had freed a resisting voice. In 2016, following Trump's election, patriarchy had become visible as a crude, mysterious, and powerful force alive not only in the politics of our country but also in the private lives of our students.

3 Why Didn't We See It?

There was something we among others did not see in the Trump campaign. Despite the mass rallies, we overlooked the resonance his voice had for many Americans. If anything, we thought the crudeness of his comments about his penis size and his power and the vulgarity of his comments about women, would do him in. What we missed was the shift in the framework. We were looking at Trump through a framework of democracy, but for Trump patriarchy was the frame. Gender was no longer one issue among many (race, class, sexuality, etc.) as it is within a democratic framework where the concern is equal voice or equality. Gender – its binary and hierarchy – had become the lens through which everyone and everything were seen. Democracy with its value of equality is one concern within a patriarchal framework, but the primary concern is manhood. It was the perceived loss of power that white American men had suffered under the presidency of Barack Obama and presumably would suffer under Hillary Clinton, and Trump's promise to restore that power that carried him into the White House. It wasn't politically correct – there was no appeal to democratic values – and this was precisely the point. What was missed by us along with others for whom democratic values are the point, was that the fight was precisely about the framework. But the shift in the framework made it hard to argue about this because the grounds of the argument kept shifting.

What now becomes clear is how in the Republican primary, Trump systematically dispensed with his opponents in patriarchal terms as insufficiently masculine or manly: little Marco wasn't big enough to be the president, low energy Jeb wasn't aggressive enough, lying Ted wasn't courageous enough to face the truth. Whether or not any of this was true didn't matter. What mattered was to cast doubt on their manhood, so that in the end, he was the only man standing. And then, he took on Hillary in terms so familiar to the disparagement of women within patriarchy that the only surprise is the extent to which it surprised us.

Untrustworthy? – that's the oldest epithet hurled against women. Think of Eve, not to mention Delilah. Hillary was untrustworthy – crooked and nasty. Her qualifications were irrelevant.

Patriarchy is a powerful lens and Trump used it so effectively that it is hard now to remember that Hillary won the popular vote or to take in the magnitude of the difference: close to 3 million more Americans voted for Hillary than voted for Trump. In patriarchal terms, all that matters is that she was the loser. To a surprising extent, it doesn't even matter how she lost, only that she lost. And for that, we blame her.

There it was; patriarchy in plain sight. The gender binary and hierarchy were the yardsticks Trump used in measuring his opponents, and they all came up wanting. Not a real man, not a good woman. Democracy with its rule of law and great principles of liberty, equality and justice was beside the point. Was not the point. And it took us a long time to see this because the framework is what frames a conversation; in itself, it is invisible.

Put simply, Trump shifted the culture; he changed the grounds of political discourse. By democratic standards, he broke all the rules. Within a patriarchal framework, that didn't matter. What mattered was his claim to manhood, which was his claim to power and authority. He was a man not a woman, masculine not feminine, rough and tough not gentle, someone who because of his power could, as he said, get away with anything. He could shoot someone in plain sight on 5th Avenue and the people who voted for him would still vote for him.

It has taken a while for this to sink in. The truth of this statement and the fact that he meant it. This prompted the analogies to dictators, fascism, and military takeovers, but it was the shift in the framework that has made it hard both to see and to come to terms with what happened. Trump put his family on display to show himself as the patriarch, the father, and as the father, he was the voice of morality and law. One of the tell-tale signs of the patriarchal frame was that the children whom he prominently displayed, Ivanka most centrally, never mentioned their mother.

The evolutionary anthropologist Sarah Blaffer Hrdy put it this way.[1] Although patriarchy often masquerades as nature, it is not in fact natural to us as humans. We survived as a species because of our capacity for mutual understanding: for empathy, mind-reading, and cooperation, all of which, as Hrdy notes, are present in rudimentary form practically from birth. In contrast, as she writes, "patriarchal ideologies that focused on the chastity of women and the perpetuation and augmentation of male lineages undercut the long-standing priority of putting children's well-being first."[2] Rather than being linked with human survival, patriarchy puts our survival in danger.

We see this in the Trump administration: the determination not to care about the future, to dispense with health care, to end efforts to protect the environment, to cut the budget for education, to risk nuclear warfare rather than be shamed by North Korea, a small nation that within Trump's patriarchal way of seeing does not deserve to have power or to be taken seriously. Like Mexicans and Muslims, like blacks and women.

And maybe we didn't see it because in fact we were taking them seriously. Within a democratic framework where equal voice is paramount, our attention is drawn to those who don't have a voice or whose voices have found little or no resonance, people who have not been taken seriously or listened to. The democratic advances of the mid-twentieth century were largely reparative: hearing the voices of those who had had no voice in shaping their destiny, no rights, no say in what was happening to them, those without the resources to pursue life, liberty, and happiness. Black Lives Matter is a current iteration. But within a patriarchal framework none of this matters. What matters is the voice of the father; his power and his authority.

Listening to Trump, you can hear it. The seduction, the appeal of the father. Trust me. I will protect you. It doesn't matter that his promises are empty. He is the leader. Father is back.

Trump, one senses without a second thought, had made patriarchy the frame and then was surprised, one gathers, by the resonance he encountered, largely from other men who like himself were preoccupied with issues of honor and shame. Which then only encouraged him to go further in shifting the terms of the conversation. When we wrote our 2008 book, we thought that patriarchy could only have force when it hid itself in ostensibly democratic argument. That gender – commonly marginalized in serious discussions of politics – had the power Trump's politics showed it to have surprised even us, but it was gender invoked not in the service of equality and a greater realization of democratic values; it was gender evoked with an eye to dispensing with democratic values and restoring patriarchal privilege. Seen in this light, it doesn't matter that some have health care while others do not or that tax breaks go to the very rich; it doesn't matter that the most vulnerable are to be afflicted. They are the losers. If anything, they should pay more.

Our thesis was more powerful than even we had supposed; our argument – in which patriarchy is central – was indeed prophetic in ways we had not anticipated. Trump's campaigning voice was heard as authentic by his followers because it was not "politically correct." But we would add, it sounded authentic because in fact it was authentic: authentically patriarchal. Unflinching in giving voice to a masculinity defined in terms of roughness and toughness, a masculinity that was above all not feminine, that claimed superiority (America First) without apology, that promised to undo shame and restore honor to those, mainly white men and their white wives, who felt that they had lost their dignity by losing what they had considered to be their rightful position in the racist and patriarchal scheme of things. Trump promised to make America great again, meaning not only white again but also patriarchal again. And this for the most part was not seen. In part because within a democratic framework, it was literally inconceivable.

In 2016, manhood became the call and patriarchy was the frame. Just listen for the gender binary, the sharp division between masculine and feminine, the either/or categorization that bars anything queer or transgender or bisexual, that brands gay men as not really men and lesbians as not real women. In the terms of the gender binary and hierarchy, any deviation from or variant of what can be thought of as the missionary position becomes a cause for hysteria. Because in fact the whole patriarchal order is at stake in women having a voice of their own and not becoming selfless or submissive or men choosing in the vernacular of the 1960s to make love not war.

Trump's triumphalism was unequivocally patriarchal; he trumpeted his success as a business leader. He appealed to us versus them, winners versus losers, strength versus weakness; he scapegoated those whom he perceived as lesser, as losers – ethnic and religious minorities; he chastised women and focused on their attractiveness to men, their sexuality; and, most alarming of all, he saw violence as the remedy, the way to undo shaming and restore manhood at whatever cost. Supporters of Trump find his voice authentic, and indeed it is: authentically patriarchal.

In the transition from patriarchy to democracy, manhood and womanhood are on the line. We've seen this played out in the culture wars that followed the resistance movements of the 1960s and 1970s. One of us (Gilligan) asked, in *The Birth of Pleasure*,[3] was it possible to be a man without being a soldier or preparing oneself for war? Was it possible to be a woman without being a mother, or at least preparing oneself to bear and raise children? Soldiers and mothers are the patriarchal couple, honored for their willingness to sacrifice themselves. One of us (Richards) asked, in *Disarming Manhood*,[4] was it possible for a man to be a man and also to embrace nonviolence as an ethical stance? Separately and together, we turned our focus to the force of love and its power to uproot patriarchy. Love is legendary as a force that crosses the binaries of race, class, gender, and religion and upsets the hierarchies that hold a patriarchal order in place.

In *Joining the Resistance*,[5] one of us (Gilligan) writes about a healthy resistance to betraying love or silencing the self – a resistance associated with psychological resilience. This healthy resistance to moral injury is comparable to the body's immune system; the healthy psyche like the healthy body resists infection. But this healthy resistance to betraying what's right becomes a political resistance to demands of patriarchy. In *Why Love Leads to Justice*,[6] one of us (Richards) writes about how love that crosses the boundaries by resisting the Love Laws of patriarchy frees an ethically resisting voice, a voice that resists injustice including the injustices of racism, sexism, homophobia, anti-Semitism, caste, and class; the list is endless.

Love which was so palpably in our midst during the Obama presidency – Barack's love for Michelle, for his daughters, and also for America and its democracy – was suddenly missing from our public life: displaced by cruelty and lies, by a discourse of hate and contempt. The quest for a more perfect union had given way to a divisiveness that seemingly knew no bounds. And everywhere, the tell-tale markers: the binaries and the hierarchies – givers and takers, winners and losers, America First. Our public conversation was no longer governed by democratic ideals and values.

In the 2016 presidential election, the battle between democracy and patriarchy was out in the open and perhaps it is fitting, given that we were in the presence of two warring paradigms, that Clinton won the popular vote while Trump won the electoral college vote and the presidency. In this respect, although Trump became president, the election was something of a stand-off.

In a telling paper, Moira Weigel shows that opposition to "political correctness," as a term of American political rhetoric, began in the 1990s, and "has proved a highly effective form of crypto-politics. It transforms the political landscape by acting as if it is not political at all."[7] The campaign against political correctness began as a criticism of the country's universities on the grounds that they were allegedly no longer open to free debate. It was then taken up and used by right-wing politicians to counter liberal argument as such and to undermine its appeal to university-educated young people. To this extent, opposition to political correctness was a disguised attempt to criticize the cogency and persuasiveness of liberal argument without engaging with the argument: hence, a "form of crypto-politics."

The argument against political correctness was raised by Donald Trump to an altogether more inflammatory level, because it was used to frame his cruelty toward women and his attacks on Mexicans and Muslims as an exercise of freedom. It allowed cruelty to masquerade as authenticity. Trump *trumpeted* his political incorrectness and his authenticity. He was authentic, but in the falsifying way that nationalist leaders in the nineteenth and twentieth centuries had been, forging a sense of national identity and unity by appealing to the tropes of racism including anti-Semitism (we are reminded of Adorno's searing critical attack on the role "the jargon of authenticity" played in Heidegger's philosophy and his appalling endorsement of Hitler's fascism[8]). Trump's appeal was certainly not because of his arguments. He himself has little investment in truth or in policy, or for that matter in the rule of law or in democracy. There was, for example, no basis in law for his charges against Hillary Clinton that brought crowds to their feet chanting: "Lock her up." Such populist appeals are redolent of fascism. The depths of cynicism that had fueled the attacks against Clinton only became fully apparent following the election when it came to light that many in Trump's entourage including those in the White House were themselves using private email servers. But by then nobody seemed to care.

Trump's campaign illustrates the kind of populist propaganda and demagoguery (use of half-truths and even flat lies) that Jason Stanley has analyzed and condemned as masking the anti-democratic forces that motivate them.[9] As an example, Stanley cites the way in which the Republican strategist, Lee Attwater, used welfare as a code word for racist slurs.[10] Ian Haney Lopez has documented other cogent examples,[11] including what the Nixon advisor John Ehrlichman acknowledged as the basis for Nixon's War on Crime: "We knew we couldn't make it illegal to be either against the war or blacks ... but by getting the public to associate the hippies with marijuana and blacks with heroin, and then criminalizing both heavily, we could disrupt these communities."[12] Some commentators argue Trump's success requires closer study of the rise of German fascism.[13] In this connection, when Adorno and his colleagues studied the authoritarian personality in the American context, they drew a distinction between *pseudo-democratic* rather than *openly antidemocratic* appeals.[14] In their view, an authoritarian personality could make openly anti-Semitic appeals in Hitler's Germany, but in the United States, such appeals were pseudo-democratic, which is to say covert, as Jason Stanley's has claimed. And yet, in the Trump-era Charlottesville demonstrations, the anti-Semitism was in fact open. What makes Trump's populist politics so alarming is not simply its openly anti-democratic character but the resonance it has created for what had previously been unspeakable.

What is it about gender that makes it difficult to talk about, even when a gender dynamic is playing out right in front of our eyes? Why are Americans still in general more comfortable blaming Hillary Clinton than examining the gendered forces that were brought into play against her election?

When Barack Obama was running for president in 2008, he gave a speech on race in America that confronted the issue with remarkable intellectual and political force. Hillary Clinton made no comparable speech on gender either in 2008 or 2016. Obama is, after all, bi-racial: the son of a white mother and a black father, and one could say on that basis, he is qualified to speak about racial animosities in a way that others are not. Especially because he identifies as black. Hillary is a woman; she is not a man. She is the daughter of a woman and a man, but it's a stretch to imagine the voice in which she could have spoken about animosities between women and men without sounding shrill, or being heard as a man-hater. In this we can see the force of the gender binary and understand why transgender people are met with such a sense of alarm. Along with many other things, the 2016 election calls us to challenge any easy race–gender analogy, and it's possible that the tendency to assimilate gender to race may have been one of the mistakes made by those who advised Hillary and crafted her strategy.

That a women's march, the largest such march on record, took place only after Hillary was defeated and without honoring her as among the foremothers in whose steps they were walking in some ways makes the point. Gender could be appealed to – it was after all a women's march – but only when it could no longer influence the outcome of the election. The omission of Hillary's name, the deliberate non-mention of the first woman in American history to run for president as the candidate of a major political party, suggests to us that in the eyes of the planners the march was intended to protest Trump's election and Hillary was held responsible for his victory. In other words, it was her fault.

The familiar tropes are tiring. She is to blame; it's all her fault. We find unconvincing the explanatory narrative of Clinton's electoral failure in the book, *Shattered*.[15] This narrative was largely informed by the views of those in her campaign who relied on the data analytics that they considered responsible for Obama's election in shaping Hillary's strategy. But whereas Obama and those who ran his campaign addressed the issue of race forthrightly and skillfully, gender, despite its obvious presence remained somewhat submerged, perhaps deliberately so, even in Clinton's 2016 bid for the presidency. To take an obvious example, attention was if anything diverted from the gender dynamics of the second debate despite Trump following Hillary around the stage and looming over her while she spoke. She kept smiling stalwartly while, in the eyes of many watching the debate, he was stalking her. How could her smile be perceived as authentic? What was so egregious and offensive in Trump's behavior thus had the effect of contributing to the reading of Hillary as inauthentic.

Upon reflection, it is possible that she, like we, had assumed that gender would be covertly present as an issue in the campaign rather than blatantly on display in Trump's behavior. Or perhaps she assumed or was advised that the best way for a woman seeking power to deal with a man's offensive behavior is to ignore it – to act as if it isn't happening or doesn't bother her (studies show that both women's ambition and their anger in politics are unfavorably perceived in contrast to men's).[16] In *What Happened*, Hillary says she regrets this.[17] Reviewing her book in the *New Yorker*, David Remnick observes:

> In conversation and in the book, Clinton's pain is manifest. When it comes to feminism and her role in the woman's movement, she says, she never figured out "how to tell the story right." And the country she believes is not ready to hear it. Or, at least, not from her. "That's not who we are," she writes. "Not yet."[18]

In *The Destruction of Hillary Clinton*,[19] Susan Bordo comes closer to reckoning with the role gender played in Clinton's loss of the presidency. Bordo charts the multiple ways in which the double standard was used against her. For example, although Comey had information about Russian interference in the election that would have been relevant for voters, his two interventions in the campaign, both of which violated FBI standards of professional conduct were at Hillary's expense.[20] Clinton herself takes this view, and her heartbreak at the injustice is shared by many who worked on her campaign.[21]

If there was a problem in Hillary Clinton's campaign, it was a problem of voice. In patriarchal terms, the problem is insoluble. A woman seeking power either sounds muted (selfless, a good woman) or shrill (power-seeking). If she competes with a man for a position of leadership and wins, she robs him of his manhood. She becomes a castrating bitch. To be authentic – to be herself – she has to challenge the framework. As Clinton did in the third debate. When she challenged Trump's framing of late abortions, she sounded authentic because she was being authentic. She saw that his way of framing the problem made it impossible to see what in fact she knew to be true and she refused to enter his framework. Instead she changed the terms of the argument to reflect the experiences of women in that situation.

By framing the election in patriarchal terms, Trump rendered Hillary's candidacy unwinnable, which makes it more remarkable that she came as close as she did to winning. But it also explains why we didn't see what was coming because looking through a democratic lens, it was Trump whose candidacy appeared unwinnable

One of the more heartening events of 2017 was the number of men who joined the women's march following Trump's inauguration.

With their feet, they were saying, to paraphrase Hillary Clinton, that women's concerns are human concerns and human concerns are women's concerns. The ethic of care, as one of us (Gilligan) has written, is a human necessity, integral to survival and a requisite both for love and for democracy.[22] Because the ethic of care is the ethic that prevents moral injury, it is the ethic of resistance to patriarchy.

This became obvious in 2016. Above all, it was the caring of the Obama administration that Trump set out to dismantle, beginning with Obamacare and extending to the Environmental Protection Agency. To the department of education, he appointed an opponent of public education; to the department of health and human services, he appointed someone who regarded human services as not the government's responsibility. The startling thing is that there was no disguise, no effort to hide the intention or to back off when it became clear how many people would suffer as a result of these policies. Because despite the populist appeal, this was not government by or for the people. It was government by the father who knew best and who said he would take care of us and protect us. In fact, it was government for the 1 percent, those at the very top of the patriarchal ladder.

Among the things we didn't see is how many people felt that Trump would take care of them. In their eyes, he saw their situation (the shame and the loss of human dignity they felt) and shared their anger (he too had been shamed by the cultural elite). He assured them that he would fix the problem, make great deals and clean up the swamp. They believed him even when all the available evidence made it clear that Trump was not someone who kept his word. Did the people who voted for him want to believe something that within themselves they knew not to be true? This question takes us back to the insights of our students.

In the shadow of Trump's victory, they recognized how insidiously patriarchy can insert itself into the subconscious, becoming a force that acts upon us without a conscious thought. In their own lives, they had sacrificed love or silenced themselves or undergone a night of torture for the sake of a manhood or a womanhood that would leave them "rightfully depressed" – rightfully because deep down inside, they knew that they had betrayed what was right. Following Trump's election, a third of the students in the Resisting Injustice seminar chose to explore their own personal sense of betrayal in their final papers. In their eyes, the election of Trump signified a betrayal of what's right on a national scale.

In David Remnick's book *The Bridge*,[23] the Obama presidency was seen as the legacy of the civil rights movement. Similarly, Clinton's running for president can be seen as a legacy of second-wave feminism – women's rights are human rights, women's voices can make a difference.

That it didn't happen, that she lost the presidency was immediately attributed to her personal shortcomings and to the animosity toward her felt by the white women who voted for Trump and the Bernie Sanders supporters who voted for Jill Stern or simply didn't vote at all. In this view, she was defeated by herself, by other white women, and by the left.

Feminism, insofar as it was discussed at all, was taken to be a women's issue and a white women's issue at that. Yet what the 2016 election revealed, and what feminists or at least some feminists have known from the beginning, is that gender is also an issue for men and patriarchy is harmful to men, along with everyone else. This is something we have both written about separately and together at some length.

Still it was striking to us how forthright Trump was in his appeal to gender, in particular to the codes of male honor. It was as if he knew what Hillary could not speak of: that gender was the heart of the matter in the 2016 presidential election. Gender was, Trump saw, the key to everything. His own family, including the children from his two former marriages, were used as a moniker of the patriarchal family, with Trump, the father, the patriarch defined in the terms of the gender binary as strong (not weak), dominant (not submissive), aggressive (not passive), independent (not dependent), potent (not impotent), successful (not a loser). He was by his own definition right not wrong; his authority was in his own eyes unquestioned. In patriarchal terms, it didn't matter – in fact it accrued to his credit, a further proof of his manhood – that Trump had gone through two wives, each of whom he had discarded for a younger woman. This was accepted as the way things are, or something a man can get away with if he is a star. This deeply sexist man would also use gender against Hillary Clinton by holding her responsible for her husband's infidelities and shaming her as a woman who had been unable to satisfy her man.

It is instructive to compare Trump's use of his family with Obama's very different political framing of his family as, basically, a nuclear family with a husband and wife and two children. Obama never brought out how highly anti-patriarchal his background and his family actually were. He was brought up without a father, by his mother and her parents; he and Michelle (clearly his equal) were raising their children with the help of her mother who, once he was president, lived with them in the White House. Obama was deeply aware of the damage patriarchy inflicts on men, having observed it in his own father.[24] Yet he may have sensed that America, although ready to some extent for a black president and even a black first family, was not ready for a family that was not visibly patriarchal. Michelle's mother, although plainly living in the White House, was for all practical purposes invisible. As though she were not there.

There is a political psychology here, and it centers on gender. Trump's own sense of shamed manhood – never being taken seriously by New York City elites – elicited a response in many of the white men who voted for him because his rage and shame resonated with theirs. These men and their wives had assumed a hierarchy now very much under threat both from people of color and from trade agreements which led jobs to be moved overseas.[25] There is, of course, a stark irrationalism in white men directing their rage at blacks and women, professionals and gays, but not at Donald Trump. It was evident, or should have been evident, that Trump's policies would be less in the interest of many who voted for him than those of Hillary Clinton. But it was not rational self-interest that drove his election.

We are dealing here not with deliberative argument or ideas but with powerful emotions: shame and rage. It's why the question of truth or the prevalence of lies became, much to the astonishment of many, irrelevant. Beside the point. As Arlie Hochschild made clear, "the Great Paradox"[26] was the tendency of people to vote against policies that were clearly in their interest (for example, environmental protection). This makes sense, however, only if patriarchy remains very much intact. Donald Trump, a self-absorbed man, who, in contrast to Hillary Clinton, had little record of concern for others, had been imaginatively transformed into the charismatic patriarch, who these voters, men and women, desperately believed would save them from shame and by aiding them in their economic distress, restore the dignity of their manhood or their marriage.[27]

An important American play, *Sweat*, by the African American playwright, Lynn Nottage,[28] premiered in New York City at the Public Theater shortly before the election. Nottage sets her play in Reading, Pennsylvania, where she spent two and a half years listening to the workers, many of whose jobs were vanishing. The action takes place in a bar where steelworkers assemble. Two women friends are the protagonists: Cynthia, who is black, and Tracey, who is white. Their sons, respectively black and white, are also good friends. Racism only enters in after economic tensions erupt when Cynthia, the black woman, wins out over Tracey, the white woman, for the job in management they both had applied for and layoffs begin because the company has decided to move jobs to Mexico.

"Most folks think it's the guilt or rage that destroys us. But I know it's shame that eats us away until we disappear,"[29] one of the sons observes. His insight follows the explosion of violence that destroyed the friendships and left the bartender maimed. Nottage was as shocked by the election result as anyone, but, she explains, "what wasn't shocking was the extent of the pain . . . These were people who felt helpless, who felt like the American dream they had so deeply invested in had been suddenly ripped away. I was sitting with these white men, and I thought, You sound like people of color in America."[30]

Vulnerability to the shaming of their manhood is what men, black and white, share. What Nottage, a brilliant playwright and close observer of American culture, dramatized was the psychological power of this shaming of manhood and the violence it unleashes and justifies. Why did Nottage see what the Democratic Party including Obama and Clinton seemed not to have seen? Was it because she was a black *woman*? Wasn't it three black women (Alicia Garza, Patrisse Cullops, and Opal Tometi) who founded Black Lives Matter?[31] Nottage's play, written before the election, was an early warning signal. More than anyone, she recognized the dynamic that was about to play out right in front of our eyes.

What is psychologically crucial here is the vulnerability of people to shame when they are in danger of losing the very ground of their being: their sense of themselves as a person of worth. The election of Trump in 2016 showed white men and their wives to be most invested in the restoration of patriarchy. Obama's stunning victory in 2008 and again in 2012 left many Americans with a renewed sense of hope that in the end we would care for one another and justice would prevail. But then seemingly out of nowhere, in 2016, there was Trump.

Trump's imaginative appeal turned in part on his full-hearted and authentically patriarchal stance, which some Americans took as proof of his manhood and hence as a strength. They were exhausted, he would save them: from the liberals, from Wall Street, from themselves. His candidacy exposed a culture of patriarchy whose existence many had denied or written off as outdated. A framework of patriarchy and manhood that predated the *Oresteia*, was driving the 2016 presidential election, in part by keeping us from seeing what was right in front of our eyes. As our student Adam put it, "the culprit was a ghost."

There is yet another confirmation of the role patriarchy played in Trump's unexpected victory: namely, his hypocritical alliance with fundamentalist constitutional conservatives and his commitment to appoint justices on the model of the recently deceased Justice Antonin Scalia. This commitment was made with particular reference to Scalia's hostility to *Roe* v. *Wade* and the role he played in interpreting the Second Amendment of the Bill of Rights to limit gun control laws. Both issues, but particularly the latter, were central to the refusal of the Republican majority in the United States Senate, under the leadership of Senator Mitch McConnell, even to give a hearing to then President Barack Obama's nomination of an eminently qualified jurist, Merrick Garland. McConnell egregiously violated Senate precedent in not even giving a hearing to the appointment of Judge Garland; in doing so, he ruled out any public discussion of whatever issues Garland's appointment might raise for the Republican senators, and why, in contrast, some appointment more on the model of Justice Scalia seemed to them more reasonable.

There was no such public discussion because Republicans in the Senate and Trump in his campaign were not willing or able to engage in such discussion, which means they are ideologically unfit to do their duty under the Constitution of the United States. Rather, the entire issue was to be politicized in the worst possible way, mobilizing ardent minorities opposed to *Roe* v. *Wade* and in favor of gun rights. Both issues, are, of course, highly gendered.

It is striking that men, when it comes to choices analogous to the choice of abortion for women (for example, frozen embryo cases, surrogacy contracts, post-mortem pregnancies), make such choices on similar grounds to those of women who choose to have abortions.[32] No one thinks of demonizing men when they face such choices and make them as responsible moral agents. Women making the choice to abort are in the same position, and only the continuing power of American patriarchy renders them invisible (indeed, demonizes them as non-persons) when their choices challenge men's control over their sexuality. Men, being patriarchs, enjoy their freedom in sexual matters, as they always have.

Aside from sectarian religious views of abortion, even women who do not share these views are vulnerable to what Wendy Davis has called "wolf whistle politics." Under the impact of such politics, they align themselves with right-wing patriarchal men because of the freedom from constraints on women's sexuality, which they believe a right to abortion endorses.[33] The politics of abortion touches on the conception of motherhood, and pro-life politicians, dominantly men, forge false narratives that pro-choice women are not and cannot be good mothers.[34]

The ideal of a right to guns is also highly gendered, as it plays into and appeals to a conception of a manhood forged on a man's ability to protect his family and defend his honor.[35] But it also plays on a dynamic of shame that mandates violence as its redress. It is against this background that gun control laws make so much sense. The current defense of the Second Amendment is questionable on both historical and textual grounds,[36] but it draws psychological support, as it did in the Trump election and still does in our politics, from the continuing force in American culture of the gender binary and hierarchy.

The work of Justice Scalia on the Supreme Court was not without distinction, but neither his almost hysterical hostility to *Roe* v. *Wade* nor his ardent support for a right to guns under the Second Amendment are supported by his vaunted originalism. Originalism cannot explain either the political theory of the Founders of the United States Constitution or the authoritative judicial interpretations of the Constitution over time. No justice, including Scalia, has ever confined his interpretations to how the Founders might have applied the relevant words or clauses, nor did Scalia ever explain why he adopted this approach in some areas but not in others. At bottom, what lies behind Scalia's choices is neither text nor history, for there are powerful arguments of both text and history against his interpretations.[37] What is at work are his own preferences as a patriarchal man, including his Catholic moral conservativism, and the anger and at times contempt in his opinions as a justice of the Supreme Court at those who dared to challenge traditional patriarchal authority.

Scalia's willingness to express his rage both on and off the Supreme Court may well have appealed to the many men and some women still wedded to American patriarchy. His anger at cultural changes resonated with and rationalized their own. His opposition was the force Senator McConnell and his Republican colleagues appealed to as the politics that would support their refusal to give a hearing to Judge Merrick Garland.

Trump himself held up Justice Scalia as the model for his judicial appointments. There was never any serious discussion of constitutional interpretation either by McConnell or Trump. In fact, Trump remitted his choice of judicial appointees, including Justice Gorsuch, to the religious sectarianism that evidently has motivated the leader of the Federalist Society on whom Trump relied.[38] And now Justice Gorsuch appears ready to do the work of his patriarchal masters, and to pave the way for a Supreme Court supinely hostage to their values.[39]

So when Trump embraces Scalia as a model for judicial appointments, he displays yet again the prominent role that patriarchy plays in his own views and in his alliances with those he relies on.[40] The appeal of Scalia for Trump is undoubtedly that Trump is drawn to precisely the most belligerent conservative man on the Supreme Court of the United States, something of a bully, who would not allow women justices on the Court to speak without constantly interrupting them.[41] This is what Trump believes to be good judging – not ethical impartiality and fairness to minorities, but a machismo that, despite Scalia's personal friendship with Ruth Bader Ginsberg, discounts any claim to gender equality or gay rights or responsible gun control as unmanly. Unmanly because they resist the gender codes of patriarchal manhood.

But the most dramatic confirmation of the hold patriarchy continues to have on the American polity and psyche was the rejection of Hillary Clinton's challenge to the patriarchal gender binary and hierarchy – the sheer chutzpah of her not only running for president but coming so close to victory. As we watch the memory of her near-victory fade and the blaming of her take over, as we hear the adjective "shrill" now transferred to Elizabeth Warren and Nancy Pelosi, it is clear to us that something systemic is at work. The obsessional focus on matters (Clinton's email server as Secretary of State) that did not bear the fair weight they were supposed to have is further evidence that the argument was spurious. What it was ostensibly about is not what it was really about.

Why is a woman who stays with a flawed man the subject of such rancor? Why were voters angry at her rather than at Trump who cheated on and then left two wives? What about Trump's marital history? Why was that never mentioned? Once again, only patriarchy can account for this darkening of ethical and political intelligence.

Why was Clinton's competence celebrated when she was Secretary of State, but not when she was seeking the presidency? Is it simply that, as Secretary of State, she occupied her proper role in the gender hierarchy below a man whom she was serving (President Obama)? Was it that Americans would not acknowledge her competence when she ran on her own? When she was seeking power rather than serving others (though conceivably her move to become president could have been seen as serving the American people, which is how Obama cast himself, as did Bill Clinton). Is the gender hierarchy this powerful in American culture? More forceful and blinding than we had supposed? The failure to treat Hillary Clinton fairly, the failure to see her, one might say, as a person in her own right, perhaps more dramatically than any other point, shows the limitations of American democracy and the hold patriarchy continues to have on the American psyche.

4 Why Now?

Why the resurgence of patriarchy now? Why did it have the appeal it did? Why did its appeal mute resistance?

Nothing has been more prominent in the populist politics of Trump than anger verging on, if not spilling over into, violence. Where is this anger rooted? What is driving it?

ANGER, VIOLENCE, AND THE SHAMING OF MANHOOD

Shame is the link between men's anger and violence, the psychiatrist James Gilligan observes in *Violence: Reflections on a National Epidemic*.[1] Shame is the proximal cause of violence, he writes, the necessary although not sufficient condition for violent behavior. To put it succinctly, when manhood is shamed, violence is imminent.

Listening to Trump's campaign rhetoric, it was hard to miss the prominence of concerns with honor and shame. In his promise to make America great again, he played on people's fears of being laughed at. He would restore American men and in particular white American men to a position of superiority. His appeal was to the white men whose jobs had gone overseas in various trade agreements, who were committing suicide in unprecedented numbers, who had become addicted to opioids and alcohol, the men who weren't for the most part filling our prisons but who were at home with their white wives, who also felt shamed and were living with despair – they were Trump's base. Trump's promise to make America great again was a thinly coded message: he would make America patriarchal again by restoring white men to what had been their unquestioned position of superiority over men of color and immigrants, not to mention gays, transgender people, and women.

Why in 2016? Because for the past eight years a black man had been president, a man who had distinguished himself by opposing the war in Iraq, who as far as we know did not own a gun, who had married a

woman who was at least his equal, whose policies were guided by an ethic
of care. And because in 2016, Americans for the first time were actually
facing the prospect of a woman becoming our commander in chief.
On both counts, democracy was outpacing patriarchy, which was in
danger of becoming truly a relic, archaic, a thing of the past.

It was Jim Gilligan who drew our attention to the way in which Hitler
came to power on the campaign promise to "undo the shame of
Versailles," who underscored the power of shame in marshaling support
for the misguided war in Iraq (Obama being one of the very few who
were impervious to the appeal). George W. Bush had taken the country to
war in Iraq on grounds that were demonstrably false but fueled by
the promise to undo the shaming of American manhood by the attacks
of 9/11, just as the attacks themselves, as Jim Gilligan also pointed out,
were explained by Osama Bin Laden as payback for over eighty years of
humiliation and degradation that the Islamic world has suffered at the
hands of the West.

In this light, it is easy to see how Trump came to power on the promise
to undo the shaming of American manhood, by which he meant white
American manhood. And given this, it's not so surprising that
white married women, meaning the women who live with men who
feeling shamed are prone to violence, also gave a majority of their votes
to Trump, who, perhaps in their eyes, offered to remedy their situation.

Backlash is something we are familiar with, so why in 2016 did it
come as a surprise? Why do we suddenly find ourselves talking about a
potential for fascism as something that not only happened in Germany
and Italy in the twentieth century but could happen here in America now?
Why rereading Margaret Atwood's *The Handmaid's Tale* did it no longer
read like science fiction but as depicting a world we are conceivably four
steps away from?[2]

In *The Deepening Darkness* we showed that the political fascism of
Mussolini in Italy and Hitler in Germany was devoid of serious political
theory. "The fist," as a fascist militant asserted in 1920, "is the synthesis of
our theory."[3] What made Hitler's fascism so psychologically powerful was
that his appeal to Aryan pride resonated so strongly with the Germans
who elected him that it overrode and suppressed the religious and philo-
sophical culture with its appeal to feelings of guilt and respect for human
rights, perhaps most brilliantly expressed in the moral philosophy of
Immanuel Kant. In Hitler's Germany, the blinding force of patriarchal
gender codes in politics was never more palpable, fueling a quasi-political
religion to which people surrendered their consciences.[4]

Hitler, himself, was a deeply shame-ridden man. He mobilized
Germans as Captain Ahab mobilized his whaling crew in Melville's *Moby*

Dick: by appealing to their manhood. If this could happen in one of the most advanced cultures of Europe presumably it could happen anywhere. But why this threat in America now?

Undoubtedly, the most brilliant analysis of fascist politics is Hannah Arendt's *Origins of Totalitarianism*.[5] Arendt had observed the rise of fascism at firsthand as a student of Heidegger. What she found common to both German fascism and Soviet communism was the anti-scientific certitude of, in Hitler's case, racist science and, in Stalin's case, the laws of history. Both rationalized the authority of the leader, the *Führer*, as a kind of priest-god, uniquely attuned to apodictic scientific and historical truth, including whatever murders such truth required.[6] This political psychology required the suppression of any voice that might reasonably challenge its authority, a challenge all the more threatening because its claims were so untenable, both scientifically and ethically. Arendt highlighted this feature as central to totalitarian politics in the passage we chose as our epigraph and have quoted previously, but its importance is such that we quote it again because it so aptly characterizes the Trump supporters.

> The ideal subject of totalitarian rule is not the convinced Nazi or the convinced Communist, but people for whom the distinction between fact and fiction (i.e., the reality of experience) and the distinction between true and false (i.e., the standards of thought) no longer exist.[7]

By asking Why now?, however, we ask a further question: What keeps people from distinguishing fact from fiction – that is, from acknowledging "the reality of experience"? What undermines "the standards of thought"? Arendt's answer is terror; the sheer power of fear in the face of real danger can make it difficult for people to see what is real or to think clearly about what we are seeing. As an additional feature of totalitarian regimes, propaganda is deliberately designed to confuse people's ability to think about their experience.

We have seen these strategies deployed by Trump and Bannon. Propaganda is another word for fake news, and fear of Mexican immigrants and Muslim terrorists has been deliberately stoked along with the fear of being shamed: laughed at or taken advantage of by others.

There is a comparably illuminating analysis of the underlying psychology of fascism in the study by T. W. Adorno and his colleagues of the authoritarian personality.[8] Adorno's work was inspired by the psychoanalyst Erich Fromm, who introduced the concept of authoritarian personality in an effort to understand how fascism could have arisen from and taken over German democracy.[9] Like Arendt and Adorno, Fromm – a Jew – had fled his homeland, and then tried to make sense of what had happened. Why had Germans come to fear the freedoms of democracy, in particular its respect for the inalienable right to conscience, and ceded ethical judgment to "irrational overestimation and admiration"[10] of a totalitarian leader?

Fromm observes the role of gender in Hitler's rhetoric: "[T]he satisfaction the masses have in domination;"[11] as Hitler puts it, is "[l]ike a woman ... who will submit to the strong man rather than dominate the weakling."[12] There is a psychological disorder here, Fromm argues, a disorder in love, because "Love is based on equality and freedom."[13]

Adorno's study is of the American authoritarian personality. Like Arendt, he does not explicitly bring patriarchy into his analysis; but, the F-scale (the potential fascism scale) measures a patriarchal psychology with its emphasis on submission and aggression, opposition to the subjective, stereotypes of power and "toughness," destructiveness and cynicism, projection of dangerous impulses onto others, and exaggerated concern with sex (including homophobia).[14] Authoritarian psychology is marked by hierarchy (as opposed to equality),[15] and by a rigid gender binary,[16] by moralism,[17] as well as by an intolerance of ambiguity,[18] and by an associated belief in pseudo-science.[19] Bob Altemeyer's more recent confirmation and elaboration of this psychology identifies three features of "right-wing authoritarianism," namely, authoritarian submission, authoritarian aggression, and conventionalism.[20]

Neither Arendt nor Adorno, among the very best political scientists of their time, see, let alone acknowledge, the role gender plays in the phenomena they otherwise investigate so trenchantly. We need to understand how democratic peoples sometimes espouse what William James called in his own time American "stupidity and injustice," arising from what he called an ethical "blindness with which we all are afflicted in regard to the feelings of creatures and people different from ourselves."[21] When James wrote, as was also true in the later time of Arendt and Adorno, gender was marginalized in serious intellectual discourse, and he did not investigate the role gender plays in our "blindness."

Woolf sees it because, as her novel *Mrs. Dalloway* makes quite clear, she connects the plight of the traumatized war veteran Septimus Warren Smith with the plight of Mrs. Dalloway, who in her own way has sacrificed her life to the demands of the patriarchy.[22] Septimus suffers from flashbacks of the death of his beloved friend Evans; Mrs. Dalloway suffers from the death of herself. It is only in the very last word of the novel that we learn her name, Clarissa. Having become in society's terms a good woman, she, too, is haunted by flashbacks, that take her back to the moments when she did not follow her heart.[23] Woolf had been sexually abused by her older half-brother, which can at least in part explain why she was able to see so clearly the links between patriarchy and fascism. But it was her genius as an artist that led to her insights into how the aftermath of trauma (whether war trauma or sexual trauma) and the dynamics of gender play out in the lives of both women and men.

Unreal divisions between thought (masculine) and emotion (feminine) feed into unreal loyalties, as Arendt and others have seen.[24] They damage our ability to register within ourselves the reality of our experience and to pick up the experience of others. Hence we lose touch with the distinction between fact and fiction. Advances in neuroscience have shown clearly that in the absence of brain injury or trauma, our thoughts are connected to our emotions; in the words of Joseph LeDoux, our brain is an "emotional brain."[25] Or as Damasio, also a neuroscientist, explains: in our bodies and our emotions we register our experience from moment to moment, picking up the music or the feeling of what happens, which then plays in our minds and thoughts.[26] When we split thought from emotion and separate our minds from our bodies, we retain the capacity to think deductively and solve logical problems, but we lose touch with the voice of experience. Our ability to think inductively, to reason from experience is challenged, and we become unable to think intelligently about what on the basis of experience we know.

Thus we can extend both Arendt's understanding of totalitarianism and Woolf's implication of patriarchy in fascism by showing the mechanism that undermines what otherwise are basic human capacities: our ability to register the reality of our experience and the emotional intelligence that enables us to read the human social world accurately. It is the initiation into patriarchy, and more specifically the internalization of its gender binaries and hierarchy, that, like placing a stick in a wheel, impedes or brings to a halt our capacity to function as human beings. From research on trauma we now know that the splitting of reason from emotion, like the separation of the self from relationships, rather than being markers of progress or development are manifestations of injury or trauma. From research on development we have come to see that the induction into patriarchy with its gendered splits and hierarchies, bears some of the hallmarks of trauma: a loss of pleasure and a change in voice.

A growing chorus of voices within the human sciences – neuroscientists, evolutionary anthropologists, primatologists, and experts on trauma along with developmental psychologists – now make it plain that the claims of patriarchy are based on false authority. The nuclear family was not the original human family despite the dioramas in natural history museums that would have us see it as such; the hunting hypothesis with its "sex contract" (whereby a man as hunter provides for his mate who repays him with sexual fidelity so the provider can be sure that the children he supports will carry his genes) has been discredited, along with the assumption that the best possible environment in which to raise children is one of continual and exclusive maternal contact, meaning a full-time, stay at home mother.[27] The research of Michael Tomasello and others has shown that children flourish best when they have at least three relationships that convey the clear message: you will be cared for no matter what. It is not the mother per se but the assurance of being cared for that is essential.[28]

As the evidence mounts, the question becomes: why do we hold onto what we know is not true? How do we become blinded to reality, incapable of thinking intelligently, wedded to patriarchy, vulnerable to fascism and totalitarian leaders? For Arendt, false authority is the nerve of totalitarian politics. It is this phenomenon in Trump's politics and its appeal for many Americans that suggests fascism may be now more alive in our midst than many of us would like to believe or can be brought to admit.

The heart of its darkness is not merely falsifying but killing ethical experience, which rests on empathy and respect for the equal dignity of all persons. Patriarchy fuels this dynamic, this blindness in our personal and political lives. As Americans, we are loathe to admit – to see and acknowledge that this is not new in our politics, which have never been immune from this threat.[29] Drawn as we are to the authority of our Founders, we might well be inspired that James Madison, the leading Founder, so clearly saw this potential in democratic group psychology. What he called "faction," was, in his view, the central challenge to constructing a constitutional democracy that would respect human rights.[30] It is extraordinary that a form of constitutional originalism, which fails even to see this challenge and its significance, should now, in Trump's admiration for Justice Scalia, be the standard for appointment of justices to the Supreme Court.[31]

THE RESURGENCE OF PATRIARCHY

It is by now a familiar feature of recent American history that presidential elections have been won by a reactionary politics that sets out to limit and even reverse what had been celebrated as important ethical and constitutional advances. The resistance movements of the 1960s and 1970s – the civil rights movement, the anti-war movement, second-wave feminism, and the gay/lesbian liberation movement – form the backdrop against which the election of 2016 can best be understood.

All these resistance movements signify ethical advances because all of them rest on democratic values, including the value placed on free and equal voice. For example, resistance to the Vietnam War began among soldiers who in protesting the injustice of the war they had been called upon to fight, were resisting the authority of the patriarchs, the fathers, the so-called best and the brightest who had led the country into the war.[32] The civil rights movement, led by the Reverend Dr. Martin Luther King, Jr, challenged racist injustice not through a resort to violence, but through an ethical voice that his father had opposed – a voice which in advocating nonviolence challenged the canons of patriarchal masculinity.[33] Second-wave feminism and later gay rights directly challenged patriarchal norms of sexism and homophobia.

We are by now familiar with the reactionary politics of leaders of the Republican Party, who sought to limit or reverse these ethical advances. In response to the civil rights movement and its legislative successes (the Civil Rights Act of 1964 and the Voting Rights Act of 1965) and the growing credibility of the anti-Vietnam War movement, Nixon initiated the war on drugs, continued by Reagan and both Bushes. Nixon's advisor, John Ehrlichman, acknowledged the racist basis for Nixon's war on drugs. The policies were never based on a coherent view of the harms of drug use (which criminalization exacerbated). Rather the war on drugs drew support from the racist associations that Ehrlichman frankly spelled out, and the anti-drug laws have been disproportionately enforced against people of color. The consequence over time was mass incarceration, which disproportionately imprisons people of color. The harm is not only from criminal laws that are themselves substantively unjust (laws that themselves exacerbate harms), but from appalling prison and jail conditions, including those recently made public in the exposure of what was going on in New York City's Rikers Island jail.[34] The conditions of imprisonment clearly do not reform; if anything, they foment recidivism. Since those imprisoned, overwhelmingly people of color, when released, lose their right to vote and have little access to employment, the criminal justice system has been aptly named by Michelle Alexander as "the new Jim Crow."[35]

How could this happen? All the ethical movements of the mid-twentieth century were forms of resistance to patriarchy. Was it because their resistance was so unprecedented? In his presidency, Barack Obama embraced and sought to deepen and expand democratic values, including a feminist ethic of care that prominently increased access to health care to cover 20 million more people.[36] Obama's resistance to patriarchy elicited a reactionary politics not only in the Republican Congress, which set out deliberately to oppose his policies, including those they otherwise had agreed with, but in the campaign and election of Donald Trump, a man whose political ambitions were evidently, at least in part, modeled on his admiration for Nixon.[37] To understand how and why this happened in the 2016 election, we turn to the central theme of the Trump campaign, Make America Great Again – an appeal to America First nationalism that can be placed in the larger framework of the political psychology of fascism.

Trump's brand of nationalism was developed by his campaign advisor and, eventually, manager, Stephen K. Bannon, a man who, like Trump, has always liked a fight (both men went to military schools). Like Trump, Bannon "had cycled through multiple marriages and was rich, brash, charismatic, volcanic, opinionated, and never ruffled by doubt."[38] Unlike Trump, however, Bannon has strong intellectual interests and loves to read and discuss ideas. There is no doubt he is a man of strong convictions leading to a distinctive form of disruptive conservative polit- ics well outside the mainstream of American conservative thought and practice. Bannon has always sought out and celebrated (through making documentaries) counter-culturally conservative men or women (Ronald Reagan and Sarah Palin) who might carry his populist nationalism to power.[39] Through Breitbart News, which he ran after Breitbart's death, he supported Trump's candidacy and excoriated his opponents. In particular, he promoted conservative groups that aimed to discredit Hillary Clinton,[40] including the book *Clinton Cash*, which was apparently influen- tial in discrediting Clinton for alleged conflicts of interest.[41]

Breitbart was substantially funded by the wealthy, conservative Long Island family of Robert Mercer, notably his daughter Rebecca Mercer, who would also financially support the Trump campaign.[42] One of Bannon's leading allies was then Senator Jeff Sessions, who joined Bannon at Breitbart in their successful opposition to Republican attempts at immigra- tion reform, a success which led Bannon and Sessions to appreciate the political force of ground-up populism. Sessions, who became Trump's Attorney General, was one of the first senators to support him.

Bannon's nationalism is rooted in his family's traditional Irish Catholicism, which opposed reforms within Catholicism:

> As the Roman Catholic Church took steps to modernize after the Vatican II reforms of 1962–1965, the Bannons were drawn in the opposite direction, toward a deep connection with Church tradition and the mysteries and beauties of its ancient rituals. After Pope John Paul II permitted limited use of the Latin-only Tridentine Mass, which was banned by the Second Vatican Council, the older Bannons became Tridentine Catholics. "When [the Roman Catholic Church] first started allowing it in the mid-eighties," Steve Bannon recalled, "we left our parish that we'd been in for years and went and joined St. Joseph's in Richmond, which offers a Tridentine Mass."[43]

The Bannons sent all three of their sons to Benedictine, the private Roman Catholic military academy in Richmond, which "stood as a bulwark against a liberalizing world":[44]

> "We were a right-wing military Catholic high school," said John Pudner, a childhood friend of the Bannons who grew up two blocks away and attended Benedictine. "We were very small, just four hundred kids at a time. It was a very close-knit community . . . We were all taught that Western civilization was saved five hundred years ago in Spain, when Ferdinand and Isabella defeated the Moors," said Pudner. "The lesson was, here's where Muslims could have taken over the world. And here was the great stand where they were stopped. We were taught a worldview: 'This is how Catholicism survived.' I think that shaped all of us. But what Steve took away, I think, was a belief that you've got to be willing to identify the threat. When we were growing up, the threat was the atheist Soviet Union . . . Now Muslims are trying to blow us up."[45]

By every account, Bannon prized – even relished – this identity; he was a born believer with a quickness to take passionate sides. More often than not, he was the one who would throw the first punch with a group of rich prep schoolers. But he was also taken with the much larger idea, imparted at Benedictine that Western civilization had to be constantly and vigilantly defended against shadowy, shape-shifting enemies, and he was prone to viewing contemporary struggles, even minor ones, as critical junctures of historical significance. This fed a grandiose image of himself as someone galloping to defend not just a class but Western civilization itself.[46]

Bannon regards his religion, socially conservative pro-life Catholicism, as the core of what America is, now very much under threat by Islam in general and Islamic terrorism in particular as well as by American secularism.[47] While Bannon is interested in history, he is captivated by academically marginal cyclical theories of history in which cataclysm and war are likely, if not inevitable.[48] For a man interested in history, he has no interest in the role the Crusades played in fueling religious wars on Islamic powers and the reactionary impact these wars had on Islam, leading to the Ottoman Empire's conquest of the Christian Empire of Byzantium and its nearly successful conquest of the rest of Europe.[49]

In Bannon's imagination, America is now under threat in the same way Vienna was once under threat by Islamic armies at its gates. The analogy comes to mind of the way Hitler's anti-Semitism transformed victims into aggressors, requiring the pre-emptive strike of genocide. Bannon shaped and stage managed a political campaign that prominently featured not only attacks on illegal immigrants, but on immigrants from

Muslim countries (all "terrorists"). That these appeals had the populist resonance they had bespeaks the forces at work in Trump's victory. As in the electoral success of Brexit in Britain and the rise of far right movements in Europe, anti-immigrant sentiment was the heart of the populist nationalism that swept Trump into power.

Bannon's America First nationalism is rooted in patriarchy, and exemplifies as well the three ingredients of authoritarianism – authoritarian submission, authoritarian aggression, and conventionalism. Its conventionalism is its now visibly anachronistic holding onto American cultural patriarchy as the measure of all good things in the American experiment; its submission is to the leader who both embodies patriarchal values and can defend them; and its aggression is against anyone who would contest or dilute these values. There is a conviction in people such as Bannon that, with the collapse of traditional patriarchal authority in American religion and politics, we face moral nihilism. As patriarchal supports collapse or are under threat – the shaming of manhood elicits violence against scapegoats (in Bannon's case, Islam as a religion). That both Bannon and Trump like fighting – as the mark of what it is to be a man – makes psychological sense. It may well be that Trump – a secular New Yorker – is not exactly the patriarch Bannon would have ideologically preferred, but he is patriarchal enough and, what is more important to Bannon, politically successful. In Trump, Bannon found the vehicle he had long been seeking, the means to realize his ideological dream.

This account explains the potent role of shaming and honor, the appeals to a certain construction of manhood and the sanctioning of violence in Bannon and Trump's politics. It offers a way of understanding why its unapologetic misogyny had the appeal it did in the attempt to reestablish the shame culture of patriarchy and cover over or marginalize the guilt culture of concern with harming others or trampling the rights of persons. Hillary Clinton – the first credible woman candidate for president in American history – was the object of this misogyny, which took the form of holding her to the double standard from which men have always been exempt – so that every mistake must be fatal, and every success degraded. Bannon had long been involved, as were the Mercers, in supporting groups and authors attacking Clinton.[50] Even the Access Hollywood tapes, in which Trump boasted of his sexual abuse of women,[51] were countered in the second debate by the presence of a panel of women alleged to have been sexually harassed or exploited by Bill Clinton. Their visual presence at the debate implied an equivalency and had the effect of making Hillary appear culpable for her husband's sexual behavior. It was Bannon who had engineered the panel.[52]

Bannon comes from a working class background (as did the other boys at Benedictine). He carried his sensitivity to the shaming of class inferiority in the United States through his upwardly mobile life and powerfully brought it to bear on Trump's campaign, uniting his social conservatism with feeling for the working class, against "rich guys protecting their tax breaks."[53] Trump himself comes from a very different background though not without the sense of being shamed by his better educated and more established Manhattan peers (Trump was from Queens). What is remarkable is that someone like Trump with Bannon's advice succeeded in bringing the angry voice of shamed manhood to bear on issues that had resonance for many working class white men and women. Trump could not have done this alone. The quite visible use of misogyny by Trump against Clinton, however, may well have been decisive. Trump stoked the rage of working class men and women but a rage coming from experiences of injustice that Trump, unlike Clinton, stood little chance of taking seriously, let alone rectifying. Thus, the irrationalism of the election's political psychology. It was necessary to reject Clinton not on the grounds of her policies, but rather on account of her gender, which rendered her unacceptable as president. Hence the personal nature of Trump's attacks on her: she was crooked, she was nasty. It didn't matter if it was true or false. She was not a good woman, and besides, as a woman, she was weak, prone to illness and fainting, incapable of being our leader.

TRUMP'S APPEAL

Trump is certainly neither Hitler nor Stalin, and he wholly lacks the terrifying grandeur of Ahab. What Marx said of Napoleon I and Napoleon III might be said of Trump: history repeats itself, "[o]nce as tragedy, then as farce."[54] Trump's rather astonishing self-certainty – his lack of interest in critical thinking about policy and his appeal to American nationalism – aligns him with the politics of fascism. At the heart of this appeal is the darkness of American patriarchy. All its tell-tale markers are present: the sensitivity of manhood to shaming, pseudo-science, propensities to violence against outsiders, all triggered by a gender binary and hierarchy now more under threat than ever.

With the presidency of Barack Obama and the potential presidency of Hillary Clinton, the gender binary and hierarchy were severely challenged. What was new about Trump was the authenticity of his patriarchal voice. It was the very visibility of patriarchy in Trump's politics – his political incorrectness – that was the psychological basis of his appeal.

If we had thought that patriarchy would calmly withdraw from the hegemonic role it had historically played in American politics and culture, we were wrong. Our surprise was at how viciously it reasserted its presence and power. No longer framed by democratic principles or rhetoric, patriarchy had itself become the frame. Trump's twitter feed became a daily barometer of where things stood on its scale of measurement.

Matters were not helped by the degree to which Hillary Clinton's campaign, whether intentionally or not, ignored this shift in the framework. There was something valiant about her soldiering on, articulating democratic ideals and values, while a systematic distortion had been fed into the sound system. It was impossible for her to be heard in her own right or on her own terms, because the terms themselves had been called into question. As if equality was for the weak and only losers were concerned about justice.

The question that haunts us is why couldn't this be talked about? Couldn't the shift in frame have been acknowledged? This is how the world looks when seen through the lens of democracy; this is how things look when patriarchy becomes the lens, when the gender binary divides everything into either masculine or feminine and the hierarchy elevates men who are in patriarchy's terms "real men" over other men and also over women, who in terms that are meaningful to men are divided into the good (the chaste and the selfless) and the bad. Would this be so hard to explain?

Why did gender for the most part remain the elephant in the room – never engaged directly in the way Barack Obama engaged race in his campaign? Why was the women's march held after rather than before the election? And why for that matter was Clinton herself, the first woman ever nominated for president by a major American political party, not counted by the organizers of the march among their foremothers?

HOW TRUMP'S POLITICS MUTED RESISTANCE

The papers of our students that we discussed in Chapter 2 reveal an awareness of an unconscious complicity with the forces that led to the election of a man they detest. Can we make psychological sense of this? Why was there not more resistance to Trump when resistance, as we now see, was clearly needed? Did his politics – or perhaps more accurately his patriarchal framing of political discourse – mute resistance?

To investigate this, we begin with the question: why has patriarchy lasted so long, or, as one of us (Gilligan) and Naomi Snider put it in the subtitle of a recent paper, "The Loss of Pleasure, or Why We are Still Talking about Oedipus" – "a tale of male violence and female silence."[55]

Drawing on the studies of the Harvard Project on Women's Psychology and Girls' Development and the new studies of boys' development and of men and the work with couples that followed in their wake, Gilligan and Snider argue that the earlier timing of boys' initiation into patriarchy (between the ages of four and seven rather than as with girls, at the time of their adolescence) affects the capacity for resistance. The initiation of boys into the codes of patriarchal masculinity at the time when they are entering formal schooling and learning about the way things are means that they are more likely to accept the gender binary and hierarchy as just how things are. Whereas girls being initiated later, when they are more cognitively sophisticated and have had more experience, can see the framework they are entering in becoming young woman not as how things are but as the way things are said to be. In fact, it was the awareness among girls of this gap between how things are and how things are said to be that aroused their suspicion and fueled their resistance. When what they were being told about the world, including about women and men, did not ring true to their experience, they had more resources to draw on in finding ways to stay with what they know.

Girls' later induction into the gender codes and scripts of patriarchal manhood and womanhood thus makes it easier for them to spot their falsity: that is, to see, for example the disparity between the way men and women are and the way they are said to be. It is easier for them to see the framework, to see that they are being asked to shift the framework – to see and to speak in a way that rings false to them but is widely taken to be true. Like the notion that men don't care about relationships and women don't know what they think. Summing up the ravages of patriarchy on the human psyche as they affect the lives of women and men, Gilligan and Snider observe that both men and women are pressed into falsity, men into "the pseudo-independence of masculine detachment"[56] and women into "the pseudo-relationships of feminine goodness."

Connecting the developmental studies of Gilligan and her colleagues with John Bowlby's studies of attachment and loss,[57] Gilligan and Snider came to a startling discovery: the gender ideals of patriarchal manhood and womanhood correspond to what Bowlby identifies as pathological responses to loss. Pathological in that they compound loss by standing in the way of relationships.

What's more, this observation prompted a further discovery: the initiation into the gender codes of patriarchy subverts the very capacities we rely on in order to live in relationships: that is, our ability to repair the ruptures that are an inescapable part of the everyday. Relationships are not steady states; in the normal course of things, we move in and out of touch with ourselves and with others, finding and losing and finding again. It is when loss becomes irreparable that love becomes tragic. But when boys in the course of becoming "boys" learn to shield their emotional sensitivity and cover their vulnerability, they become insensitive to the loss of connection or unable to register what they or others are feeling. Within the codes of patriarchal masculinity, the human need for somebody to "be there for you," as one of the boys in Niobe Way's studies put it, becomes "sissy-like," that is, girly or gay. Not a need that a real boy would acknowledge, or at least not in front of other boys or in public. Thus the move to repair ruptures in relationships, which requires registering the loss of connection, comes to be seen as unmanly and subjected to shaming.

For girls, it is an honest voice – the voice that says what they are feeling and thinking – that comes to be heard as unseemly. When a girl can't say what she is feeling and thinking without her voice sounding too loud, or angry, or stupid, or rude, or without being told she is crazy – that what she sees happening is not really happening – then her ability to repair ruptures in relationships is jeopardized. Her moves to repair in response to losing touch or feeling out of connection become subjected to shaming. Thus the relational capacities that are essential to love and also integral to democracy – our ability to live with integrity, in touch with ourselves and in connection with others – are at risk in the course of our initiation into the gender codes of patriarchy.

Gilligan and Snider conclude that patriarchy persists because it inflicts a loss of relationship and then renders that loss irreparable. Detachment or seeming independence on the part of men and what Bowlby terms "compulsive caregiving" in women, the selfless care-giving that has been held up as the epitome of feminine goodness, render relationships either seemingly unnecessary for men or as requiring a woman, paradoxically, to give up her desire to be herself in a relationship for the sake of having "relationships." For a woman then it becomes necessary for her not to be herself in order to be someone others want to be with.[58]

The Gilligan-Snider argument thus builds on Gilligan's previous exploration of the psychological consequences of the earlier timing of boys' initiation into patriarchy and the later timing of girls' initiation, including her explanation of why women's voices are essential to resisting patriarchy. Although resistance is in the interest of both women and men, women's participation is crucial because if women don't speak then it's likely that nobody will speak about the loss of relationship that patriarchy inflicts.

The key discoveries Gilligan and Snider came to arise from the realization that patriarchy although psychologically unstable (because it falsifies the reality of experience) is held in place because both the pseudo-independence and detachment of patriarchal manhood and the compulsive care-giving and self-silencing of patriarchal womanhood are defenses against the loss of authentic relationship that patriarchy inflicts. What's more, these defenses against loss render the loss of relationship irreparable. Hence the stability and the persistence of patriarchy, despite its psychological costs.

So it comes to pass that the losses patriarchy inflicts are not acknowledged, let alone resisted, but accepted as in the very nature of things. The consequence in men is that the shaming of manhood becomes incendiary and can justify violence against those who are perceived as the source of dishonor. In women, shaming leads to the silencing of voice, the very voices that might reasonably challenge the injustice of patriarchal demands. The consequence for both men and women – psychologically locked into patriarchal demands set by the terms of the gender binary and hierarchy – is impairment of their capacity to see, let alone repair, the relationships that patriarchy breaks. In effect, our capacity to love and feel empathy across the barriers imposed by the various iterations of the gender binary and hierarchy (the racism, sexism, homophobia, xenophobia, class stratification, and anti-Semitism, and on and on) is impaired or shattered.

The Gilligan-Snider thesis explains and clarifies both the larger question of how and why patriarchy has historically lasted for so long, and the more immediate question concerning the 2016 election: how and why was resistance muted? By deliberately or, we suspect, without a conscious thought, shifting the framework – by making patriarchy his frame, the lens through which he viewed the world – Trump managed, to everyone's surprise including his own, to undercut the resistance. This was the surprise of the election. Very few people saw it coming.

The larger historical question is posed by perhaps the most successful patriarchal imperialism in human history, the Roman Empire, a history we study at length in *The Deepening Darkness*. The Romans were highly patriarchal not only in their public but in their privates lives (for example, public speech by women was, following Greek tradition, largely silenced).[59] The central strategy of Roman imperialism focused on its enemies: divide and conquer. It was not enough for a successful imperialism that it create enemies where none existed (thus rationalizing Rome's unjust wars), but, to be successful, it must divide its enemies from one another so that they could not jointly resist such domination. To achieve this end, Roman patriarchy cultivated and encouraged patriarchy in its enemies, dividing them from one another (despite their common danger) so that they vied for supremacy over one another. What has made this strategy of divide and conquer so successful in the history of imperialism is what the Romans learned from the experience of their civil wars: it destroys democracy (thus Augustus ended the Republic and established the Roman imperial autocracy). Having learned this psychology from bitter internal experience, the Romans used it externally upon their enemies, encouraging divisions that made them easier for the Roman armies to conquer.

Learning from the Romans, the British used a similar strategy to divide Hindus from Muslims in India. The catastrophic effects include the violence of partition, the continuing hostilities between the two resulting states, and their internal problems (both states suffer from inter-religious violence that can be traced, in part, to the trauma of partition).[60]

The Gilligan-Snider thesis clarifies the underlying psychology of divide and conquer. The underlying assumption is that the cultures in question are all patriarchal. Consistent with the pattern of difference in the initiation of men and women into patriarchy, men embody the pseudo-independence, detachment, and aggressiveness of what has been called "the male role belief system," that is, the ideology of patriarchal manhood where being a man means being superior. It is a recipe for violence. Women then embody the compulsive care-giving, self-sacrifice, and voice-lessness of the subservient feminine role. Thus initiated, neither men nor women can resist patriarchy, but rather act out its terms. This renders them vulnerable to the Roman strategy of divide and conquer: the gender binary divides them from one another, and then conquers each separately by shaming the capacity to resist.

American women were historically vulnerable to this strategy, given the force of American racism which divided white from black women.[61] This has marginalized the power of feminism in American politics in contrast to the force it has had in other advanced constitutional democ-racies.[62] Even the legendary capacity of women to repair relationships has been impaired by their internalization of patriarchy, locking them into an experience of loss in personal relationships that they take to be in the nature of things. Under patriarchy women are put into an impossible position, because, as Hawthorne saw in *The Scarlet Letter*, the very qual-ities that enable a woman to see through the "iron framework of reasoning"[63] that upholds patriarchal privilege and power also disable her by leading her to appear in the eyes of the Puritans as an impure woman, a woman who has been adulterated. In this light, there was no way that Hillary Clinton could have been president.

Why has it been so easy for what Wendy Davis calls the "wolf whistle politics" of the Republican Party to divide women from one another? Davis was in the Texas legislature, and came to national attention when she held an eleven-hour-long filibuster to block more restrictive abortion laws in Texas. She later ran unsuccessfully for governor.[64] A single mother who went to Harvard Law School to advance herself, Davis speaks from experience when she describes the avalanche of distorted representations of her life and her arguments, all questioning how she could possibly be a good mother and also go to law school and support the right of women to choose abortions.

Texas "wolf whistle politics," mobilized largely by men to restrict abortions, uses a range of distorting stereotypes, imputing an unbridled sexual freedom and selfishness to women like Davis and suggesting that women who make more patriarchal choices than Davis have nothing in common with her. In their eyes, she is not a woman but "a slut."[65] Such politics could not have any traction if liberal arguments took on more seriously how patriarchy harms all women, as well as all men and everyone else no matter what gender, thus forging a sense of the common humanity we all share. Because patriarchal conceptions of gender remain so entrenched in our culture and also, as our student Adam notes, an unconscious force in our personal lives, we continue to feel the pull toward infidelity and silence even when our impulse and/or our conscious intention is to resist. Patriarchy silences the voices of women who align themselves with patriarchal men, but as such women also may know more starkly than anyone, it also silences the men.

The feminine icon of the self-sacrificing, care-taking women – the "Angel in the House" – is psychologically incoherent because as any care-taking person knows, a lot of self goes into caring (paying attention, listening, knowing what is needed, making decisions, taking action, being present). But so is the so-called independent man who relies on the silence of those who care for him to keep his need to be taken care of secret. The situation of the iconic patriarchal woman, the woman who in Bowlby's terms compulsively takes care of others in the hope that some-one, one day, will notice and take care of her, is aptly caught by the memorable chapter title "Doing Good and Feeling Bad," in Jean Baker Miller's *Toward a New Psychology of Women*.[66] Because to be seen as good while doing good, a woman must render herself as it were invisible.

Trump is if not the most extreme certainly the most vulgar embodi-ment of a patriarchal man to appear on the national political stage and yet he has a resonance for the men and women who elected him and have continued to support him. The strategy of divide and conquer could not have succeeded had it not conspicuously deployed gender to shame men sensitive to their loss of stature and drive the women who care for them into perceiving feminism as a threat. We see this not only in the white women who voted for Trump, but those who chose not to vote or wasted their votes mindlessly.

How could Americans come to be so divided from the better angels of our natures? How could we have elected as president a man who so openly flaunted democratic ideals and values? Trump has made visible the darkness of patriarchy, and seeing the depths of the problem, we cannot avoid the question: Where were women's voices? Or to put the question more politically, can a women's movement resist the strategy of divide and conquer?

WOMEN OF LIBERIA MASS ACTION FOR PEACE AND WOMEN WAGE PEACE (ISRAEL/PALESTINE)

In 1938 in *Three Guineas*, Virginia Woolf had taken up the question: can women help men prevent war? It was not by repeating men's words and following their methods but by finding new words and creating new methods that women could make a difference, she concluded.[67] In setting out the steps through which that might happen, she had in mind the situation of British women and more specifically, the daughters of educated men. Since then, in very different contexts, there have been actual movements of women acting in concert with one another to end armed conflict or war.

The Women of Liberia Mass Action for Peace is one example. It helped bring an end to the Second Liberian Civil War in 2003.[68] Another is Women Wage Peace, the Israeli/Palestinian, Jewish/Arab movement that was started by a group of women in 2014 following the Gaza War.[69]

Women of Liberia Mass Action for Peace began "despite Liberia having extremely limited civil rights. Thousands of Muslim and Christian women from various classes mobilized their efforts, staged silent nonviolence protests that included a sex strike and the threat of a curse."[70] In 2003, the women of the movement forced a meeting with President Charles Taylor, extracting:

> a promise from him to attend peace talks in Ghana to negotiate with the rebels from Liberians United for Reconciliation and Democracy and Movement for Democracy in Liberia. A delegate of Liberian women went to Ghana to continue to apply pressure on the warring factions during the peace process.[71]

Relying on the Liberian cultural taboo that a man who sees a woman his mother's age naked is cursed forever, the women came up with the following strategy: they would surround the place where the men were negotiating and keep them from leaving until they had reached an agreement to end the war by threatening to take off their clothes. Two hundred women, dressed in white, took up their positions and anytime the men moved to leave the negotiating room, the women would begin to undress. Some men tried to escape by jumping out of windows at the back of the building, but the women persisted, "staging a sit in outside of the Presidential Palace. They blocked all the doors and windows and prevented any from leaving the peace talks without a resolution."[72]

The women of Liberia thus became an effective political force, acting to bring an end to the civil war. They succeeded in bringing about an agreement after the peace talks had been stalled. Not only were the women, by joining with one another across various lines of divisions, able to achieve peace in Liberia after a fourteen-year civil war; they also helped to bring to power (in 2006) the country's first woman head of state, Ellen Johnson Sirleaf. When President Sirleaf first came to office, she made women's rights one of her priorities.[73]

The Nobel Peace Prize of 2011 was awarded to three women, two of whom played prominent roles in the Liberian movement, "President Ellen Johnson Sirleaf of Liberia – the first woman to be elected president in modern Africa – [and] her compatriot, the peace activist Leymah Gbowee"[74] (the third was Tawakhol Karman of Yemen, a pro-democracy campaigner). The *New York Times* reported:

> Most of the recipients in the award's 110-year history have been men, and Friday's decision seems designed to give impetus to the fight for women's rights around the world.
>
> "We cannot achieve democracy and lasting peace in the world unless women obtain the same opportunities as men to influence developments at all levels of society," said the citation read by Thorbjorn Jagland, a former Norwegian prime minister...
>
> In a subsequent interview, he described the prize as "a very important signal to women all over the world."[75]

The Israeli movement, Women Wage Peace, was inspired by women's movements in Northern Ireland and Liberia, where women of different faiths had united to help resolve the conflict. Inspiration also came from the Four Mothers movement, established in 1997, which was effective in prompting Israel's military withdrawal from South Lebanon. Organized in response to the 2014 Gaza War, Women Wage Peace was founded on the belief that the conflict could not continue, that there was a need for a new language, and that in accordance with UN Security Council Resolution 1325 women must be involved in every step of the way toward negotiating an agreement.[76]

At the very start of the movement, Rabbi Donna Kirschbaum took up the obvious questions: "Why Women and Why Now?":

democracy fits the tenor of our times, not patriarchy. And clearly it's
no wonder that our movement attracts women who wish to speak out
about a political agreement with the Palestinians (and do so by building mutually supportive relationships with other women). We are
women who believe that our voices deserve to be heard and that a
richly democratic culture could and should flourish here. Although our
movement has been criticized for being leftist (or not leftist enough),
or naïve or elitist, I am confident that we can answer these charges,
especially if we take [Carol] Gilligan's advice: learn to listen to the
conversation under the conversation. That is, learn to identify a
speaker's authentic voice often buried under the highly-scripted one
learned in a patriarchal culture that expects men and women to lose
"the basic capacity to relate."[77]

Women Wage Peace is now the largest grassroots peace movement in
Israel. In 2017, the movement organized a Journey to Peace, a two-week
journey through Israel that made its way to a tent of reconciliation in the
Judean desert where Palestinians can come without a permit. Three to
five thousand Palestinian women and five to ten thousand Israelis (the
estimates vary) and the men who joined them came together to reconcile
as the children of the Jewish and Islamic foremothers, Sarah and Hagar.
One of us (Gilligan) was among the four women who spoke in the tent, the
others being a Palestinian peace activist, an Israeli Jewish novelist, and an
Israeli Arab educator. The journey ended with a rally in Jerusalem, held in
a park near the Prime Minister's residence:

As it turned out, 30,000 people gathered in the park not far from the
Prime Minister's residence – the equivalent to 1.14 million in the US in
terms of percentage of the population. There was a stage and a program, speakers and singers, including Yael Deckelbaum and her band
playing the Prayer of the Mothers, the song she had composed for last
year's March of Hope, also organized by Women Wage Peace. Everything that was said was said both in Hebrew and in Arabic, sometimes
also in English. Among the speakers were Liora Hadar, a religious
woman from a settlement in Samaria, the northern West Bank, who
said "I believe change can come about if thousands of women decide
together they simply won't live under the conflict anymore;" Shachiv
Shnaan, a Druze former member of the Knesset who had lost his son
Kamil, a policeman, in the July Temple Mount attack. Three terrorists
had gunned him and a colleague down and injured a third person.
"We've suffered much," Shnaan said, "Israeli and Palestinian families
have lost their loved ones and we're left with wounds that cannot heal.
I'm here to say: we choose life. We're allowed to say it loud: we are
lovers of peace;" and Huda Abu Arqoub, Regional Director of the
Alliance for Middle East Peace, who said, "As a Hebron resident and

someone in contact with the people of Gaza, I'm here to tell you Gaza residents also believe in an end to the hostilities and are crying out for peace ... Wars don't have any winners. We're neither Palestinians nor Israeli – but mothers who'll do everything for a better future for our children."[78]

"A Call to Peace" was presented to the Knesset on the opening day of the winter session; a woman's Knesset was formed to bring a different voice into the discussion of the conflict. Along the route of the journey, which had continued for two weeks, the marchers had been joined by local and national politicians, including the right-wing mayors of cities such as Dimona and Tiberias, and also the mayor of Tel Aviv, who spoke at a rally held at a park in Jaffa.[79]

Are these plausible models for a resistance movement of American women and the men who would join them in resisting patriarchy? The women's march on the day following Trump's inauguration was the largest such march ever recorded, and there women joined with one another across various lines of division and also were joined by men, who, by the very act of joining a women's march, were resisting patriarchy. Three black women began Black Lives Matter, and women and men are now joining the #MeToo movement to break the patriarchally enforced silence about patterns of bullying, sexual harassment, and rape. In line with Woolf's observation that the public and the private worlds are "inseparably connected; that the tyrannies and servilities of the one are the tyrannies and servilities of the other,"[80] in line with her recognition that patriarchy and fascism are two sides of the same coin, the private and the public faces of tyranny, women's voices may indeed be crucial. As the UN Security Council resolution states, and for reasons that we are now able to understand more precisely, women can in fact help men prevent war and realize the great principles of democracy not by "repeating your words and following your methods but by finding new words and creating new methods."[81]

5 The Endgame of Patriarchy?

The therapy that proved effective for Jonathan Shay's traumatized Vietnam combat veterans turned on "communalization of the trauma."[1] Telling their stories to someone who listened and could be trusted to bring their voices into the community. One-on-one therapy was not sufficient. The therapy had to involve at least two other people, so that the betrayal of what is right would no longer remain a secret.

As Shay discovered, the veterans were suffering from moral injury, from a betrayal of what is right that had been officially sanctioned. In the words of one of the veterans: "In your heart you know it's wrong but here are your superiors telling you it's okay." Trust, the backbone of relationships and society, had been shattered and healing depended on its restoration. Shay goes to some lengths to describe a process of listening that struck one of us (Gilligan) as instantly familiar, because it was the approach she had taken in her research. And this was the first clue to the insight she came to: in the context of studying development, she had been witnessing moral injury. The initiation of children into the gender codes of patriarchy forces a betrayal of relationship, which in the eyes of children constitutes a betrayal of what is right. Yet, as in the case of Shay's veteran, confusion sets in when the children discover that this betrayal is culturally sanctioned and socially enforced.

Decades of research as well as our student papers provide vivid examples of this. Separations that once had been taken as part of growing up were recognized instead as signs of moral injury. It was in these terms that we came to understand Trump's election. His electoral victory had bestowed a cultural sanction on what had clearly been a betrayal of what is right: his cruel and contemptuous treatment of Mexicans, Muslims, women, immigrants, gold star families, and the disabled, not to mention his incitements to violence and disregard for the law. In their final papers written after the election, a third of our students, asking in effect "How could this happen," had turned inward to explore what they had come to recognize as signs of moral injury in themselves – signs they had

previously seen as badges of their manhood or womanhood. In writing
about their experiences, they were communalizing the trauma.

As one of the requirements for our seminar, the students divide into
groups and collaborate in writing and performing a short play, based on a
play included in the course readings which illuminated a central theme of
the class. For some years now, Beckett's *Endgame* has been one of the
plays we assigned.[2] Written at the end of World War II, it portrays Hamm,
blind and dying, his parents relegated to the trash (literally on stage in
trash cans), and his servant Clov, who is preparing to leave him. Endgame
refers to the final stage of a game such as chess or bridge, as for example,
"the knight is trapped in the endgame." We read Beckett's play as dramatizing the endgame of patriarchy.

In the final scene, as Clov prepares to leave Hamm, Hamm asks him to
say something before he goes: "Something . . . from your heart."

"My heart!" Clov says, and then in a toneless voice begins:

> They said to me. That's love, yes, yes, not a doubt, now you see how –
> . . . How easy, it is. They said to me. That's friendship, yes, yes, no
> question, you've found it. They said to me. Here's the place, stop, raise
> your head and look at all that beauty. That order! They said to me,
> Come now, you're not a brute beast, think upon these things and you'll
> see how all becomes clear. And simple! They said to me, What skilled
> attention they get, all these dying of their wounds. . .[3]

He then counters this voice – the voice of what they said to me – with his
voice: what he says to himself and in that moment we recognize yes, he
has a voice, although that voice has been held captive:

> I say to myself – sometimes, Clov, you must learn to suffer better than
> that if you want them to weary of punishing you – one day, I say to
> myself – sometimes, Clov, you must be there better than that if you
> want them to let you go – one day. But I feel too old, and too far, to
> form new habits. Good, it'll never end, I'll never go.
> (Pause.)
> Then one day, suddenly, it ends, it changes, I don't understand, it
> dies or it's me. I don't understand, that either. I ask the words that
> remain – sleeping, waking, morning, evening. They have nothing to say.
> (Pause.)
> I open the door of my cell and go. I am so bowed I only see my feet,
> if I open my eyes, and between my legs a little trail of black dust. I say
> to myself that the earth is extinguished, though I never saw it lit.
> (Pause.)
> It's easy going.
> (Pause.)
> When I fall I'll weep for happiness.
> (Pause. He goes toward the door.)[4]

This counterpoint of voices gripped our students in the fall following Trump's election. This passage from Beckett became the focus of the play they wrote. Over the years, students who signed up to write and perform a short play inspired by *Endgame*, had been inventive in a variety of ways. But it was only in 2016, that the seven law students who wrote the *Endgame* play zeroed in on the disparity between what was said to them and what they say to themselves.

They began with what they said to me:

"Tone it down, you need to fit in,"
    "Relax. Your voice is too strong when you speak. So – strident,"
    "When are you going to get a boyfriend?"
    "No homo,"
    "You're too emotional,"
    "Be a good girl. Not too good of a girl, but a good girl. Stay that girl – forever if you can."

They ended with what "I say to myself. . ."

MATTIE SAYS:	Knowing that no one was listening to how unhappy she [my mother] was – being forced to fight to re-enter a world she never wanted to be in in the first place, I wonder if this is what it means to be a grown up.
MATT SAYS:	It's senior year in high school.

The first guy I ever kiss outs me to my entire class
I experience a million emotions but relief floats to the surface
I'm a free man, right?
It's junior year in college
I start working out every day
If I can't be a real man on the inside
At least I can look like one on the outside.
I move to New York after undergrad, hoping to leave behind the self-hate I'd known back south
I flip on Grindr
"Masculine for masculine," "no fats, no femmes," and "straight-acting only"
Are my welcome to the city.
A seed is planted the first time a queer boy is told to act like a man
Even in spaces where women are absent, the sapling is nourished by the patriarchy
It grows into a vine
And we hang ourselves with it.

CLAUDE SAYS:	Lafayette Avenue and 9th Street, a block I have walked thousands of times ... I'm wearing a short skirt and carrying a large tote bag ... a man walking with his daughter, a girl of about 5 years old, tells me to pull my skirt down. I tell him my skirt is fine ... He crosses Lafayette ..., yelling at me about what a horrible example I am for children ... I'm stunned – What's the bad example? A woman in the street wearing a miniskirt? A woman talking back to a man? Or a father teaching his daughter that her body is shameful. That she should cover it, that men get to talk to women however they want, that strange men can police women's bodies?
ADAM SAYS:	My best friend is gay and I was probably the last to know ... It turned out he had another circle of friends I didn't even know about. A life where he could be true to himself and have real relationships. He never let the two worlds come together. Until they did. We try really hard to stay in touch now. It's harder than you can possibly imagine. I was his cover, I guess. I knew only what he wanted people to know about him, so we don't have much to talk about now. I don't know him really. I don't know my best friend.
TATIANA SAYS:	In Colombia where I am from there is a strong emphasis on beauty. That beauty sadly has transformed from a celebration of different forms of beauty to a world where every girl is expected to strive to look a certain way.[5] They had to give in to this idea of beauty to fit in or risk being outsiders ... My best friend, Diana ... and I were tomboys. We wore what we wanted, acted how we wanted ... Diana turned 15 before I did and the transformation seemed almost overnight. We were now in high school, and I was still a bit of a tomboy, but Diana had changed ... I could not relate. She sat with other girls that looked and acted like her and I found a new group of friends. At that moment I realize that what my cousins feared, becoming outsiders, was the same fear I embraced at the cost of losing my friend in order to not lose my self.
RICH SAYS:	Sitting with my older cousins listening to Hip Hop, I learned lessons on patriarchy and misogyny from the music ... But Ms. Lauryn Hill came along and taught me that everything wasn't about "That Thing" between her legs ... See despite the fact that I am supposed to be tough, I am

supposed to be relentless, I am supposed to be aggressive and assertive, and sometimes disrespectful and unworthy of her blessings, I need her.

ELIANA
SAYS:

Your voice is too strong, too strident when you speak. When you're a woman there is one acceptable tone you use, and that varies depending on the listener. A game you can't win but I have to keep trying to … I am the only person who must convince you every single time we meet that my voice is a voice worthy of being heard. And you tell me that there is a way to say what I want – the substance melting away – that I am not playing by the rules you expect by not serving coffee and answering the phone, by looking at you in the eye like an equal expecting to be heard. You are telling me that it doesn't matter what I say if I don't say it *nicely*. You ask more of me than of your male peers. You ask me to distance myself from my story, to strip my language of any indication that I, a woman, am speaking. My tone, my language, and my thoughts can't co-exist.

Following this, the students joined as a chorus and in concert repeated Clov's words:

I say to myself – sometimes, you must learn to suffer better than that if you want them to weary of punishing to you – one day, I say to myself – sometimes, you must be better than that if you want them to let you go – one day. But I feel too old, and too far, to form new habits. Good, it'll never end, I'll never go.

Then in unison they say, "We have to go." And walk out of the room.

Following Trump's election, resistance became essential. Repeating the patriarchal demands – the gender codes that had become part of their daily existence as law students – as well as those they had encountered in the course of growing up, they countered them with their own voices: what they say to themselves. Across differences in ethnicity, race, gender, class, and sexual orientation, our students had taken in the voices of patriarchy. And perhaps it was the awareness of the commonality of their struggles, heightened possibly by the experience of writing the play, that led them to join with one another in their determination to resist. "We have to go," they concluded.

In 2009 we had predicted the endgame of patriarchy: some final confrontation of the contradictions between democratic ideals and values and patriarchal privilege and power. In the fall of 2016, we found ourselves asking: was this in fact the endgame?

Having followed the struggles between democracy and patriarchy over time and across cultures, we were struck by how in the 2016 election, the concern with manhood had come to the fore. In *Manhood in the Making: Cultural Concepts of Masculinity*, David Gilmore shows the patterns of patriarchal manhood given the overriding concerns with honor and shame, to be universally fragile and fraught:

> In particular, there is a constantly recurring notion that real manhood is different from simple anatomical maleness, that it is not a natural condition that comes about spontaneously through biological maturation but rather is a precarious or artificial state that boys must win against powerful odds. This recurrent notion that manhood is problematic, a critical threshold that boys must pass through testing, is found at all levels of sociocultural development regardless of what other alternative roles are recognized. It is found among the simplest hunters and fisherman, among peasants and sophisticated urbanized peoples; it is found in all continents and environments. It is found among both warrior peoples and those who have never killed in anger.[6]

In summary, he writes that, "'being a man' does not come easily . . . Based on stringent standards of accomplishment in tribal affairs and economic pursuits, real manhood is said to be 'the Big Impossible,' an exclusive status that only the nimble can achieve."[7] Patriarchal manhood – bound to a rigid gender binary and hierarchy – is so psychologically fraught and difficult because it cuts against the range of emotions and thoughts that people as humans share. Its demands are such that the initiations into patriarchy (even those less extreme than the ones some of our students described) all bear the hallmarks of trauma.

Thus it makes sense that at times of transition, such as our own, when the cultural framework is shifting and becoming more democratic or less rigidly patriarchal, the frailties of manhood would surface. Shaming would be in the air – heightening the potential for violence, especially among white men, and also the awareness of the price men have paid for what is now recognized as toxic masculinity.

It is illuminating in this light to look at Shakespeare's four great tragedies and to notice that each bears the name of a man: Hamlet, Othello, Macbeth, and King Lear. Four men, distinguished by their sensitivity, their humanity, by being the noblest, the most loyal, the most sensitive and poetic, the most generous, become caught in the grip of a manhood that will lead to their destruction. Men who become caught in the demands of patriarchy: that Hamlet revenge his father's murder by killing Claudius; that Othello restore his honor by killing his putatively unfaithful wife and her lover; that Macbeth scale the heights of ambition and ascend to the throne by killing the king; and that Lear reclaim his patrimony, which he had given away to his daughters. All are chewed up in the struggle, which yields some of Shakespeare's most emotionally taut and evocative poetry.

King Lear, the last of the four plays, ends with the injunction: "The weight of this sad time we must obey/ Speak what we feel, not what we ought to say."[8] Beckett's play, *Endgame*, written in the wake of World War II, where he was a member of the French resistance, portrays a dying world. Lynn Nottage's play *Sweat* ends with the two young men, Chris and Jason, returning to the bar, where Oscar, the illegal immigrant, is caring for Stan, the maimed bartender. Jason says, "It's nice that you take care of him." Oscar responds, "That's how it ought to be." Stage instructions end the script:

> There's apology in their eyes, but Chris and Jason are unable to conjure words just yet. The four men, uneasy in their bodies, await the next moment in a fractured togetherness.
> Blackout.[9]

6 Maps of Resistance

Occupy Wall Street began five years before Trump's election. Many of its claims were taken up by Bernie Sanders in his campaign for the Democratic presidential nomination. He and Elizabeth Warren continue to tilt Democratic politics in a more progressive direction, arguing the need for redistributive justice.

Black Lives Matter also antedates Trump's election and has become the call for continuing struggle to resist the racism still entrenched in American society and culture. In this light it is hardly surprising that neither Trump nor Sessions, his attorney general, seem to notice or care about the structural injustice that American criminal justice continues to inflict on Black Americans and Latinos. Trump and Sessions are, after all, privileged white men, and their appointees to positions of political power have, to an astonishing extent in an increasingly diverse American landscape, been white men, and wealthy white men at that. For such men, Blacks, like Hispanics, are invisible or visible only as criminals whose claims to justice can be dismissed or ignored.

It is something of a tragedy for the cause of racial justice in the United States that during the long period of the largely Republican war on drugs, otherwise liberal whites and blacks were complicit in mass incarceration, as James Forman, Jr, argues in his recent book. Forman, a black scholar now at Yale Law School and the son of a leading civil rights advocate, shows how black leaders were drawn into complicity and makes his case on the basis of the black people he represented as a public defender in the District of Columbia. The power of the narrative is in his insistence that we see the issue from their point of view and recognize the harms that black politicians inflicted on them.[1] From our perspective, the assumptions behind such complicity, including "warrior policing,"[2] bespeak the power of patriarchy in black culture, dividing black politicians and police from blacks of lower stature. Following the election of

Barack Obama (who was critical of mass incarceration), we are now in a new period of black resistance.

There has always been a close relationship between racial and religious discrimination. Anti-Semitism was originally a Christian religious prejudice, but under Hitler and even earlier it was conceived as a racial prejudice. A pseudo-science of race rationalized the murder of six million European Jews.[3] Our constitutional traditions in the United States clearly condemn the expression of both religious and racial prejudice through law; indeed, the prohibition of religious discrimination was constitutionally explicit in the First Amendment of our Bill of Rights in 1791, in the first clauses of the Amendment, protecting free exercise and forbidding anti-establishment. In contrast, the prohibition on racial discrimination comes into our law only much later, in the Equal Protection Clause of the Fourteenth Amendment in 1868. Because the prohibition of religious discrimination is so constitutionally clear, historically and textually the Trump administration's ban on Muslim immigrants – engineered by Stephen Bannon – has been regarded as constitutionally problematic by our courts.[4] The ban was met with resistance as soon as it was announced and implemented, giving rise to the sanctuary movements at both state and local levels.[5]

Resistance to the Vietnam War began within the military and led in time, to something unprecedented in the history of imperialistic wars, namely, the withdrawal from a war that Americans had become persuaded was unjust and not in the national interest. It is very much a part of this anti-patriarchal story that the American judiciary had by the time of the Vietnam War developed a muscular protection for the freedom of speech of those who fundamentally challenged the justice of American institutions, including not only our racism (the civil rights movement) but also our racist imperialism (Vietnam), and later our sexism and homophobia.[6] What freed the ethical voices of the men who protested the war in Vietnam was their resistance to patriarchy – to the authority of fathers – and what made their voices possible and resonant was a protection for the right of free speech, which enabled them democratically, on the principle of equal voice, to address directly the American people without state censorship.

The open misogyny of Trump's campaign was followed on the day after his inauguration, by the Women's March (the largest such march in American history[7]). It is a striking feature of Trump's presidency that women are largely invisible, as if only men – white men and military and business men at that – are competent to rule, exactly what the gender binary and hierarchy require. Trump works from a rigid patriarchal script – winners versus losers, men versus women, unprecedented in recent American history. His administration shows outright hostility to the constitutional rights of women as they affect women's access to contraception and abortion,[8] and his judicial appointments are dictated by some of the most fundamentalist and deeply patriarchal religious citizens masking themselves as originalists (whose hero and indeed Trump's judicial mentor is the former Justice Scalia,[9] the most patriarchal and religiously sectarian of our recent justices of the Supreme Court).

There is every reason for women to be alarmed at such attacks on basic constitutional rights. Trump's war on women is inseparable from his war on an ethic of care that challenges the gender binary. Within patriarchy caring is gendered "feminine" and relegated to the private sphere rather than recognized for what it is: a social responsibility. It is only within the framework of patriarchy that the ethic of care and the activity of caring come to be seen as "feminine." A duty of women rather than as some of the caring men who resisted fascism described it, a "human obligation."

The women's movement of the 1960s and 1970s highlighted the issue of voice, which became key to second-wave feminism. Bringing women's voices into what had been called the human conversation, as one of us (Gilligan) had written, changes the voice of that conversation by giving voice to aspects of human experience that previously had been for the most part unspoken or unseen. In its challenge to patriarchy, second-wave feminism was aligned with democracy and the cause of equal rights, but it also implied a societal transformation: a different voice, a new way of speaking about the human condition and of framing moral conflicts.

Trump, a rich and white entrepreneurial man who prides himself on his deals, sees the world through the prism of his own business success. There is a case to be made, one Naomi Klein makes with great force, that Trump's Boys Club of economic advisors was involved both with the financial scandals leading to the depression of 2008 and with the oil industry's war on climate science.[10] As Klein sees it, a predatory business model has marginalized an ethic of care, including caring for people and for the environment.[11] As we would put the point, in the Trump Boys Club, such concerns are dismissed, as the gender binary requires, as feminine.[12]

7 The Power and Invisibility of Gender

In his recent book *Age of Anger*,[1] Pankaj Mishra argues that the rage underlying imperialistic and terroristic violence, both in the past and in the present (including the rage of fundamentalist Islamists), should be understood as rooted in an experience of humiliation, including humiliation at their backwardness in the face of Western economic abundance and consumerism.[2] What Mishra overlooks is that the forms of violence he describes also are rooted in patriarchy. We agree with Charles King, a recent reviewer of Mishra's book, who notes the gaping hole, the lacuna, at the heart of an otherwise powerful argument:

> If one were looking for a grand narrative to explain the particular forms of social mobilization exploited by Recep Tayyip Erdogan, Donald Trump, Vladimir Putin and Abu Bakr al-Baghdadi – with its admixture of machismo, self-obsession and thin-skinnedness – the most obvious one has something to do with gender. One need only be a self-aware theorist, not a feminist theorist, nor even a Freudian one, to see the entanglements of gender and sexuality with the political dispositions that Mishra catalogues so well. One wonders if an alternative genealogy – one that ran, say, from Sojourner Truth to Simone de Beauvoir, Emmeline Pankhurst to "Trump that bitch!" – might tell us something equally important about the modern condition: yet another age of angry men.[3]

Like the reviewer, we wonder at how so astute a social theorist and cultural historian as Mishra can have missed the issue of gender. The power of gender in democratic politics has always been that it is often invisible to the men motivated by its demands. And unjust wars – so harmful to the men who fight them – exemplify this dynamic quite starkly.

Our earlier discussion of the *Oresteia* (Chapter 1) showed how what we called patriarchy hiding democracy could lead to the contradictions in the argument of the play justifying, on the one hand, the Athenian democracy as a solution to the internal cycle of violence among Athenian citizens but,

80

on the other, rationalizing the unjust imperialistic wars that the democracy fought, ending, disastrously in its defeat. Athenian politics, in particular its decision to break the truce with Sparta and initiate the Peloponnesian War, illustrates the problem, as Thucydides in his classic history drily observes: "What made war inevitable was the growth of Athenian power, and the fear which this caused in Sparta."[4] In cultures still highly patriarchal, where the shaming of manhood justifies violence, the mere fact of inequality is an insult to male honor. Imperialistic wars – often wars between competing imperialisms (for example, World War I) – historically have this character. This may be a good reason to worry about Donald Trump, given his penchant to perceive insult from anyone who challenges his stature, as China now is doing on an international scale.[5]

Killing even in war is always psychologically fraught. As we now know, many soldiers refuse to kill.[6] What's more, the military training required to overcome the reluctance to kill, may itself induce post-traumatic stress disorder.[7] There is, however, another side to the psychology of men fighting in wars: the close bonds men form with one another when their manhood is not in question. As Sebastian Junger recently put the point: "What the Army sociologists, with their clipboards and their questions and their endless meta-analyses, slowly came to understand was that courage *was* love."[8]

It is the psychological force of patriarchy that, even in democracies, has enlisted men to fight unjust wars, often rationalized by perceived insults to manhood. Women can be complicit in this as some British women were in World War I, judging men unmanly when they resisted going to war on moral grounds. Many wars in human history are unjust both in their ends and means, and patriarchy – whether hiding in democracy or rationalizing autocratic regimes – can explain how both men and women, although clearly harmed by such wars, nonetheless are the instruments of such injustice.[9]

American experience illustrates why Americans in the age of Trump might and should worry about this, for we have historically not been exempt from what Thucydides observed as the propensity of Athenian democracy for fighting unjust wars. Consider in this light the Spanish-American War, World War I, the Vietnam War, and the War in Iraq.

Both the Spanish-American War and World War I must be understood in the context of the reactionary American politics of the post-Civil War period. In the late nineteenth and early twentieth centuries, America was at a moment of transition away from the anti-racism of the Reconstruction Amendments to an increasingly racist culture (supported both by politicians and by the Supreme Court in *Plessy* v. *Ferguson*[10]). Americans were attracted for this reason to European models of racist imperialism and to its own version of imperialism.[11] The North and South, which had fought a civil war ultimately over slavery and the cultural racism that rationalized it, buried its enduring ethical meaning. Instead, white men in the North and South found common ground in racist imperialist ventures abroad.[12] The rather extreme and populist racism of this period explains how Americans could be and were drawn into unjust imperialistic wars. America First nationalism – in which gender played a central role – was at the heart of this politics.

The appeals to gender that provoked Americans into imperialistic wars are shockingly visible in both the Spanish-American and Philippine-American Wars. Theodore Roosevelt's conflicted psychology of manhood played a pivotal role, as many scholars have observed.[13] Roosevelt had had to struggle to conform to then dominant conceptions of manhood; when he first appeared as a legislator in the New York Assembly, both his clothes and his manner and voice had led "the newcomer [to] quickly become known as 'Oscar Wilde,' after the famous fop who, coincidentally, had arrived in America earlier the same day."[14] After the deaths of both his mother and his wife at roughly the same time, he recovered his always fragile sense of manly self by a physically demanding period of hunting and riding in the American West.[15] He would later publish a multi-volume study about this, *The Winning of the West.*[16]

Roosevelt had no patience with and indeed turned on any man with "a certain feminine reticence." Accordingly, "he would write of Henry Adams and that other 'little emasculated mass of inanity,' Henry James, that they were 'charming men, but exceedingly undesirable companions for any man not of strong nature.'"[17] Roosevelt supported the Spanish-American War in rhetorical terms that William James, who had taught Roosevelt at Harvard, observed: "Not a word of the cause, – one foe is as good as another, for aught he tells us ... He swamps everything together in one flood of bellicose emotion." Of his former student, "he is still mentally in the *Sturm und Drang* period of early adolescence."[18] Roosevelt was a passionate anglophile, which can explain his modeling of American manhood along imperialistic lines, as well as his later advocacy for entering World War I on Britain's side. He urged his sons to serve, one of whom was killed.[19]

However, even during this period there was notable resistance to America's propensity to initiate unjust wars, as the examples of William James and also Mark Twain clearly show.[20] Both men had lived for long periods in Europe (James as a boy;[21] Twain as an established author[22]), and were accordingly skeptical of Theodore Roosevelt's America First nationalism. In contrast, Roosevelt, like other Americans of his period (including Woodrow Wilson[23]) publicly inveighed against recent immigrants from abroad because of their "hyphenated Americanism"[24]; the threat was "a flabby cosmopolitanism that led in turn to flabby patriotism."[25] Wilson was also a virulent racist, which informs his version of America First nationalism.[26]

Patriarchy both uses and enforces gendered stereotypes (here "flabby" immigrants) in rationalizing imperialistic wars. No one of this period better recognized "the stupidity and injustice" of such thinking than William James, who saw it, as we have noted, as feeding an ethical "blindness with which we all are afflicted in regard to the feelings of creatures and people different from ourselves."[27] And no one better debunked the anti-immigrant stereotypes than a feminist woman of this period, Jane Addams, who worked closely at Hull House with immigrants, finding among them "an unquenchable desire that charity and simple justice shall regulate men's relations."[28] Addams went on to connect what she had experienced with anti-militarism, putting "a limit to revenge."[29]

It was never clear that World War I – a war among competing European imperialisms – was just either in its ends or means, and our entry into that war was probably unjustified, as perhaps most Americans in that period believed. Once the United States declared war, the Wilson administration – sensing the illegitimacy of its decision to enter the war – turned on any opponents of the war, perhaps the most egregious violation of free speech in American history, as our constitutional law has now come to regard it.[30] The consequence was such outrage at Wilson's policies that Americans after the war refused to endorse the League of Nations. A resurgent America First nationalism made us an isolationist power.[31]

Wilson's mismanagement of the terms of peace – imposing extraordinary demands for reparations on a defeated Germany – so insulted Germans that "the shame of Versailles," as John Maynard Keynes warned it might,[32] fueled the rise of fascism in Italy and Germany, as well as in Spain and Japan. America's isolationism made politically impossible any reasonable attempt, of the sort Churchill urged on the British parliament,[33] to stop such aggressive nationalism before it was too late. It was too late, leading to the catastrophe of World War II.

Americans did clearly resist our entrance into World War I, and there was also resistance in Great Britain, notably, by the philosopher Bertrand Russell and by the literary historian, Lytton Strachey, as well as the poet and war hero, Siegfried Sassoon, both gay men, who for this reason might be considered to stand in a different relation to patriarchal masculinity.

Throughout his life, Lytton Strachey had endured taunts directed against his gender-bending conception and style of manhood. Perhaps for this reason, he was unmoved by the taunts directed at his ethical

petition for conscientious objector status. Strachey was in a position
reasonably to contest the terms of the patriarchal gender binary directed
against him: namely, that it was manly to fight but not manly to think for
oneself and to resist demands to use violence. To understand the depth of
Strachey's convictions on the matter, there was no chance, in light of his
poor health, of his being called up after compulsory military service had
been introduced in Britain (he was ultimately exempted on health
grounds). However, he objected to conscription in principle, had worked
for the No Conscription Fellowship, and, after the passing of the Military
Service Bill, registered as a conscientious objector. On March 7, 1916 he
appeared as a claimant for exemption before the Hampstead Advisory
Committee, and read the following statement:

> I have a conscientious objection to assisting, by any deliberate action
> of mine, in carrying on the war. The objection is not based upon
> religious belief, but upon moral considerations, at which I arrive after
> long and careful thought. I do not wish to assert the extremely general
> proposition that I should never, in any circumstances, be justified in
> taking part in any conceivable war; to dogmatize so absolutely upon a
> point so abstract would appear to me to be unreasonable. At the same
> time, my feeling that the whole system by which it is sought to settle
> international disputes by force is profoundly evil; and that, so far as
> I am concerned, I should be doing wrong to take any active part in it.
>
> These considerations have crystallized in my mind since the out-
> break of war. Before that time, I was principally occupied with literary
> and speculative matters; but, with the war, the supreme importance of
> international questions was forced upon my attention. My opinions in
> general have been for many years strongly critical of the whole struc-
> ture of society; and, after a study of the diplomatic situation, and of the
> literature, both controversial and philosophical, arising out of the war,
> they developed naturally with those which I now hold. My convictions
> as to my duty with regard to the war have not been formed either
> rashly or lightly; and I shall not act against those convictions, whatever
> the consequences may be.[34]

The committee rejected his claim. As a gesture of support, Strachey later
attended Bertrand Russell's trial for publishing an article advocating
acceptance of a peace offer recently made by Germany. Russell was
convicted and sentenced to six months' imprisonment in Brixton jail.[35]

As his statement makes clear, Strachey had come to believe that
Britain's willingness to go to war and its conscription policy had made
him "strongly critical of the whole structure of society." In an essay
"Militarism and Theology" published in 1918 he argues that this structure
had made the most terrifying and bloodthirsty militarism perfectly

acceptable to "the great mass of ordinary, solid, humdrum, respectable persons" who remain "the dominating force in human affairs."[36] The analogy explored by Strachey is the certainty underlying intolerance in religion. This makes exactly the right point about the role Roman patriarchy had played in shaping the Christianity of the West in its own image – the Christianity to which most of the antagonists (the Ottoman Empire excepted) in World War I appealed. Strachey had found his vocation as an analyst of the role patriarchy played in so shaping the conception of manhood and womanhood in Britain. He saw the ways that a patriarchal political psychology had made such violence and injustice acceptable. What Wyndham Lewis would parody in Strachey as "asserting his revolutionary pseudo-manhood"[37] was a profound investigation of what had made patriarchal manhood and womanhood so dominant in Britain and so dangerous, something a more conventional man like Lewis could not comprehend.

The poet Siegfried Sassoon came to the recognition of the injustice of World War I later than Strachey and his friends. Sassoon had fought with notable bravery in the war, but he, like his fellow soldier, poet, and friend, Robert Graves, was shocked that the war with its extraordinary level of casualties was allowed to continue. In the autumn of 1916, the government had been "offered peace terms on the basis of *status quo ante*," an offer rejected "by the 'Win-the-War' Coalition Government of Lloyd George."[38] Both Sassoon and Graves "could no longer see the War as one between trade-rivals; its continuance seemed merely a sacrifice of the idealistic younger generation to the stupidity and self-protective alarm of the elder."[39] Sassoon, unlike Graves, was moved to an act of public resistance, writing a letter to his commanding officer about why he could no longer serve:

> I am making this statement as an act of willful defiance of military authority, because I believe that the war is being deliberately prolonged by those who have the power to end it.
>
> I am a soldier, convinced that I am acting on behalf of soldiers. I believe that this war, upon which I entered as a war of defence and liberation, has now become a war of aggression and conquest. I believe that the purposes for which I and my fellow-soldiers entered upon the war should have been so clearly stated as to have made it impossible to change them, and that, had this been done, the objects which actuated us would now be attainable by negotiation.
>
> I have seen and endured the sufferings of the troops, and I can no longer be a party to prolong these sufferings for ends which I believe to be evil and unjust.[40]

It was at this point that Graves, who agreed with Sassoon's views but was concerned for his future (such a public statement – and Sassoon's letter had been published – even by a war hero, was cause for court-martial), intervened to get a medical board appointed. He himself testi-fied, "[t]hough conscious of a betrayal of truth" that Sassoon was not sane and required medical care.[41] Sassoon was sent for care to Craiglockhart where he was treated by the psychiatrist W. H. R. Rivers; he eventually returned to the front to fight with his men until the war ended.[42] Sassoon condemned what Graves had done: "[A] man of courage would not acqui-esce as [Graves] did." Graves could not remember his reply.[43]

In her novel *Regeneration*, Pat Barker explores Sassoon's experience with W. H. R. Rivers at Craiglockhart, bringing to life the relationship between these two remarkable men.[44] Rivers is haunted by his role as therapist of the war-resister. In a scene set in a church, he reflects on the stained glass windows portraying God's sacrifice of his Son, and Abraham's binding of Isaac: "[T]he two bloody bargains on which a civilization claims to be based. *The* bargain, Rivers thought, looking at Abraham and Isaac. The one on which all patriarchal societies are founded."[45]

He thinks of his own relationship to his father, a priest and a speech therapist. As a boy, Rivers had suffered from a stammer. His father would pay attention only to the stammer and not to what he said until "he'd dared suggest that Genesis was no more than the creation myth of a Bronze Age people."[46] The analogy is that as a military psychiatrist Rivers felt pressured to treat Sassoon's resistance as a disorder, rather than listening to what he said and taking seriously his objections to the war as a "senseless slaughter." In coming to see this, Rivers recognizes that this blindness is part of the bargain upon which all patriarchal societies are founded.

The most stark and instructive recent example in American history of what Rivers came to see about World War I – namely, its psychological roots in patriarchy – is the role that was played by what David Halberstam called "the best and the brightest" in initiating and continuing the war in Vietnam.[47] Halberstam's is an appalling narrative of how some of the best educated and most liberal minded American men, first in the Kennedy and then the Johnson administration, led us into and escalated this war on the basis of false assumptions. Both the background of the war and the character of the enemy were never critically examined by these other-wise intelligent men until the dimensions of their miscalculations and their lies to the American people became apparent. And even then, the appropriate response under the Nixon administration was unduly delayed, costing many more American and Asian lives.

The great moral problem for Americans posed by Vietnam started at the end of World War II when America faced the question of how to deal with its allies, notably Britain and France. Both were still wedded to forms of colonialism in Asia and elsewhere. President Franklin Roosevelt was quite hostile to colonialism, an issue that divided him from his greatest European ally, Winston Churchill, who was passionately committed to the British Empire in general and to its role in India, in particular.[48] Churchill was, however, defeated in British elections after World War II, and the new British government was to negotiate the end of British rule in India in 1947. France, however, tenaciously held on to its imperial rule in Indochina.

Facing a nationalist insurgency led by Ho Chi Minh, France withdrew from Indochina after being defeated by Minh's forces at Dien Bien Phu in 1954 during the Eisenhower presidency. The French had underestimated the nationalist appeal of an indigenous guerrilla resistance to a Western imperial power, and Americans were to make the same mistake. Basically, they took on France's mantle as an imperialist power during the administrations of Eisenhower, Kennedy, and, most disastrously, Johnson. How could Americans, whose own revolution had rejected British imperialism, make such a mistake?

The great problem for Americans was that Ho Chi Minh, though a nationalist was a Communist. In 1949, Mao's communists had taken power in China after defeating the nationalist forces of Chiang Kai-shek. Halberstam observes:

> The State Department knew the crunch was coming; in August 1949 it published its White Paper on China, a document designed to show that the fall of China was the fault of Chiang and that the United States had gone as far as an ally could go. What is remarkable about the White Paper in retrospect is the intelligence and quality of the reporting.[49]

America was, however, now in the midst of the Cold War with the Soviet Union, and Senator Joseph R. McCarthy, Republican from Wisconsin, in February 1950:

> made the first of his major, red-baiting Communist-conspiracy claims ... His timing could not have been better, in four months the Korean War began, and because the China experts were already in disrepute, the State Department did not heed their warnings on what American moves might bring the Chinese into the war. The warnings unheeded, the Chinese entered, and the anti-Communist passions against the China experts mounted. It was a Greek thing.[50]

By 1954, McCarthy was finished, "but the fears he had created would live long after him ... He had also made the foreign policy of the United States even more rigid, both then and later. The country would in particular pay the price for this in Vietnam. The legacy of it all was poison." Eisenhower, for example, "said in his inaugural in January 1953 that the French soldier in Indochina and the American soldier in Korea were fighting the same thing."[51]

Eisenhower's assimilation of the Chinese in Korea to Ho's insurgency in Vietnam was false. The Vietnamese were nationalists first, and despised the Chinese as imperialists as much as they despised Western imperial powers. Americans were always surprised, as were the French, that the Vietnamese fought on: "[T]he truth of the war never entered the upper-level American calculations; that this was a revolutionary war, and that the other side held title to the revolution because of the colonial war which has just ended."[52] Their movement in Vietnam was genuinely revolutionary and anti-feudal. It enjoyed the indigenous support of the Vietnamese people, who were prepared to endure losses and were resilient in ways that were not taken seriously either by the French or the Americans. They thought their superior technology would be, indeed must be, decisive.

The failure of American leaders – especially in the Kennedy and Johnson administration – to take the ethical claims of the Vietnamese people seriously is the heart of the American darkness during this period. As Chester Bowles wrote in his diary in "one of the most prophetic analyses of the new [Kennedy] administration":[53] "[I]t lacks a genuine sense of conviction about what is right and what is wrong."[54]

As we have seen, the issue of manhood has been implicit in critiques of American politics for some time, but never more vividly than in David Halberstam's analysis of what went wrong in regard to Vietnam. *The Best and The Brightest* is an indictment of men who had risen to the very top of the hierarchy; men whose claim to authority and judgment had been unquestioned, which became part of the problem. Because as patriarchal men, when their judgment was questioned, their manhood, contingent on being superior – the best and the brightest – was subjected to shaming. Rather than listening to the critics and ending the war, they responded, as patriarchal men are primed to do, with violence: that is by escalating the war in the name of defending their own and America's honor. That it had the opposite effect of disgracing both themselves and their country is a lesson that has come to feel very contemporary and urgent, which we examine in detail.

It was not a matter of liberalism (these men were among the most politically liberal people of their period), nor of intelligence (they were intellectually brilliant), nor of education (they had gone to the best schools and were at the top of their classes), nor, even of experience (the military leaders had often served the nation bravely and well in World War II, as had President Kennedy himself and others in his administration, and McNamara was a highly successful business leader at Ford). They were, as Halberstam rightly calls them, "the best and the brightest," meaning they had reached the pinnacle of what counted in America as successful and accomplished manhood.

What immediately strikes us is how rigidly this successful manhood adhered to the terms of the gender binary and hierarchy. Their much vaunted rationality – exemplified by the civilians, McGeorge Bundy[55] and Robert McNamara,[56] and the military men, Maxwell Taylor[57] and General Westmoreland[58] – is the hard rationality of cost effective means-end reasoning, mathematically displayed in flow charts and body counts. Hard not soft, masculine not effeminate. Rationality was, for them, cold, heartlessly cold; "[c]onviction and certitude without emotion. When he [McNamara] finished everyone knew what to do. The modern man."[59] Maxwell Taylor was "[a]ll business, all ambition, cold as ice."[60]

Taking this conception of rationality as all that rationality could or should mean, these men at the top bonded to one another. They did not think to listen to – indeed they dismissed – those who presumed to question their judgment. McGeorge Bundy referred to George Ball disparagingly as "the theologian," because Ball raised moral questions about ends. An insular and ultimately irrational arrogance[61] had led the American military to lie to civilian authorities about our losses and defeats and to deny the resilience of the Vietnamese.[62] Later, this same arrogance led embattled civilian leaders, including Robert McNamara and President Johnson, to lie both to Congress and the American people about what they were doing. Thus they secured the Tonkin Gulf Resolution authorizing military escalation[63] and then concealed the dimensions of the escalations.[64]

Men who had risen to the very top could not question what they took to be their successful lives. This rendered them acutely sensitive to the shaming of manhood. Any intimation of defeat, of being seen as less than the best and the brightest, was an insult they found insufferable. This psychology was most starkly displayed by President Johnson himself. He refused to believe that Ho Chi Minh, the leader of a small and technologically backward nation, could withstand let alone defeat America's industrial and military superiority ("'Raggedy-ass little fourth-rate country,' Lyndon Johnson called Vietnam during the great debates"[65]). Speaking to reporters, he characterized America's response to alleged attacks by the Vietnamese at Tonkin Bay in terms that suggest his sexual anxieties: "I didn't just screw Ho Chi Minh, . . . I cut his pecker off."[66]

Halberstam concludes:

> machismo was no small part of it. [Johnson] has always been haunted
> by the idea that he would be judged as being insufficiently manly for

the job, that he would lack courage at a crucial moment. More than a little insecure himself, he very much wanted to be seen as a man; it was a conscious thing. He was very much aware of machismo in himself and those around him, and at a moment like this [escalating military force in Vietnam] he wanted the respect of men who were tough, real men, and they would turn out to be the hawks. He had always unconsciously divided the people around him between men and boys. Men were activists, doers, who conquered business empires, who acted instead of talked, who made it in the world of other men and had the respect of other men. Boys were the talkers and the writers and the intellectuals, who sat around thinking and criticizing and doubting instead of doing . . .

Doubt itself, he thought, was an almost feminine quality, doubts were for women; on another issue, when Lady Bird raised her doubts, Johnson had said of course she was doubtful, it was like a woman to be uncertain. Thus as Vietnam came to the edge of decision, the sides were unfair, given Johnson's make-up. The doubters were not the people he respected; the men who were activists were hawks, and he took sustenance and reassurance that the real men were for going ahead.[67]

It was always Johnson's sense, following Kennedy's assassination, that "the best and brightest" supported him. Yet he was as much hostage to their worship of manly success as they were to his.[68] "[Johnson] was a relentless man who pushed himself and all others with the same severity and demanded, above all other qualities, total loyalty, not loyalty in the traditional sense, not positive loyalty, . . . but total loyalty, not just to office or party or concept, but loyalty first and foremost to Lyndon Johnson."[69] Since Johnson was older and therefore closer to the political impact of McCarthy and his conspiracy theory about the loss of China, he was more vulnerable than the men around him to the confusion of China and Vietnam. Still, their support after Kennedy's death strengthened Johnson's confusion with consequences not only in Vietnam but for his poverty programs and the future of the Democratic Party as a liberal and progressive party that could win elections. Men (this band of brothers with Johnson at its head demanding total loyalty) stood together over Vietnam, disastrously so for them and us. At the end, the damage to ethical intelligence was all too evident: few acknowledged mistakes: "[T]here was no sense of remorse, not even on why they failed to estimate correctly . . . The faults, it seemed, were not theirs, the fault was with this country which was not worthy of them."[70]

The analogy to Hitler, who at the end turned on the German people, is inescapable. How, psychologically, could this happen, and in admired liberal leaders of the United States of America, rightly still honored, as by us, for their domestic achievements designed to remedy longstanding injustices of race and poverty? Is it just, as Johnson's biographer Robert A. Caro observes, that "Ruthlessness, secretiveness, deceit – significant elements in every previous stage of Lyndon Johnson's life" here destroyed him? Caro goes on to comment: "Not always, however ... sometimes these other elements – the anger at injustice, the sympathy, empathy, identification with the underdog that added up to compassion – had been expressed, by this master of the political gesture, in gestures ... deeply meaningful."[71] So, why Vietnam?

The problem, at bottom, was the killing of ethical conscience itself in their fear that their manhood would be subjected to shaming., and the contempt for moral leadership articulated by Dean Rusk, the Secretary of State: "I wouldn't make the smallest concession for moral leadership. It's much overrated."[72] Halberstam recalls a "young White House aide" who "remembered the conversation, which shocked him, and from then on always thought of Rusk in this context; he thought that when Rusk died that should be inscribed on his tombstone, his epitaph."[73] He is then reminded of something that Kennedy had said about Stevenson:

> What was it Jack Kennedy had said about Adlai Stevenson during the Cuban missile crisis when he had mocked Stevenson's softness – that you had to admire the way Stevenson was willing to fight for his convictions when everyone else in the room was against him. The irony of that statement was missing for Kennedy and it was missing for Johnson as well.[74]

In the American experience of unjust wars, the Vietnam War is remarkable not for the fact of resistance in itself (which had occurred earlier), but because the resistance, like Siegfried Sassoon's resistance to World War I, originated among the soldiers fighting the war. For the first time in American history, the resistance to war was widespread, resonant, and effective – the American people were persuaded the war must be brought to an end even without victory. It was the resistance to the war by the soldiers serving in Vietnam, giving voice to their experience of the war, that was so psychologically powerful. Men such as Tim O'Brien who had struggled with their consciences over whether to serve in Vietnam and had ended up serving, came to see and write about the moral injury they had suffered in betraying what is right. O'Brien writes: "My conscience told me to run, but some irrational and powerful force was resisting, like a weight pushing me toward the war."[75]

We are struck by the consistency in men's description of the force that impels them to act against their better nature. Tolstoy refers to it as crude, powerful and mysterious. Our student Adam refers to it as massive and intangible; O'Brien as powerful and irrational. All had felt unable to resist it. As O'Brien came to see, its force was rooted in cowardice. Its power lay in the shaming of manhood.[76] The conflict was between his vulnerability to the shaming of his manhood and his guilt arising from a conscience concerned with harm to others. This is the realization Tolstoy – a man who had fought in Russian wars – also came to, leading him ultimately to resistance, which in his case took the form of pacifism.[77]

Unlike in World War I, by the time of Vietnam the American law of free speech had evolved so that anti-war speech was fully protected constitutionally.[78] The anti-Vietnam war resistance was also connected to the civil rights movement, whose leader, Martin Luther King, Jr, had come out in opposition to the war.[79] What was the connection?

Both the anti-Vietnam war resistance movement, which began within the military, and the civil rights movement with its commitment to non-violence were challenging the honor codes of American manhood. More specifically, they were challenging the assumption that violence or the use of force is the way that men can undo shaming and restore honor. In this, the anti-war movement was questioning the core assumption of patriarchal manhood.

Seen in this light, it is no accident that the resurgence of patriarchy in the present is manifest in Trump surrounding himself with military men and seeking an increase in the military budget while at the same time further restricting women's access to birth control and abortion and protections against sexual assault. Plus reinstating a rigid gender binary in his opposition to any policies that would recognize the human rights of LGBTQ Americans or grant them constitutional protection as citizens.

As Trump girds himself for war, and at times seems eager to provoke it at whatever cost, we can take instruction from the American ethical leaders who, in an earlier historical period, worried about America's propensity to initiate unjust wars, namely William James and Jane Addams. James protested both American imperialism[80] and the virulent racism of American lynchings.[81] In his 1910 essay, "The Moral Equivalent of War,"[82] he was particularly concerned with the mindless militarism he condemned in the policies of Theodore Roosevelt. Yet after considering pacifist (Tolstoy) and feminist alternatives, he concludes that the "war-party is assuredly right in affirming and reaffirming that the martial virtues, although originally gained by the race through war, are absolute and permanent human goods."[83] He then proposes a moral equivalent of war, namely, mandatory public service for young people as a way of redirecting and civilizing these "virtues." James clearly sees the role that the gender binary plays in framing these issues but, working within the terms of the binary, looks forward "to a future when acts of war shall be formally outlawed between civilized peoples."[84]

In contrast, the ethical and psychological brilliance of Jane Addams's framing of the same issue (American aggressive militarism) arises from the way she investigates the question through her close study of recent immigrants she knew from her work at Hull House. These are precisely the immigrants that Theodore Roosevelt and Woodrow Wilson would condemn as "hyphenated Americans." What Addams saw in her experience of these immigrants was not a threat, but an ethical impulse of care and concern arising from "the opportunity and necessity for breaking through the tribal bond."[85] In a period when immigrants were demonized as "the scum of Europe,"[86] Addams closely observed and appreciated the humane capacities she saw in the immigrants she knew at firsthand – the "old German potter … his life … illumined with the artist's prerogative of direct creation," the humane relationality of Southern Italians "congregate[d] in cities where their inherited and elaborate knowledge of agricultural processes is unutilized,"[87] the courage of Russian immigrant victims of religious and political persecution with their experience of "the bittersweet of martyrdom,"[88] and "the most recently immigrated Jews" with their "refreshing insistence upon the reality of the inner life."[89]

Entering into the worlds of these people, Addams came to understand their struggles in a new environment and was aware of how little their struggles and gifts were taken seriously or appreciated. Addams also saw in American immigrants:

> the power of association which comes from daily contact with those who are unlike each other in all save the universal characteristics of man, … suggestions of a new peace and holiness. It would seem as if our final help and healing were about to issue forth from broken human nature itself, out of the pathetic striving of ordinary men, who make up the common substance of life: from those who have been driven by economic pressure or governmental oppression out of a score of nations.[90]

Addams argues that what she discovered from working with and listening to immigrants is an alternative to William James's search for a moral equivalent to war: the "substitution of nurture for warfare … analogous to that world-wide effort to put a limit to revenge."[91] She finds the psychological root of a militarism also in the American criminal justice system, including prisons.[92] Unlike James, Addams challenges the gender binary itself, and frames her argument in terms of an ethic of care that substitutes nurture for warfare and puts "a limit to revenge."

A central feature of Trump's America First nationalism was the Muslim travel ban, followed closely by his draconian approach to illegal immigrants. The stark inconsistency between the now visible patriarchy and the values of constitutional democracy and universal human rights is in itself grounds for concern. For a man as patriarchal as Trump, the very fact that the power of America is no longer hegemonic (for example, the rise of China upsetting what once might have been regarded as the rightful hierarchy among nations) may register as a personal insult and thus a justification for violence.[93] For a man who venerates power and strength above all, human rights barely register. This is what makes Trump's America First populism so ethically vacuous and dangerous, along with his unconcern for the most vulnerable among us. As Jane Addams observed, "emotional pity and kindness are always found in greatest degree among the unsuccessful,"[94] and Trump's worship of success accordingly evinces little kindness and less pity. It is not an ethical answer to appeal to power, as the Athenians did when the Melians protested their injustice: "[I]n fact the strong do what they have the power to do and the weak accepted what they have to accept."[95] Have we learned nothing about how democracies lose their ethical footing?

We return then to the issue of gender: Why is it so difficult to see the pivotal importance of gender? In Charles King's review of Pankaj Mishra's book *Age of Anger*, we saw the glimmer of an answer. At the same time that King flags the missing issue of gender in Mishra's analysis of the rise to power of Trump and his ilk (Erdogan, Putin, and Abu Bakr al-Baghdadi), noting that "the admixture of machismo, self-obsession and thin-skinnedness ... has something to do with gender," he then goes on to say: "One need only be a self-aware theorist, not a feminist theorist, nor even a Freudian one, to see the entanglements of gender and sexuality with the political disposition that Mishra catalogues so well."[96]

Why "not a feminist theorist"?

Is it because King sees feminism as only for women? Is it because despite writing about gender, he himself is blinded by the gender binary and hierarchy so that a movement, feminism, perceived as in the interest of women cannot, given the terms of the binary, also be in the interest of men? Or given the hierarchy, a women's liberation movement cannot ultimately be taken as the basis for the "grand narrative" that King is looking for? This is a problem all too common. Yet two great American artists, Nathaniel Hawthorne and Herman Melville, in their prophetic mid-nineteenth-century novels, *The Scarlet Letter* and *Moby Dick*, illuminated the entanglements with gender that are at the root of our current situation.

8 *Democracy's Future*

HAWTHORNE AND MELVILLE: *THE SCARLET LETTER* AND *MOBY DICK* AS PROPHETIC NOVELS

In *The Scarlet Letter*, written in a rush of emotion in the six months following his mother's death. Hawthorne explores the problem of patriarchy. He shows us its effects on men, and then imagines resistance in the voice of a woman who is living outside its frame. Hawthorne's masterpiece along with his relationship with Melville inspired *Moby Dick*, published a year later in 1851 and also *Billy Budd*, published posthumously in 1924. All three works expose the force of patriarchy, albeit in quite different ways, Hawthorne's focusing on the problem of love, Melville's on the problem of violence. What makes these works so remarkable is their study of the contradictions between patriarchy and democracy. They are prophetic in showing what we are still reluctant to see: the toll patriarchy takes on American manhood.

The Scarlet Letter is, of course, a self-conscious work on and about patriarchy, a term Hawthorne uses repeatedly throughout the novel.[1] We know that his sister-in-law, Elizabeth Peabody, was an abolitionist feminist, opposing not only American slavery and racism but also sexism. The abolitionist feminists linked both racism and sexism to the force of patriarchy in American religion and ethics as well as in American politics.[2] *The Scarlet Letter* brilliantly exposes Puritan hypocrisy but also the internal contradictions that led the very same scarlet A that branded Hester Prynne as a woman who had committed adultery to be perceived by many as standing for "Able; so strong was Hester Prynne, with a woman's strength."[3] On this view, which one of us (Gilligan) first developed,[4] *The Scarlet Letter* is a resistance novel, and the resistance is to patriarchy; in particular, to the damage patriarchy does to relations between women and men. At the end of the novel, Hester assures the people who come to her for counsel and comfort of her firm belief that at some future time, when the world has grown ripe for it, "A new truth will be revealed in order to establish the whole relation between man and woman on a surer ground of mutual happiness."[5]

Melville's *Moby Dick* and *Billy Budd* are decidedly not about patriarchal constraints on women (there are few women in the former, none in the latter), but both zero in on how patriarchy destroys men. And how difficult, if not impossible, it is for men to resist.[6] Hawthorne makes the same point in *The Scarlet Letter* with his two central male characters, Dimmesdale (Hester's minister and lover) and Chillingworth (Hester's husband). Writing about moral injury, one of us (Gilligan) has suggested that the adulterous women in both Tolstoy's *Anna Karenina* and Hawthorne's *The Scarlet Letter* "are so dazzling, so vibrant, that our eye fixes on them ... We want to know what happens to them. It is almost as if they serve as decoys to distract us from what Tolstoy and Hawthorne are showing us about what happens to men under patriarchy."[7] One reason readers may focus on the dazzling adulterous women, is that what these artists are showing us about men's infidelity is more challenging to see. It counters the assumption that in privileging men and giving them power, patriarchy is in men's interest. Instead, we are shown how it destroys them.

Dimmesdale and Chillingworth are both described as unusually sensitive, intelligent, and humane men. In the character of Dimmesdale, Hawthorne reveals how a man of nature (of dale) becomes dim, and in the character of Chillingworth, how a man of worth becomes chilling. It is the force of patriarchy that leads the Reverend Dimmesdale, a man who loves the truth, to betray himself by living a lie, and Mr. Chillingworth, whom we feel comes to love Dimmesdale, to devote himself to destroying his soul.

In Melville, the homoeroticism among men is more explicit. In *Moby Dick*, the love between Queequeg and Ishmael *is compared to a marriage* ("hugging a fellow male in that matrimonial sort of style"[8]). In *Billy Budd*, it surfaces in the twisted repressed homosexuality of Claggart and the feelings of Captain Vere and Billy for one another.

Hawthorne's interest in how patriarchy deforms men, including good men, is, of course, continuous with the similarly probing psychological investigations of other great artists (notably Shakespeare), especially in periods of cultural change like the transition in Britain from the medieval religious consensus to the more open questioning of the Renaissance and Reformation.[9] Britain under Elizabeth remained an absolute monarchy, even more starkly so under the Stuarts, whose political views, and perhaps Shakespeare's, called for hierarchy: "Observe degree, priority, and place."[10] But questions about patriarchy are raised in many of

Shakespeare's plays, including the history plays and the tragedies. These questions were to culminate in the emergence of arguments for toleration, free speech, and constitutional democracy in the English Civil War, and, after the Glorious Revolution, in the development of British democratic constitutionalism, all of which framed the American Revolution and the Constitution of 1787 and Bill of Rights of 1791.[11]

Hawthorne situates his novel in Puritan New England, founded on Puritan resistance to Charles I's claims to absolutism in both religion and politics. The novel studies the psychology of men and women in transition, not from absolutism, but within a more democratic culture that had resisted absolutism both in religion and politics and yet had remained patriarchal, as Hawthorne reminds us repeatedly ("patriarchal personage ... patriarchal privilege ... patriarchal power ... patriarchal deacon"[12]). It was Puritan resistance that first led to the idea of written constitutions protecting basic human rights, initially suggested in Britain and later institutionalized in the United States.[13] The underlying ethical impulse was, with the printing press and mass literacy and the translation of the Bible into the vernacular, that all persons including women could themselves read basic ethical and religious works and form their own convictions without the intermediary of a priesthood. It was this ethical impulse that inspired Puritan resistance to hierarchy in both religion and politics, and the impulse to democracy based on equality and human rights.

The brilliance of *The Scarlet Letter* is that the voice of ethical resistance is the prophetic voice of Hester Prynne, who sees the role that patriarchy plays in deforming human nature in both women and men. Her revelation is that what has come to seem "like nature" is in fact not nature but a culture that grounds the whole relation between man and woman in mutual unhappiness. Read and taught as a tragic love story or a cautionary tale about the wages of sin, *The Scarlet Letter* is far more radical. It's not the love between Hester Prynne and Arthur Dimmesdale that is tragic, although within the culture of puritanism it becomes a tragedy and a sin. It is "an iron framework of reasoning"[14] that imprisons them – a cultural framework in which women are either goodwives or witches and men are trapped by patriarchal privilege and power into living a lie.

The novel plays constantly with shifting the frame, starting with the introductory chapter where the unnamed narrator, studying "this patriarchal personage," the "Father of the Custom-House," with "a livelier curiosity than any other form of humanity there presented to my notice," finds that "he was, in truth, a rare phenomenon; so perfect in one point of view; so shallow, so delusive, so impalpable, such an absolute nonentity, in every other."[15] In the chapter "Another View of Hester,"[16] we discover that Hester, because of the scarlet A, is outside the iron framework of puritanism. As an adulteress, she cannot be a goodwife; as the mother of Pearl she cannot be a witch without having the Puritans take her child away. Thus her mind is free to roam, and living outside the framework, she sees the frame.

The Puritan settlement was once a forest floor: built up in one way it could be "torn down and built up anew."[17] "Men of the sword had over-thrown nobles and kings. Men bolder than these had overthrown and rearranged – not actually, but within the sphere of theory, ... the whole system of ancient prejudice ... Hester Prynne imbibed this spirt."[18] For a woman to find her fair and suitable place in the new society – that is, for a woman to be included within the framework of democracy – "the very nature of the opposite sex, or its long hereditary habit, which has become like nature, is to be essentially modified,"[19] and that of woman too (woman "cannot take advantage of these preliminary reforms, until she herself shall have undergone a still mightier change"[20]). In short, what Hester sees is that a political transformation (the change from a patri-archal to a democratic society) hinges on a psychological transformation, whereby what has become through long hereditary habit "like nature," must be essentially modified. The revelation of *The Scarlet Letter* is that in the absence of this transformation, not only is democracy comprom-ised but love becomes tragic.

This extraordinary intellectual insight and freedom of Hester Prynne is often missed in the focus on what from a patriarchal stand-point is her unredeemable sin. Despite the cues strewn along the way – "in one point of view ... in every other," "another view of Hester," the change in the meaning of the letter A; and in the end the question never resolved as to whether there was, as some people attest, a scarlet A on Dimmesdale's chest, or whether there was no A there, as others, who were also there and saw his bare chest affirm – the shifting of the framework is overlooked. *The Scarlet Letter* shows us both how a patriarchal framework, even one seemingly cast in iron, can shift, and also the forces holding it in place. A woman, we are told, must bring the new truth, but there is a catch-22, because with the stunning economy of the letter A, Hawthorne captures how the "lawless pas-sion"[21] that releases Hester from the iron framework of puritanism rendering her Able to see the frame, also disables her because it renders her, in the eyes of the Puritans, an impure woman, a woman who has been Adulterated.

Hawthorne refers to Hester Prynne as "hand in hand with Ann Hutchinson, as the foundress of a religious sect. She might, in one of her phases, have been a prophetess."[22] But Hester's prophesies remain in her own mind, and, though she persuades her lover Dimmesdale to join her in leaving, and though he publicly acknowledges his love for Hester and Pearl, he is not heard, and in the end he does not leave, but dies consumed by guilt and confessing his remorse for betraying the Father. Chillingworth, although driven to hound Dimmesdale like a fiend, so riddled by shame at being dishonored by another man and determined is he to expose his secret, in the end leaves his estate, which was "very considerable,"[23] to Pearl, freeing the daughter who was not his own to live her own life and by doing so, becoming, in effect, her good father. In their own way, each of these men, Dimmesdale and Chillingworth, resists the strictures of patriarchy, and yet in the end both are tormented – one might say tortured – by its bonds. Dimmesdale, despite his emotional sensitivity and passion, becomes dim, and Chillingworth, despite his intelligence and his feeling for Pearl and for the Native Americans, becomes chilling.

The effects of patriarchy on men is the very center of what arrests our attention in Melville's two masterpieces. Like *The Scarlet Letter*, *Moby Dick* is an antebellum novel framed by the intimation, in the early 1850s, of a national tragedy very much in the offing (and erupting in the Civil War). The British novelist, E. M. Forster, rightly called Melville's study of evil prophetic, reaching "straight back into the universal, to a blackness and sadness so transcending our own that they are indistinguishable from glory."[24] If Hester Prynne is a prophetess of how patriarchy can be transformed by love, *Moby Dick* is prophetic of the catastrophic consequences for democracy when patriarchy is hegemonic. The *Pequod*, a model of the ship of state, is led by a monstrous patriarch, Captain Ahab, whose unquellable rage arises from the insult to his manhood by his loss of a leg to the white whale he was hunting. The novel shows us the lucrative American whaling industry run by Quakers, nonviolent in their religion and politics, but here engaged in a business that lives off the killing and dismembering not of fish, but of mammals, who, along with porpoises and dolphins, are among the most intelligent of such creatures. In his early novels based on his South Sea adventures, Melville tried to show the humane features even of cannibals, who horrified America's proselytizing clergy.[25] In *Moby Dick* he exposes the hypocrisy of nonviolent Quakers cannibalizing mammals – a horror shown in vivid detail.

But at the center of the novel we see not only Ahab's narcissistic rage, but also how the men he leads, including Starbuck, who perceives the irrationality of the venture, follow him even unto their deaths. As Starbuck sees clearly, Ahab's pursuit of the white whale is utterly irrational, distracting the ship from what its Quaker owners regard as the only rational object of this business, making money off the parts of the whale for which there was a market. Yet the insult to Ahab's manhood and his personal obsession with revenge ("I'd strike the sun if it insulted me"[26]), fuels a psychology that the men of the *Pequod*, including Starbuck, cannot and will not resist. What Melville shows us is an interlinked personal and political psychology that, under patriarchy, mobilizes seemingly unstoppable violence. Similar in this sense to the antebellum South where any threat to the racist hierarchy of American slavery elicits violence against people of color as scapegoats (Ahab may be modeled on Calhoun[27]), or to Hitler's appeal to the shame of Versailles that led to the murder of six million European Jews,[28] Melville reveals the scapegoat of insulted patriarchal manhood, a projected emptiness, a white whale, who could be anyone, the more innocent and vulnerable the better.

The ship, the *Bellipotent*, in *Billy Budd* is also a model of the patriarchal state, only here a British military vessel at war with France in the Napoleonic War, a war between two imperialisms. The contrast between the rigid hierarchical order of the patriarchal state and its alternative is starkly drawn as Billy, commandeered from his ship, *Rights-of-Man*, to serve on the *Bellipotent* says: "And good-bye to you too, old *Rights-of-Man*,"[29] "a terrible breach of naval decorum."[30] Why "terrible"? Even to mention the rights of man, the basis of democracy, in such a context is to provoke terror in the patriarchal order, the kind of insult to patriarchal manhood that demands and justifies violence. And Billy is killed.

With *Billy Budd* Melville's carries his interest in the effects of patriarchy on men into their psyches, to wit, the psyches of men who are sexually attracted to and sometimes love men. The text could not be clearer: Billy, "the Handsome Sailor,"[31] is loved by everyone, but it is Claggart's repressed sexual desire for Billy that is transformed into violence, leading to the death of both. Homophobia transforms homosexual desire into shame, an insult to one's manhood. The insult to manhood then elicits violence in the absence of love or guilt, as Jim Gilligan's work so clearly shows.[32]

What is of interest in *Billy Budd* is not only exposing the damaging effects of patriarchy on a man like Claggart, but its effects on the patriarch of the *Bellipotent*, Captain Vere, a man portrayed as perceptive, scholarly, and humane – as humane and learned as Hawthorne's Dimmesdale and Chillingworth. It is Captain Vere who ultimately condemns Billy to death, but his route to this end is not direct. Once Billy has struck Claggart dead, Vere (for whom "forms, measured forms are everything,")[33] "vehemently exclaimed, 'Struck dead by an angel of God! Yet the angel must hang!'"[34]

Richard Weisberg has shown that both the procedure and substance of Billy's conviction and death penalty violate legal norms, norms with which Melville, a former seaman, was well familiar.[35] Even Vere's officers express doubt that Vere is following the proper legal rules and procedure; they convict and condemn Billy to death at Vere's insistence, concerned otherwise, as Vere puts it, that mutiny would be encouraged.[36] In fact, it is Billy's execution that nearly provokes mutiny among the men who loved him.[37] Vere's compulsion to kill Billy is put by him in two revealing ways: the decision must not rest on "the feminine in man"[38] and must follow "the imperial one"[39] required by law. Appeal to the gender binary shows we are within patriarchy, and the effects of patriarchy on men are evident not only in Claggart, but in Vere, and even in Billy's acceptance of his death, exclaiming, "God bless Captain Vere!"[40]

The novella tells us that Captain Vere talks privately with Billy about his condemnation to death, but we are not told what was said. Presumably, what was said must explain Billy's blessing of Vere before his death. What we are told, however, is this:

> Captain Vere in the end may have developed the passion sometimes latent under an exterior stoical or indifferent. He was old enough to have been Billy's father. The austere devotee of military duty, letting himself melt back into what remains primeval in our formalized humanity, may in the end have caught Billy to his heart, even as Abraham may have caught Isaac on the brink of resolutely offering him up in obedience to the exacting behest.[41]

It is clear that Vere was emotionally engaged by Billy: "[L]etting himself melt back into what remains primeval in our formalized humanity,"[42] namely, the intimate relationship between father and son. Billy is an orphan, fatherless; and Vere is certainly not Billy's father. But the relationship is put in the patriarchal terms of the Abraham-Isaac story, in which a father is prepared to kill his son to prove his devotion to God. Isaac, however, is not killed. Yet Vere believes himself compelled, contrary to his feelings and to the skepticism of his fellow officers about the legality of what he is doing, to condemn the innocent boy to death, and Billy embraces his death as he may have believed that through his acceptance he was embracing the father he never had.

Billy Budd was published posthumously, years after Melville's death, suggesting that it explored painfully personal and shameful issues for Melville that he could not expose in his lifetime. The playwright Eugene O'Neill's insistence that his greatest and most personal play, *Long Day's Journey Into Night*, only be played after his death comes to mind as an analogy. Melville's sense of personal pain is clearly rooted in his guilt and remorse over the suicide of his eldest son, Malcolm.[43] Melville was as bad a father as he was a husband,[44] and the rage, which he exposed earlier in Ahab, is here explored in one of the most intimate of personal relationships under patriarchy. There were undoubtedly many other violently abusive husbands and fathers under American patriarchy,[45] but none had the artistic talent and integrity to explore the problem in the way Melville courageously does in his last work. In *Billy Budd*, he overcomes his shame through confessing a sense of a guilt that he had come to believe should be more broadly understood and shared

There is, however, another painful and shameful personal issue that may be implicit in *Billy Budd*, and is quite explicit in the opera based on the novella composed by Benjamin Britten to a text written in part by the British novelist E. M. Forster – namely, repressed homosexuality.[46] Britten's interest in setting Melville's novella arose from E. M. Forster's desire to collaborate with Britten on a new opera. "The men were not close, though Britten felt a sense of gratitude toward Forster for introducing him to Crabbe's poetry, repaying him by dedicating his comic opera *Albert Herring* 'to E. M. Forster, in admiration'."[47] Britten was much more courageous in dealing with explicit gay themes than Forster, whose gay novel, *Maurice*, written in 1913, was only published after Forster's death. But the men, both gay and in loving relationships (Forster with a policeman, Britten with the singer, Peter Pears), shared a common sensibility about the value of gay love and friendship. Unsurprisingly, it was Britten who proposed *Billy Budd* to Forster.

Billy Budd appealed to Britten as a parable about how patriarchy destroys love and legitimates violence. To recapitulate and flesh out the story, its hero is an honest and handsome sailor who had been impressed into the British navy at the time of the French Revolution. Budd is beloved of everyone who knows him except for John Claggart, the master-at-arms. Claggart, twisted by homophobia, is sexually attracted to Budd, and for that reason maliciously decides to destroy him – a counterphobic response to the very idea of gay love, destroying, as homophobia requires, the thing one loves. As the very idea of loving the boy leads Claggart to destroy the boy and himself, Claggart falsely accuses Budd of mutiny. Budd, who has a stammer, cannot express his indignation in words, and instinctively strikes out at Claggart, killing him. Captain Vere, the scholarly captain of the ship, understands perfectly well Claggart's malice, and "fully comprehends that Claggart's vindictive attraction to Billy is the real crime."[48] When Claggart dies, however, Vere follows his duty as captain of a ship at war, and convenes the required court to apply to the letter the Mutiny Act, which he supposes (wrongly) would condemn Budd to death. Budd is found guilty, and hanged. Claggart is buried at sea with full military honors.

Forster began work on a libretto (Eric Crozier, who assisted, was initially skeptical: "Who had ever heard of an opera with an all-male cast?"[49]). Though he preserved much of Melville's dialogue, Forster's most important change was to keep Vere alive after the events in the novella, thus making the opera a memory drama in which Vere, now an old man, reflects with remorse on what he had done. He had performed the role imperial patriarchy required of him and killed a boy whom he, along with others, loved.

The collaboration between Forster and Britten was tempestuous. Some of it was age: "Forster was seventy-one and slowing down,"[50] Britten was in his mid-30s; Forster "could not comprehend Britten's fast pace and full diary."[51] Not a musician, he could not appreciate the orchestral colors of the orchestration Britten intended for Forster's setting of Claggart's aria, where he gives voice to his motives for destroying Billy. Britten had played for him only the piano version, but Forster, in a letter to Britten, objected:

> I want *passion* – love constricted, perverted, poisoned, but nevertheless *flowing* down its agonizing channel; a sexual discharge gone evil. Not soggy depression or growling remorse. I seemed [to be] turning from one musical discomfort to another, and was dissatisfied.[52]

Britten was deeply hurt and crippled in his work, and sought solace from Pears and others. With the exception of Auden, Britten had never worked with a librettist as much his artistic equal as Forster, and, as for Forster, "[n]othing in his previous friendship with Britten prepared him for the composer's single-mindedness."[53] Nonetheless, they continued to collaborate as composer and writer, leading to a work that "has legitimate claim to being Britten's greatest opera."[54]

What Britten and Forster show us in *Billy Budd*, in which Peter Pears (Britten's lover and a resister to his own family's military background) sang the role of Captain Vere, is nothing less than the politics and psychology of patriarchy. Through the microcosm of an imperial ship at war with the rights of man, we are shown an authority structure rigidly organized in terms of the gender binary and hierarchy. This extends not only to the hierarchically ordered roles of the men and boys on the warship, but to their psyches. When Billy is publicly executed, after exclaiming (in the opera) "Starry Vere, God bless you," the music explodes, a delayed expression of the crew's inarticulate rage and indignation, which is then silenced by the officers who sense their authority at threat. The opera ends with Forster's setting of Vere as an old man, realizing that he is as guilty as Claggart, responsible for the death of a boy whom he loved and whose love had saved him.

> I could have saved him ... But he has saved me, and blessed me, and the love that passeth understanding has come to me. I was lost on the infinite sea, but I've sighted a sail in the storm ... There's a land where she'll anchor for ever.[55]

The music swells into an anthem of a world in which men's love including men's love of men can be freely expressed, a world that Britten and Forster see as coming and celebrate, joined as the great artists they were, in this remarkable work that premiered in Britain in 1951.

The question for us is not whether Melville exposed the ravages of American patriarchy in *Moby Dick* and of its offshoot, American homophobia, in *Billy Budd*; he clearly did. The question, rather, is how psychologically – despite his background in a distinguished American family that traced its lineage to heroes of the American Revolution – his creativity came as far as it did in exploring, exposing, and resisting American patriarchy. In *Why Love Leads to Justice*, David argued that the key to such creativity – in both heterosexual and homosexual couples – is that falling in love across the boundaries that patriarchy enforces (and thus resisting its Love Laws), frees a voice that otherwise tends to be shamed into silence.

It seems plausible to us, as others have suggested, that meeting Hawthorne during the period when he was working on *Moby Dick* led Melville to fall in love with a man who was also a great artist (Hershel Parker, perhaps Melville's most insightful biographer, writes that Melville was "more than a little febrile – excited intellectually, emotionally, and sexually – sexual arousal being for Melville an integral part of such intensely creative phases"[56]). As a free and equal person (unlike Melville's wife) and an artist, Hawthorne opened Melville's mind and heart to men, and introduced him as well to literary ways of exploring the unconscious;[57] *Moby Dick* is dedicated to Hawthorne. Whatever experiences of sex or love with men Melville may have had in the South Seas, he had never, as an artist, loved a man as a free man and artist on the terms of freedom and equality that he loved Hawthorne. What Hawthorne had come to mean to Melville is quite explicit in his anonymously published encomium to Hawthorne's genius as an American Shakespeare, "Hawthorne and His Moses."[58] Melville, composing anonymously, as a Virginian spending July in Vermont, writes in the heat of a kind of sexual ecstasy: "I feel that this Hawthorne has dropped germanous seeds into my soul. He expands and deepens down, the more I contemplate him; and further and further, shoots his strong New-England roots into the hot soil of my Southern soul."[59]

Among the works by Hawthorne he admires, Melville mentions *The Scarlet Letter*.[60]

Hawthorne's insights into the harms patriarchy inflicts on Dimmesdale and Chillingworth may well have opened Melville's artistic heart and mind. The astonishing study of the psychological damage patriarchy inflicts on men that he undertakes in *Moby Dick* and then carries further in *Billy Budd* goes beyond anything Hawthorne had written. At the same time, by focusing solely on men, Melville cannot see what Hawthorne came to see through his character of Hester: that only when men can join women, who have freed their love from patriarchal constraints, can men free themselves from the imprisonment of patriarchy and expose their love, which otherwise remains a secret.

The search for loving relationships between men has been cited by Robert Martin as at the very heart of Melville's development as an artist.[61] If Martin is right, and we believe he is, it may be for this reason that, in contrast to Hawthorne's anti-abolitionism as well as racism and even anti-Semitism,[62] Melville's narratives explore love between men across the boundaries of race and religion (notably, Ishmael and Queequeg). His last great narrative, *Billy Budd*, prefaces the introduction of Billy himself by noting others who fit the persona of the "Handsome Sailor," including a handsome black sailor.[63] The injustice to Billy may thus reflect an injustice to black men quite like that done to Billy (for example, lynchings).[64] These are injustices not on Hawthorne's ethical radar. What Melville's work shows us is how ethically illuminating it can be to extend the critical analysis of patriarchy and resistance to patriarchy from loving relationships between a man and a woman to relationships of men to men (and also of women to women), including those that cross racial and religious divides.[65]

Melville thus deepens Hawthorne's insight that patriarchy is damaging to men as well as to women. Through his love for Hawthorne, he may have found the voice to write the most terrifying study of the damage and the destruction to which patriarchy can lead men, both in their personal and political lives. As a man, Melville may have more deeply experienced this damage than Hawthorne, but his love of Hawthorne and his attraction to him, however resisted by Hawthorne, may have been reparative, enabling him to find an artistic voice in which to express what he knew. Nothing Melville had written before *Moby Dick* had this Shakespearean power, a power he had found in Hawthorne's work and perhaps more fully realized in this novel than any American artist before or since. Love resisting patriarchy thus inspires courage.

And this legacy from Hawthorne may also have made possible *Billy Budd*, much later in Melville's life (after he had abandoned his literary career and long after Hawthorne's death). At the end of his life, unrecognized as the great artist he was and full of regret and remorse, Melville returned to the experience that always inspired his greatest work, a world of men bound together on a ship, subject to the rigid hierarchies that patriarchy enforces but also subject to love, which like the sea is a force of nature.

Love, Hawthorne writes, "whether newly born, or aroused from a deathlike slumber, must always create sunshine, filling the heart so full of radiance, that it overflows upon the outward world."[66] He also observes that "No man, for any considerable period, can wear one face to himself and another to the multitude, without finally getting bewildered as to which may be the true."[67]

We don't associate these insights with *The Scarlet Letter*, but that too is Hawthorne's point: to see what he came to see about love and patriarchy and man and woman, it was necessary first to shift the frame.

AUGUST WILSON ON NONVIOLENCE AND VIOLENCE

It is striking that Melville in *Billy Budd* should crystallize the tragedy of patriarchy for democracy in the relationship between a father and son (Captain Vere and Billy). Melville makes his point in terms of the Abraham-Isaac narrative tragically conceived, because unlike in the Biblical narrative, Vere actually kills Billy in the name of maintaining order. Over a century later, another great American artist, the African American playwright August Wilson, takes up the relationship between father and son in *Jitney*, written in the 1970s though unlike Wilson's other Pittsburg plays, not performed on Broadway until 2017. Wilson sets his play in the period of the civil rights movement portraying a conflict between father and son, joined in their resistance to American racism, but divided by how their resistance relates to American patriarchy.

The father, Becker, runs a gypsy taxi company in Pittsburgh, the city in which Wilson lived and in which he set most of his plays dealing with black lives in periods of cultural transition over race in American society. Becker's son, Booster, was both intelligent and ambitious. Excelling in science, he had been admitted on scholarship to the University of Pittsburgh, an achievement in which his father took enormous pride. There Booster met a white girl, the daughter of a wealthy executive at Gulf Oil, who had bought his daughter a car.

The girl would chauffeur Booster around town, but she had kept secret from her father her relationship with a man of color. One day, however, the father spotted his daughter's car. Coming closer, he saw Booster and his daughter making love in the car and he "went crazy." Booster had never met the girl's father. All he knew was "some crazy white man ... opened the door and was screaming his head off. He proceeded to beat the man half to death."[68]

When the young woman then tells the police that Booster had raped her, it's Booster who goes crazy. Shamed by the woman, he kills her, and then is convicted of murder and sentenced to death, which in turn kills his mother. With two women dead and Booster now returning from prison (his sentence had been commuted to life and after twenty years he was released) father and son face off.

In the scene that ends the first act of the play, Booster arrives at the Jitney station looking for his father. Becker wants nothing to do with him: "You ain't got nothing," he tells him. Booster responds by saying that in effect Becker is also nothing, just "the boss of a jitney station." Becker straightens with pride:

> I am the boss of a jitney station. I'm a deacon down at the church. Got me a little house. It ain't much but it's mine. I worked twenty-seven years at the mill – got me a pension. I got a wife. I got respect. I can walk anywhere and hold my head up high. What I ain't got is a son that did me honor ... The Bible say "honor thy father and mother." I ain't got that. I ain't got a son I can be proud of. That's what I ain't got. A son to come up behind me ... living a good, honest decent life. I got a son who people point to and say. "That's Becker's boy. The one that killed that gal. That's Becker's boy. The one they gave the electric chair. That's Becker's boy."

The terms are set: respect and honor, and pride and decency, and by implication, masculinity. What it means to be a man. Booster says: "I did what I had to do and I paid for it." Becker, moving away from him, is incredulous:

> What you had to do! What you had to do! What law is there say you have to kill somebody if they tell a lie on you? Where does it say that? If somebody tell a lie on you, you have to kill them? Who taught you that? It was a lie! That girl told a lie! If it was the truth then go ahead and kill yourself. Go on and throw your life away. But it was a lie! (Moves toward BOOSTER.) We could have fought the lie. I'd already lined up a lawyer ... together we could have fought the lie.[69]

The clash is explicit: a patriarchal framing of manhood is a lie. "Who taught you," Becker asks, "that if somebody tell a lie on you, you have to kill them?" There is a democratic process for fighting a lie: "We could have fought the lie. I'd already lined up a lawyer ... together we could have fought the lie."

In the name of manhood, Booster had thrown his life away, he had killed his mother and robbed his father of what he had worked so hard for: a son who would do him honor. "What I ain't got is a son that did me honor," he tells Booster; "I ain't got a son I can be proud of. That's what I ain't got. A son to come up behind me ... living a good, honest decent life." The argument is about manhood; the clash is between a patriarchal vs. a democratic construction of manhood, and violence hangs in the balance, along with respect for life.

BECKER.   That girl lying didn't make you wrong in the world. A lie
           don't make you wrong in the world.
BOOSTER.   It don't make you right either. Right is right and right don't
           wrong anybody. You taught me that.
BECKER.   I taught you to respect life. I taught you all of life is precious.[70]

Booster is trapped in a skein of patriarchal assumptions having to do with feelings of shame. As a child he had felt ashamed seeing his father, who in his eyes was "a big man. Everywhere you went people treated you like a big man,"[71] insulted by the white landlord who belittled him for not paying the rent. Becker had responded with his dignity intact, saying that he would pay next month but Booster experienced his father as diminished by the landlord's assault – diminished also by not responding in kind. "You didn't seem so big no more. You were the same as everybody else." In Booster's eyes, a big man would have stood up to the landlord.

When he met the white girl and her successful father:

That's when I felt like I was somebody ... Then when she told that lie on me that's when I woke up. That when I realized that I wasn't big from the inside. I wasn't big on my own. When she told that lie it made me small. I wanted to do something that said I wasn't just another nigger ... that I was Clarence Becker. I wanted to make them remember my name ... I realize it was my chance to make the Beckers big again ... my chance to show what I had learned on my own. I thought you would understand. I thought you would be proud of me.

Becker responds: "Proud of you for killing somebody!" and Booster says: "No, Pop. For being a warrior. For dealing with the world in ways that you didn't or couldn't or wouldn't."[72]

Wilson, writing in the 1970s, is dramatizing the argument that had taken place over the civil rights movement in the late 1960s, after King was assassinated. How do you stand up to violence? How does a man stand up and be a man when faced with insult, when assaulted, treated as little rather than big, not a somebody but a nobody?

Becker stands, facing Booster: "Boy, you trying to say I had something to do with you pulling that trigger. You trying to say that it's my fault because I didn't knock Mr. Rand on his ass so I could keep a roof over your head. So you wouldn't have to sleep in the street, in the cold and the snow."

Booster backs off: "No Pop. I did it." But Becker won't let the point drop. He is not moved by the appeal to black power. He is not persuaded that violence is the solution. "You gonna knock Mr Rand on his ass for me by killing that girl?" Yet for Booster, killing was, or rather had been the solution, and he had paid the price. Not only he, as he now realizes, but also his mother and his father. "No Pop, it was for me. I did it for myself. But it didn't add up the way I thought it would. I was wrong. I see that now."[73]

Becker had never visited Booster during the twenty years that he was in prison. He couldn't, he explains; not after Booster had not only killed his mother by having done what he did but also had been cold at her funeral. In Becker's eyes, this is not how a man behaves. He tells Booster now why as a man he had not responded with violence to the landlord's taunts:

> You wanna know why? I'll tell you why. Because I had your black ass crying to be fed ... Because I had a family. I had responsibility ... I done what I had to do. I swallowed my pride and let him mess over me, all the time saying "You bastards got it coming. Look out! Becker's boy coming to straighten this shit out...Watch out for Becker's boy!" (He has worked himself into a frenzy and is now near tears.) And I get, huh? You tell me. What I get! Tell me what I get! What I get, huh?

There is a basic flaw in the patriarchal conception of manhood: an assumption of separateness that flies in the face of the truth. Becker had a child to feed, he had a family to take care of, responsibilities to others as well as to himself. He could swallow his pride in dealing with the landlord because he had other sources of pride, a son who would "straighten this [racist] shit out." And it's the magnanimity of this vision of human connection that finally wins out.

"Pop..." Booster says, moving toward his father.

But Becker is not so easily appeased: "Stay away from me! What I get huh? What I get? Tell me? (BOOSTER is silent.) I get a murderer, that's what...A murderer... "[74]

Jitney is a play about manhood. About what it means and what it takes to be a man, to be a black man in America. It dramatizes the debate that broke out within the civil rights movement over the efficacy of nonviolence as a response to violence; it dramatizes what was initially the debate between Martin Luther King and Malcolm X, the debate over violent vs. nonviolent resistance, over *satyagraha* – the power of truth – vs. black power. At its core, the entire play with its almost all male cast dramatizes the debate over manhood within the black community and within America at large.

Perhaps in this light it makes sense that of all Wilson's plays set in Pittsburgh, the so-called hill plays, *Jitney* was the last to be performed on

Broadway and that it opened in the year when Trump became president. At the end of the play, following Becker's death in an industrial accident, Booster takes over the Jitney station. Answering the phone as the curtain goes down, he has come to his father's understanding of dignity and manhood.

FEMINISM THROUGH THE LENS OF PATRIARCHY

When seen through the lens of patriarchy, feminism itself ironically becomes captive to the very gender binary and hierarchy it contests. What is in the interest of women cannot, by definition as it were, be in the interest of men. Power is a zero sum game. When one goes higher, the other goes lower. There is always a bottom and a top.

Thus feminism has been systematically distorted; misperceived as a movement to advance women and women's rights in the name of justice but at men's expense. It's a short step to perceiving feminists as "man-haters" and one reason for the reluctance especially of young women to ally themselves with feminism.

George Lakoff, the cognitive linguist, has recently argued that the mistake made by Hillary Clinton's campaign in running against Donald Trump was to emphasize policies as opposed to values.[75] Lakoff is politically liberal and progressive. In *Moral Politics*, he writes of the different ways in which American liberals and conservatives think about moral issues – offering two contrasting family images: liberals as nurturant parents, conservatives as strict fathers.[76] In several recent books, Lakoff contends that the progressive liberal politicians he supports (including Barack Obama and Hillary Clinton) have made a mistake in not taking more seriously and emphasizing these contrasting moral frameworks rather than relying on the ostensibly more rational arguments about choices among policies.[77] In his eyes, conservatives, including George W. Bush as well as Donald Trump, have won elections because they framed their campaign in moral terms, whereas Barack Obama, in Lakoff's view, would have been even more politically successful (for example, not losing the House of Representatives) had he placed less emphasis on rational arguments for policies and appealed more to their underlying moral framework. Hillary Clinton's emphasis on policy was, for Lakoff, her political undoing.

Our interest in Lakoff's arguments is twofold. First, his earlier book, *Moral Politics*, tracks the divide we see between the strands of American politics which are still patriarchal (the strict father) and those that are democratic (the nurturant parent). And second, his more recent books try to advise the more democratic politicians he supports as to how they might better appeal to the American people by shifting their focus from policy to moral framework. Republican politicians have in these terms done a better job at winning elections at both the state and federal levels because they appeal more forthrightly to the moral framework of American patriarchy: the strict father. As we observed earlier, Trump conspicuously, compulsively one might say, displayed his patriarchal family with the emphasis always on himself as the all-powerful father. Obama was in fact the nurturant parent along with Michelle, but Lakoff in not noting that one of his moral frameworks (strict father) is gendered while the other (nurturant parents) is not, misses a crucial point.

Lakoff is dealing not simply with alternative moral frameworks but with a paradigm shift. The very meaning of the word "morality" changes when the framework is patriarchal than when it is democratic, as Wilson dramatized so forcefully in his play. Because patriarchy justifies violence as a response to insult whereas democracy emphasizes relationship. "We could have fought the lie," Becker tells Booster; "together we could have fought the lie." Because more trenchantly, patriarchy rests on a lie, or an evasion. The other thing Lakoff does not notice in contrasting his two moral frameworks is the absence of the mother – her silence one might say – within the moral framework of the patriarchal family.

Why is it that gender, at once so obvious, remains something we are reluctant to see or discuss? Why does feminism, in spite all that has been said and written to the contrary, continue to be viewed as a movement advocating for women at men's expense? Or to put it starkly: why do the gender binary and hierarchy retain their grip on our perception?

Second-wave feminism from the beginning has vied with the perception that if something is advantageous to women it cannot be good for men. One of us (Gilligan) has written explicitly that feminism, understood as the movement to free democracy from patriarchy, is in the interest of everyone, including men, since patriarchy with its gender binary and hierarchy deforms human nature. In the 1970s, Carol's work, along with that of Jean Baker Miller,[78] Dorothy Dinnerstein,[79] and Nancy Chodorow[80] underscored this point. Yet the central claim of these works – that patriarchy harms men as well as women, albeit in different ways – has been distorted across the political spectrum. Seen from the right, feminism is engaged in a war against boys and men.[81] Seen from the center, feminism is questionable in what is perceived as its intention to replace patriarchy with matriarchy.[82] From the left, the headline, "Gilligan's island" that appeared on the cover of both the *Nation* and the *New Republic* to characterize the Harvard Project research on girls' development sums it up: women and girls are a marginal concern, an island apart, not in the mainstream.[83]

Feminism has been not only repeatedly proclaimed dead, in the spirit of wish-fulfillment as Gloria Steinem observed, but has also been consistently misunderstood in a way that obscures its transformational vision.[84] Assimilated to the very binary and hierarchy it challenges, it becomes a movement for women only, dividing women from men and also from one another on the basis of race, class, sexuality, religion, what have you, and in effect by deploying its strategy of divide and conquer leaving patriarchy intact.

Asking why feminism is still so divisive, Ariel Levy observes: "It's as if feminism were plagued by a kind of false-memory syndrome. There are political consequences to remembering things that never happened and forgetting things that did."[85] Not least what we have forgotten are advances once within our grasp: "Like so many other ideals of the sixties and seventies, the state-backed egalitarian family has gone from seeming – to both political parties – practical and inevitable to seeming utterly beyond the pale."[86] Levy reminds us that:

> In 1971, a bipartisan group of senators, led by Walter Mondale, came up with legislation that would have established both early-education programs and after-school care across the country. Tuition would be on a sliding scale based on a family's income bracket, and the program would be available to everyone but participation was required of no one. Both houses of Congress passed the bill.
>
> Nobody remembers this, because, later that year, President Nixon vetoed the Comprehensive Child Development Act, declaring that it "would commit the vast moral authority of the National Government to the side of communal approaches to child rearing" and undermine "the family-centered approach." He meant "the traditional-family-centered approach," which requires women to forsake every ambition apart from motherhood.[87]

The "cultural memory disorder," as Levy points out has kept us from recalling the radical insight that the politics of equality are incompatible with the structure of the traditional family. The goal of full citizenship for women implied a societal transformation that would have, as Levy points out, "changed the country on a cellular level." Child care was the bone of contention:

> If the father works and the mother works, nobody is left to watch the kids. Either government acknowledges the situation and helps provide child care (as many European countries do), or child care becomes a luxury affordable by the affluent, and a major problem for everyone else.[88]

As one of us (Gilligan) has written:

> the lines of division were predicable; feminism became identified with the interests of privileged, mostly white women, who then divided

among themselves over whether it is possible to defend traditional structures and still call oneself a feminist – as Sarah Palin does – or whether feminism implies a transformation on a societal level.[89]

To a large extent, both feminism and the American history of feminism have been viewed through the prism of patriarchy. This should have been evident for some time, but the argument about gender and differences has proceeded without considering the question of how it is being framed. Trump's election in bringing the framework to the forefront led several of our students to see more clearly how a patriarchal construction of manhood or womanhood was in fact shaping their lives, without a conscious thought or despite their best intentions.

FREEING DEMOCRACY FROM PATRIARCHY

In early November 2017, roughly a year after Trump's election, an opera, *The Exterminating Angel*, opened at the Metropolitan Opera in New York based on the 1962 movie of the great Spanish director, Luis Bunuel. Both the opera and the movie give voice to resisting the darkness of fascism and freeing democracy from patriarchy. Why now?

The movie is a surrealistic study of the fascism of the Spanish elites who stood by and not only did not resist but celebrated the attack on and ending of the Spanish Republic. Bunuel had been anti-fascist, anti-clerical, and a republican, and the movie is a kind of nightmare about the destructive force, the exterminating angel, fascism had unleashed on the Spanish people, portrayed as lambs going to the slaughter. In the film, members of the elite attend a celebratory dinner but are shocked when the servants abandon them. Psychologically frozen and unable to leave the room, they turn on one another: men fight women, a loving young couple commits suicide, a man dies, behavior is increasingly feral, and the nightmare culminates with the host of the dinner singled out as a scapegoat who must be murdered and offers instead to kill himself as a sacrifice. The nightmare ends only to repeat itself later in the church where they celebrate their release from the house, followed by a scene of soldiers killing people in the streets.[90]

The libretto of the opera, written by Tom Cairns in collaboration with the composer, adds material not in the screenplay by Bunuel. The most important and trenchant of these additions comes at the end when Leticia "sees a vision of home, far away in Jerusalem." Dissonance falls away as the music shifts; marked "transfigured" it appears to have broken the grasp of the invisible angel. Leticia's voice, like that of a Valkyrie (as her character is nicknamed), takes wing. She sings words from the early-twelfth-century Zionide by Toledo-born poet Yehuda Halevi, who died shortly after arriving in the Promised Land.[91] Sung by the soprano in very high tessitura, the words are as follows:

> My home, do you ask of my peace, who asks for yours?
> To re-ascend your mountains,
> Bedew them with my tears,
> Press my face into your earth,
> Kiss your soil and your rocks.
> I'd leave great Spain for one glimpse of your dust.
>
> We, your scattered sheep, prisoners of desire
> From the four ends of the earth
> Our dreaming spirits yearn.
> I am the wail of jackals.
> My heart is with you, the rest is here.
>
> If I'd eagles' wings I'd fly to you.
> Your air is alive with souls,
> Your light not of the sun, nor the moon, nor the stars.
> Happy we the chosen, who live so see you dawn.
> In its light
> We are restored.[92]

It is the moment when the dinner guests are released from the hold of the evil force that has held them collectively in thrall. Why these words? – the words of a twelfth-century Sephardic Jew in a Spain already notorious for its political anti-Semitism against the Jews who settled in Spain after the Roman destruction of Jerusalem: thus, "your scattered sheep, prisoners of desire," "dreaming spirits," "I am the wail of jackals." The opera at its end takes us into the psyche of the most persecuted religious group in human history, and it is their experience that gives voice to these words of resistance.

Why this terrifying, nightmarish opera by a British composer now – in Salzburg, London, and now New York, a year after Trump's victory? Fascism is on the minds of Europeans and Americans in a way it has not been since World War II. A contemporary artist Thomas Ades, the composer of the opera, was moved to present in the great repositories, the operatic museums of the highest expressions of Western musical dramatic art and Enlightenment values (Monteverdi, Handel, Mozart, Beethoven, Verdi), his sense of the destructive psychological forces at work in our politics and our culture. Art should be alarming when culture has become alarming as it was for Bunuel in the Spanish Civil War and is for Ades and us today.

9 Why Feminism and Why Now?

In an op-ed piece in the *New York Times*, Jill Filipovic observes that with Trump's election it has become clear that "American manhood is reshaping itself in two opposing directions and both archetypes are ones we've never seen before:" Drawing out the contrast, she writes:

> If Barack Obama embodied the new ideal of the progressive man – a hands-on dad and self-identified feminist married to a high-achieving woman who was once his boss – who is also well mannered and protective of his family, then Mr Trump is his antithesis, an old-school chauvinist embracing a new code of adolescent anarchy. He is a paradigm of reckless male entitlement, embracing male power while abnegating the traditional masculine requirements of chivalry, courtesy and responsibility.[1]

Obama, the "self-identified feminist," embodies a manhood not bound by the gender binary and hierarchy, a manhood that, in Filipovic's observation, "had increasingly taken root." The crisis of Trump's election in her eyes reflects a crisis in American manhood, and in labeling one archetype chauvinist and the other feminist, she identifies feminism – in its construction of manhood – as key to replacing a "paradigm of reckless male entitlement" with a new ideal of the progressive man.

We hesitate to use the language of paradigm shift and yet it is apropos. In contrasting patriarchy with democracy, we are not talking about alternatives within a single framework, as, for example, patriarchy and matriarchy are alternative forms of hierarchy. We are talking about a fundamental shift: a change in the framework that affects how and what we see, what we do and do not say – in short, a change in the way in which we perceive and speak about reality.

The puzzle of Trump's election stems in part from the failure to recognize the shift in the framework. In Trump's world view, gender is the lens through which everything is perceived. The yardstick is

115

patriarchal: is a man big enough, a winner; does a woman measure up in the eyes of the fathers? Equality, fairness, equal respect, the rule of law are beside the point. It may be rough – one of Trump's words – or even sad, another favorite, but it's how it is: some men are bigger than others; some women don't measure up. That's reality.

Why feminism and why now? Because the Trump election has sounded an alarm. Asking why Americans were attracted by Trump's paradigm, Filipovic notes it was not because of his policies which most Americans in fact oppose (think of his health care proposals, not to mention the unbuilt wall), but rather because of the manhood he represents – his resurrection of the patriarchal ideal:

> This happened while, in homes across America, the Obama model of manhood had increasingly taken root. Yes, powerful men do abuse their positions to extract sexual services from women or to remind us that no matter how mighty and successful we are, we can be reduced to simply objects of predatory male sexuality. The past few weeks have been a stark reminder that these abuses don't fall along partisan lines, with the Harvey Weinstein revelations and stories across industries and continents still unfolding in their wake.
>
> Most men also continue to fall short when it comes to household responsibilities, and men still tend to out-earn women. But, in much of America, men's and women's lives look more similar than they ever have. Women do more work for pay, and men do more care work than they previously have done. Feminists have insisted that women and men alike can and should embody the characteristics we positively associate with both masculinity (power, respect, dependability, providing) and femininity (caregiving, devotion, compassion), and many of our lives have crept closer to this ideal.
>
> To Mr Trump and many of his increasingly nihilistic supporters, this is a threat to their fantasy of masculinity. We could have guessed that men who believe in gender equality would do more housework than men with conservative views, and it is not news that white conservatives overwhelmingly vote Republican. What is different from generations before is that many of the men making up Mr Trump's base are less attached to the institutions that required responsibility – unions, church, marriage, school, independent living. In the face of women's success, many of them have fallen behind on adult obligations and fallen back to misogyny.[2]

Thus there is not only a clash between opposing masculinities but a breakdown within patriarchal masculinity, and Trump's "grasp of white male aspiration and identity," explains his appeal. To "those who want power without the shackles of responsibility," Trump's own life and actions paint an appealing picture of masculine entitlement ... He may not be the smartest or most qualified guy in just about any room, but his money allows him to marry and reproduce with a succession of models, star in a reality television show, live in vulgar gold-plated glory, say whatever offensive things danced through his brain and still make a successful run for president ...

Resentful of the changing order of things, some men have simply leaned in to chaos: If the system no longer serves them, it will at least be fun to blow it all up. Which is exactly why the old rules of political engagement don't work with Mr Trump or his base.

The president is a perfect figurehead for this bizarre moment: a man who carries all of the negative characteristics of stereotypical masculinity while adopting almost none of the virtues, occupying the most powerful and exclusively male seat of power in the nation (and perhaps in the world), who ascended in large part because a yawning fear of female power kept one of the best-qualified candidates in history out of office. He is ego unchecked, narcissism in place of dignity.[3]

Against the backdrop of the once hegemonic cultural patriarchy in America, traditional masculinity is today more fragile and contested than it has ever been. Gender binaries have become more obviously porous, challenged by queer and transgender Americans. Not only women's but also men's lives have become less constrained by gender, no longer dichotomous but a fluid spectrum.[4] Trump's racism and misogyny mobilized a reactionary politics that relied on bullying, lies, and violence to reverse these developments. Without in any way seeking to mask his intention, Trump set out to repudiate everything that Obama had stood for and represented: his race, his feminism, his embrace of the Constitution in its deepest intention, and above all, his manhood.

Seen in this light, Obama's presidency was the culmination not only of the bridge from Selma – the civil rights movement and Martin Luther King – but of all the resistance movements of the 1960s and 1970s. Although these movements differed in their focus – civil rights, the Vietnam War, women's liberation, gay rights – they all dismantled the culture of patriarchy, its politics and its psychology. The new progressive manhood of Obama was aligned with Martin Luther King's conviction that in the end the force of truth and the power of justice will prevail. It was also arguably inspired by the role resistance to patriarchy played in Obama's development, as the son of a mother who had resisted white racist patriarchy.[5] We can see the consequences of such resistance not only in the more democratic manhood of men such as Obama, but the resonance such manhood had for the Americans who elected him by majorities much larger than those of Donald Trump. In fact, despite his assertions to the contrary, Trump, like George W. Bush in the election of

2000, received fewer votes than his opponent. In the more fluid gender arrangements that are now a reality for more people, we see the potential for a truly feminist resistance in that Americans, including American men, may now be more open to ending patriarchy than ever before in American history.

Obama barely knew his Kenyan father, though he had a lively imagination about him; when he did actually meet him on his father's short visit to Honolulu, he soon "began to count the days until my father would leave."[6] Obama developed his liberal and humane values in relationship with his mother and her parents, Toot and Gramps, and to the second man his mother married, the Indonesian Lolo, with whom they lived in Indonesia for several years. Obama's mother was not only passionately committed to the resistance movements of the 1960s, a passion she imparted to her son, but she had broken the patriarchal Love Laws by marrying a black man. In patriarchal terms, she had committed a high crime and misdemeanor by falling in love with and marrying a man of color – not once but twice.

In his remarkable autobiography, written before he entered politics, Obama writes movingly of how, observing his disappointment in his father, his mother explains to him the pressures his father, a Kenyan man, was under. He had abandoned the marriage in part because his Kenyan family "didn't want Obama blood sullied by a white woman"[7] and in part because his ambition drove him to accept an offer to attend Harvard that did not cover the expenses of bringing his wife and baby. What strikes Obama after all these years is the kind of love his mother had for his father: "[T]he love of someone who knows your life in the round, a love that will survive disappointment."[8]

Obama clearly came to see and understand his mother as a whole human being with sexual interests, including "fantasies that had been forbidden to a white middle-class girl from Kansas, the promise of another life, warm, sensual, exotic, different."[9] The autobiography also tells us that his mother and her parents were devoted to his education, wanting him to go to the best private school in Honolulu, Punahou. And it was Obama's mother who, when he was a boy, woke him early each morning to teach him English lessons for three hours before he went to school. When he bridled at this regime, her response was: "This is no picnic for me either, buster."[10]

There are, however, two features of his mother and father that Obama understates in his autobiography. First, in David Remnick's recent study of Obama's life, Obama's mother, Ann Dunham, emerges as a serious, demanding, and committed intellectual, "an indefatigable researcher,"[11] an anthropologist doing fieldwork in Indonesia on the lives and futures of the craftsmen of central Java for her doctoral dissertation during her son's last three years at Punahou and completing her dissertation in 1992.[12]

During this period, Dunham remained in close contact with her son, who was living with her parents; her thesis supervisor, the granddaughter of John Dewey, Alice Dewey, observed: "She *adored* that child, ... and they were in constant touch. And he adored her."[13] Her dissertation, "Peasant Blacksmithing in Indonesia: Surviving and Thriving against All Odds," was over a thousand pages in manuscript; an in depth study of "the history, beliefs, and skill of nearly every inhabitant of the village; its intricate and evolving social, religious and class structures; its cultural formation through centuries of foreign and indigenous influence."[14] While continuing work on her dissertation, Dunham worked for the Ford Foundation in the 1980s, "concerned about women's rights and their livelihoods."[15]

Second, Obama's autobiography ends with a long visit to Kenya, in which he tries to find out more about his father, now deceased. Obama does confirm the qualities his mother had observed in his father: his generosity,[16] and his universalistic ethical values[17] but he also learns about his patriarchal grandfather, called "the Terror,"[18] who had rejected Christianity for Islam because its teaching on nonviolence "was foolish sentiment, something to comfort women,"[19] and had demanded that his son leave his white wife, Obama's mother.[20] Obama learns that his father's obedience to his father reflects the wider and deeper patriarchal culture of Kenya, in which arranged marriages, polygamy, and wife beating and child beating are endemic.[21] He also learns that his father's rather American idealism conflicted with an increasingly corrupt Kenyan politics, leading to professional failure, unhappy marriages, and alcohol abuse (culminating in the auto accident in which he died). What Obama understates is what he had been spared by not living with this man who had beaten one of his wives and children in Kenya.[22] What he learned in Kenya and earlier from his Aunt Auma in the United States was, according to Remnick, "utterly at odds with ... [his] long-held myth of his father's grandeur, a myth propagated by his loving and well-meaning mother."[23] The effect on him was liberating:

> Now, as I sat in the glow of a single light bulb, rocking slightly on a hard-backed chair, that image [of my father] had suddenly vanished. Replaced by ... what? A bitter drunk? An abusive husband? A defeated, lonely bureaucrat? To think that all my life I had been wrestling with nothing more than a ghost! For a moment I felt giddy; if Auma hadn't been in the room, I would have probably laughed out loud. The king is overthrown, I thought. The emerald curtain is pulled aside. The rabble of my head is free to run riot; I can do what I damn well please. For what man, if not my own father, has the power to tell me otherwise? Whatever I do, it seems, I won't do much worse than he did.[24]

Why, in his autobiography, would Obama understate both his mother's intellectual distinction and the extent of his father's and even Lolo's violence?[25] Obama's autobiography is written very much as a struggle to find himself as a man of color whose black father was never much of a reality in his life. Calling his book *Dreams from My Father*, he frames his narrative in the patriarchal terms dominant in such narratives in our culture (men drawing their sense of ethical identity from their fathers). The truth of the matter is much more radical: it was his mother's care, joined by that of his grandparents and Lolo, that had nurtured his own ethical voice. His ethical identity was forged in a remarkably honest and unidealized relationship to a mother whom he came to see both as a sexually loving woman (challenging the patriarchal Love Laws) and as an accomplished intellectual and feminist activist. The narrative of his autobiography explodes the framework within which it is written, which is to say that it comes to see patriarchy as a lie: "The king is overthrown, I thought ... I can do what I damn well please. For what man, if not my own father, has the power to tell me otherwise?"

Obama thus experienced at firsthand both his mother's resistance to the patriarchal Love Laws, and his father's lack of resistance, opening his heart and mind to what makes such resistance so liberatory yet so difficult and the lack of resistance sometimes so tragic. What such resistance makes psychologically possible is breaking through the ethnic and other stereotypes that divide us and keep us from loving another as an individual. It was in loving relationship to such a resisting woman (who loved his father as an individual) that Obama came to accord authority to her liberal and humane values, including the moral authority of women's voices and experiences. Obama dealt with the experience of loss (the loss of his father, the feeling of separation as a man of color from his white mother and grandparents) not through identification with patriarchal stereotypes of manhood, but by staying in relationship to the real, individual people whom he loved and who loved him. Both his mother and Toot were strong, adventurous women, loving men while holding to their own ambitions and sense of themselves (Toot earned more money than her husband). Obama stayed in loving relationship to unidealized real women (including a mother who did not sacrifice her sexual or her intellectual life) and an unidealized real man, Gramps, who showed his grandson a white man who resisted his grandmother's racist fears[26] and introduced him to a black poet, who helped Obama think about and through these issues.[27]

Indeed, his mother, an anthropologist, may have imparted to her son an interpretive ability not to confuse culture and nature, and thus to be sensitive to the ways in which the power of patriarchy rests on this confusion. Through his mother and grandmother, one suspects,

Obama came to his own vibrant relationship with a strong woman, Michelle Obama, and subsequently with their two daughters. In *Dreams from My Father*, he identifies a "strong, true love" with an equal as what saves men from the "male cruelties" that destroyed his father.[28] In doing so, he shows us a manhood that is democratic, not patriarchal.

It is striking that, while describing his youth as "living out a caricature of black male adolescence, itself a caricature of swaggering American manhood,"[29] it is relationships to women who either challenge his quest for racial identity (Joyce by her search to be an individual[30]) or prod him (Regina) to greater honesty (using the name "Barack," closer to his real roots, his Kenyan father),[31] or tongue lash him into a sense of larger ethical responsibility that transcends race.[32] While both Joyce and Regina are evidently fictionalized, the underlying experience of his they reflect is clearly not that of a patriarchal man, who would not be moved in this way by the authority of women's resisting ethical voices.[33] The roots of resistance in Obama's life are clear: he writes that even when young and talking with black friends about *"white folks* this or *black folks* that," he "would suddenly remember my mother's smile, and the words that I spoke would seem awkward and false."[34] One senses as well that when in New York Obama faces the option of conventional upward mobility that so many others in his place took or would take, his choice to do community work in Chicago was very much in line with the ethical voice nourished by his remarkable mother.

It is this universalistic ethical sensitivity,[35] rooted in his mother's ethic of care, that can explain how and why it was that, for Obama, images of the civil rights movement, which predated him, "became a kind of prayer for me, bolstering my spirits, channeling my emotions in a way that words never could."[36] Obama's bi-racial background had led some American blacks who met him when he came to the mainland to study, to refer to him as "an Oreo."[37] For Obama, his choice to identify as black was very much an ethical choice made in light of what the American civil rights movement had meant to his mother and came to mean to him. It is not just that his mother was so much an expression of the civil rights movement in breaking the racist Love Laws by marrying the black man she loved and giving birth to his son. It was also that Martin Luther King, Jr, through his discovery and brilliant use of a militant nonviolent voice, had found a moving and powerful resisting ethical voice that spoke to and energized not only the people of color and others he led into nonviolent resistance, but had appeal and moral force for Americans generally. King himself described the nonviolent ethical voice of his movement as "disarming the opponent,"[38] calling to a deeper level of shared humanity and appealing to a sense of guilt over the divisions racism had allowed and sustained.

If patriarchy, as we have observed, often sustains itself through shame and violence keyed to any real or imagined transgression of the gender binary, such shame shows its power by the ways in which it wars on human relationality and rationalizes atrocity, as it did in fascist Germany and Japan. American patriarchy had supported our racism for a very long time. What King discovered and expressed, as the great ethical prophet and preacher he was, was a way through nonviolence to appeal to the underlying sense of guilt that many Americans in the South and elsewhere had felt as well. When King speaks of "disarming the opponent," he is quite precisely describing the process by which a free ethical voice resists and exposes the violence of white racist patriarchy by appealing to an ethical voice that patriarchy had silenced by shaming it as unmanly. King's voice achieved its universalistic ethical appeal because he spoke both to deeper ethical values that Americans shared (including those of their Judaeo-Christianity) and to the constitutional principles of free speech and equal protection they also held in common. Unlike Obama, King very much had a father who was in his life and a patriarchal father at that, but he bridled at many of his father's choices as a minister. Indeed, King found his ethical voice not in relationship to his father, but in relationship to the nonviolent Christianity of his mother and grandmother and in his understanding of Niebuhr and Gandhi. His resistance found its most immediately appreciative audience among courageous black women – including the women who began the Montgomery bus boycott before King appeared on the scene.[39] Obama's mother was, by contrast, spiritual, not religious in a sectarian sense, but, broadly speaking, a person rooted in the universalism of the ethic of care. As Obama put it: "Like most of my values, I learned about empathy from her."[40]

It was the force of truth that had brought Obama to national attention, his vote against the Iraq War had set him apart from his competitors for the Democratic Party's nomination, and he was a self-identified feminist, married to Michelle, a strong and outspoken and truly liberated woman, as free to be mom-in-chief as she had been to be Barack's boss and a hospital administrator. By the end of his presidency, Obama had come out in support of gay marriage.

Manhood was what the 2016 election was about. Although this couldn't be said directly, it was obvious once it became clear that despite all their talk about replacing Obamacare, when it came right down to it, the Republicans had no health care policy. It was Obama himself they were determined to replace.

Collectively speaking, we on the left don't see the problems we face as a problem of manhood. We don't speak about these problems in terms of gender. Mass incarceration, the war on drugs, the war on crime, the death penalty, solitary confinement – we know these policies disproportionately affect men but we speak of them as racist policies, policies masquerading as law and order, the new Jim Crow. The racism is spoken, the gender remains tacit even when mentioned (as in the Jim of Jim Crow). Yet we know it is Black and Latino men who are most often afflicted. It is not only racism but patriarchy that disproportionately targets black men in prison as losers unworthy of humane treatment. Their cruel and unusual punishment is rationalized and fuels the injustice, remaining invisible because the force of patriarchy, in particular when it harms men, remains invisible, as we saw in our discussion of America's unjust wars (Chapter 7).

Michael Kimmel, Tony Porter, and Terrence Real, along with Jim Gilligan, are in the forefront of those who have pinpointed the costs to men of a toxic, shame-driven masculinity – patriarchal in exposing a man to shame should he display human qualities perceived as feminine (sadness as opposed to anger) or fail to achieve or maintain a position of superiority (at the very least over women). As Jim Gilligan has written, this "male-role belief system" is a recipe for violence[41] – for suicide as well as homicide, for war as well as domestic violence, all of which predominantly lie in the province of men. Michael Kimmel has given it a name: "Guyland." In Guyland, as several of our students experienced firsthand, binge-drinking, fraternity hazing, predatory sex, and party rape are part of the rite of passage. In Guyland the gender binary and hierarchy are unquestioned. To be a man means not to be a pussy or a faggot, and manhood, its superiority and strength, is proven by a man's ability to endure what otherwise would be recognized as torture.[42] Tony Porter introduced the term "man box" to capture how a man can become trapped by patriarchy;[43] in *I Don't Want to Talk About It*, Terry Real exposes the otherwise secret legacy of male depression. In a telling chart he includes in his book, he shows how if one counts the alcoholism, the drug abuse, the emotional absence, and the reckless behavior leading to accidents as manifestations of a depression that men don't want to talk about, then the rate of depression among men is as high as it is among women.[44]

In recent work, Way and her colleagues have highlighted boys' resistance to these codes of masculinity and the association of this resistance with their psychological and social well-being, as indicated, among other things, by having close friends and doing well in school. Boys' resistance was a refusal of the emotional stoicism and independence that have been held up as badges of maturity and manliness. As one boy ruefully put it: "It might be nice to be a girl ... then you wouldn't have to be emotionless."[45]

There is more resistance among boys than common stereotypes of masculinity might lead us to expect. Holding on to emotional intimacy and close relationships with a parent, most often a mother, proved important to a boy's psychological resilience. Not surprisingly, given the culture, a high ranking on the scale of manliness allowed such robust and resilient boys more freedom to resist gender norms. Way's studies also charted the effects of culture on boys' resistance. For example, Asian boys fared badly in resistance because cultural norms stigmatized them as feminine and they tended to comply with gender norms as protection, whereas Latino boys showed higher levels of resistance both because of closer relationships with parents and because they scored higher on cultural norms of manliness.

In short, it is Obama's manhood, not Trump's, that, like a strong immune system, is associated with boys' psychological health and their ability to withstand stress.

Which brings us to feminism. Like Obama, the men leading the new men's movement are self-identified feminists. Feminists because they recognize the harm patriarchy inflicts on men. Feminists because in embracing the full range of human capacities across the gender spectrum, they reject the gender binary and hierarchy. Feminists because they see that we have to talk about gender and the patriarchal scripts of masculinity and femininity that rationalize and perpetuate injustice.

Why feminism and why now? Because it was feminism that first drew our attention to how the conversation about gender was framed. It was feminism that revealed the patriarchal framework as a framework, a way of seeing, and led us to hear the patriarchal voice as a voice: a way of speaking about things rather than a statement of how things are. To take an example close to home, it was feminism that tuned our ear to a different voice, raising implicitly the question: different from what? And thus revealing that the voice we had been taught to hear not as a voice but as the truth was in fact speaking from a patriarchal standpoint, where the gender binary and hierarchy were taken for granted. It was feminism that taught us to listen for and to hear the gender binary and hierarchy in, say, the elevation of reason (masculine) over emotion (feminine), mind over body, the self over relationships, white over black, straight over gay, culture over (mother) nature, justice over caring, and on and on.

Why feminism now? Because at this moment in history, we need both to see the framework and to free democracy from patriarchy.

The women's march that followed Trump's inauguration was joined by men who marched under the banner of feminism. The ethic of care became the umbrella that could encompass the protest against all forms of injustice. Under an ethic of care, Black Lives Matter, a movement started by three black women, and trans lives, challenging the gender binary, matter as well. The women and men of the #MeToo movement exemplify as well a resistance based on an ethic of care. Patriarchy counts on and enforces invisibility: not seeing what is before one's eyes and shaming the voices that reveal and contest its abuses.

With Trump's election, we may have reached a tipping point. In writing about Mishra's *Age of Anger*, Charles King wonders: "[I]f an alternative genealogy – one that ran, say, from Sojourner Truth to Simone de Beauvoir, Emmeline Pankhurst to 'Trump that bitch!' – might tell us something equally important about the modern condition: yet another age of angry men."[46]

To us, the answer seems obvious: feminism can tell us something about men's anger that has eluded other approaches to analyzing modernity. It shows us how centrally gender is implicated. As our student Adam put it, an ancient framework of patriarchy and manhood had forced on him a loss he regrets to this day. That in itself is a cause for anger – in his own eyes he had betrayed what is right. But as Jim Gilligan reminds us, since anger is less painful than sadness, men's anger can also serve as a cover, shielding them from the pain of loss.[47]

In the mid-1970s, one of us (Gilligan) along with other feminists, saw feminism as transformational, freeing men as well as women from the constraints of the gender binary that would render both half-human, and from a hierarchy that was antithetical not only to justice but also to love. That feminism implies a transformation at the societal as well as the psychological level is an insight that keeps getting lost and then rediscovered. The sense of surprise that accompanies the rediscovery cues us to the paradigm shift, because what was inconceivable within a patriarchal paradigm suddenly becomes obvious: patriarchy harms men as well as women. The different voice – the voice that joins rather than separates thought from emotion – is a human voice.

In *Don't Think of an Elephant*, Lakoff underscores the power of frames, which he defines as "mental structures that shape the way we see the world." How we frame things affects "the goals we set, the plans we make, the way we act, and what counts as a good or bad outcome of our actions. In politics, frames shape our social policies and the institutions we form to carry out policies. To change our frames is to change all this. Reframing is social change."[48]

For us, his most riveting observation is that frames are part of our "cognitive unconscious." As we stated earlier, you cannot see frames. As Lakoff explains, they are "structures in our brains that we cannot consciously access but know by their consequences. What we call 'common sense' is made up of unconscious, automatic, effortless inferences that follow from our unconscious frames."[49]

Feminism makes the unconscious conscious; it makes us aware of how riddled by gender our ways of making sense of the world are and have been. How automatically, effortlessly, or as our student Adam put it, how without a conscious thought, our goals, our plans, our actions, and what counts as a good and bad outcome are shaped by a force we cannot see but whose effects we live with. When patriarchy is the frame, the gender binary and hierarchy become common sense.

Lakoff himself seems unaware of this elephant in his room. His two moral frameworks are not alternative frameworks within a single paradigm; instead they signify a paradigm shift. Within the framework of patriarchy, the contrast would be framed by the gender binary: strict father vs. nurturant mother. The paradigm shift is from a framework defined by gender (strict father) to one where gender is irrelevant (nurturant parent), which is what happens when a patriarchal paradigm gives way to one that is democratic.

Hillary's loss can be chalked up to Trump's success in shifting the frame. He was the strict father who succeeded in framing her as bad – not a nurturant mother. Crooked Hillary, such a nasty woman, who could trust her? Her qualifications for the presidency became irrelevant. And nothing she said could make a difference without challenging and changing the frame.

Lakoff's analysis jibes with our own; in our eyes, he is a closet feminist. So was Foucault in his revelatory analysis of prisons, as one of us (Richards) has argued.[50] Lakoff observes that "all words are defined relative to conceptual frames," which means that when the moral framework shifts, words change their meaning. In Hawthorne's novel, not only does the scarlet A come to mean Able, but many people forget its original signification. So powerful is the effect of the frame.

Why feminism and why now? Because it is essential to free democracy from patriarchy, which in its current licentious incarnation is tinged with nihilism and edging toward fascism. But here's the rub. As a movement for women's liberation, feminism itself can get trapped in the gender binary and hierarchy, where it becomes at once a threat to men and marginal to our intellectual and political culture. Thus the power of patriarchy – its crude and mysterious force – is not confronted. Some of our most profound injustices remain invisible for this reason (take prisons or our two-tiered educational system as examples) and the carelessness of our society becomes masked by a hypocritical piety.

Only a perspective that zeroes in on the question of why there was not more effective resistance to Trump – not only among groups that voted for him (primarily white men and women) but also by those who did not vote or who threw away their votes for all practical purposes – can give rise to the resistance we now clearly need. Otherwise, the resistance one would expect within an ostensibly democratic nation will continue to be muted or subverted, as it was during Trump's campaign, and the political psychology that elected him will remain in the wings, ready to be mobilized by him or yet another demagogue. In effect, the moral injury patriarchy has inflicted on Americans of all genders sets the stage for the continuation of moral slavery.

It is feminism then, as Woolf envisioned and, around the same time, Ruth Benedict (familiar with the injustices of patriarchy in her own life) brought to bear in her pioneering studies of Japanese fascism and American racism,[51] that joins us across what we now recognize to be the full spectrum of gender, in a common struggle against patriarchy and fascism; a struggle animated by the great principles of liberty, equality, and justice. But perhaps alone among the liberation movements, feminism joins a politics with a psychology in its understanding of what keeps us enchained. Feminism with its ethic of care both pinpoints and resists the moral injury – the trauma that the gender binary and hierarchy inflict on our humanity, impeding our ability to love and compromising our ethics and our politics. As a number of our students confessed, it was the force of patriarchy and more specifically, its framing of manhood and womanhood, that had led them to acts of infidelity and silence that continue to haunt them. Why, they asked, had they betrayed their humanity? And they pointed to culturally mandated scripts of masculinity and femininity, enacted without a conscious thought and enforced through sometimes violent initiations, including bullying, sexual harassment, and rape. Finding a resisting voice together in the same way women and men in the #MeToo and other movements and high school students in the #NeverAgain movement,[52] are today raising their voices, individually and collectively, our students resisted the infidelity and silence that American patriarchy had or would inflict on them. And, unsurprisingly in view of our psychology, given women's developmental advantages in resisting patriarchy, women's breaking their silence is playing a pivotal role in a number of such resistance movements, inspiring other women as well as men to join them.[53]

We have seen the power of joining resisting voices in our work together, coming, as we do, from such different backgrounds – a straight, long-married Jewish woman, the mother of three sons, and a gay Italian-American man, who has lived with his Jewish lover for forty years. Our love arose across gender binaries and hierarchies (masculine/feminine, straight/gay) because we resisted those boundaries, as both of us had done earlier in our private and public lives. But it was feminism that was the key to joining our voices both in our first book and here – that is, our commitment again over many years to freeing democracy from patriarchy. As we came increasingly to recognize in the course of doing work that integrates psychology and politics, freeing democracy from patriarchy is inseparable from freeing love.

In our teaching we are often surprised by how little it takes to free a voice that had been held in silence. By keeping our eye on the paradigm – how issues are framed – and paying attention to resonance – what voices are enhanced or resounded and which go unheard or are silenced – our seminar has encouraged a process of discovery for our students as well as ourselves. Among the discoveries was the realization that moral injury is systemic in patriarchy – a betrayal of what is right has been folded into a process of initiation, where it readily passes as the price one pays for growing up. For our students, it was the communalization of the trauma – the discovery that a loss they had experienced was one that others also had experienced – that brought home to them their common humanity across their various differences in race and class and sexuality and nationality. As our seminar made the darkness of patriarchy visible in ways that students often had not seen before, so it also made democracy palpable. In calling forth a voice that was grounded in their experience and encouraging relationship through collaborative work, by drawing on the insights of artists as well as scholars and welcoming creative work, our classroom over time has increasingly become the kind of public arena that Arendt envisioned as a key to democracy's future.

Patriarchy has been culturally dominant for so long and resistance to it can elicit violence, repressive forces driven by the shaming of patriarchal manhood and womanhood. In the extreme, this fuels the angry nihilism that motors fascism.[54] These reactionary forces take the form they do when patriarchy is the hegemonic frame, that is, when it becomes unimaginable, indeed infuriating and terrifying, that there could be an alternative (liberal democracy) that challenges patriarchy. But our experience today (reflected in the work of our students and in the resurgent democratic resistance movements in our culture) is that there are alternative, more humane ways of living (personally and politically) now thriving among us, vibrant because the voice they express and call for is a human voice. There is no threat of nihilism here, but ways of living together that are more truly democratic. And, feminism, as we understand it in this work, is the key to real democracy because it frees a human voice from patriarchy – liberating both women and men from the harms patriarchy inflicts on their humanity.

With the darkness of patriarchy now visible, feminism becomes *the* ethical movement of our age. Resistance to patriarchy is not only critical to democracy's future as we claimed in 2008; it very likely is critical now to there being a future. For our planet to remain habitable and our species to survive, we have to attend, among other things, to the framing of manhood.

Once we can see how a particular framing of manhood and womanhood sanctions or renders invisible the betrayal of love and the silencing of a voice that resists injustice – once we recognize that this is a framing, a way of seeing, a voice or way of speaking rather than the truth or human nature – then we can envision more precisely just what it would take to free democracy from patriarchy. Why feminism and why now? Because as the movement to free democracy from patriarchy it holds a key to human survival.

Notes

Introduction

1 Carol Gilligan and David A. J. Richards, *The Deepening Darkness: Patriarchy, Resistance, and Democracy's Future* (New York: Cambridge University Press, 2008).

2 See Paul Krugman, "How Republics End," *New York Times*, December 19, 2016, p. A21.

3 See Antonio R. Damasio, *Descartes' Error: Emotion, Reason, and the Human Brain* (Orlando: Harcourt, Inc., 2003).

4 See W. E. B. Du Bois, *The Souls of Black Folk*, in Nathan Higgins, ed., *W.E.B. Du Bois: Writings* (New York: Library of America, 1986; first published 1903); *Black Reconstruction in America, 1860–1880* (New York: Atheneum, 1969; first published 1935). For commentary, see Gilligan and Richards, *The Deepening Darkness*, pp. 242–3.

5 See Richard Wright, *Black Boy*, in Arnold Rampersad, ed., *Richard Wright: Later Works* (New York: The Library of America, 1991), pp. 5–365. For commentary, see David A. J. Richards, *Women, Gays, and the Constitution: The Grounds for Feminism and Gay Rights in Culture and Law* (Chicago: University of Chicago Press, 1998), p. 275.

6 See James Baldwin, *Collected Essays* edited by Toni Morrison (New York: The Library of America, 1998); James Baldwin, *Early Novels and Stories* edited by Toni Morrison (New York: The Library of America, 1998). For commentary, see David A. J. Richards, *Why Love Leads to Justice: Love across the Boundaries* (New York: Cambridge University Press, 2016), pp. 150–81.

7 See Ida Wells-Barnett, *Selected Works of Ida B. Wells-Barnett* edited by Trudier Harris (New York: Oxford University Press, 1991). For commentary, see Richards, *Women, Gays, and the Constitution*, pp. 185–90.

8 See Jeffrey Stewart, ed., *Narrative of Sojourner Truth* (New York: Oxford University Press, 1991; first published 1850); for commentary, see Richards, *Women, Gays, and the Constitution*, pp. 115–17.

9 See Harriet A. Jacobs, *Incidents in the Life of a Slave Girl* edited by Jean Fagan Yellin (Cambridge: Harvard University Press, 1987; first published 1861). For commentary, see Richards, *Women, Gays, and the Constitution*, pp. 117–19.

10 See, for example, Toni Morrison, *Beloved* (New York: Knopf, 1987); Toni Morrison, *The Bluest Eye* (New York: Vintage, 2007); Toni Morrison, *Playing in the Dark: Whiteness and the Literary Imagination* (Cambridge: Harvard University Press, 1992); Toni Morrison, *The Origin of Others* Foreword by Ta-Nehisi Coates (Cambridge: Harvard University Press, 2017).

11 Audre Lorde, *Sister Outsider* (New York: Ten Speed Press, 2007).

12 Robin Coste Lewis, *Voyage of the Sable Venus* (New York: Knopf, 2016).

13 Michelle Cliff, *The Land of Look Behind* (Ithaca: Firebrand Books, 1985); Michelle Cliff, *Free Enterprise: A Novel of Mary Ellen Pleasant* (New York: Dutton, 2004).

14 James Gilligan, *Violence: Reflections on a National Epidemic* (New York: Vintage, 1996).
15 Virginia Woolf, *Three Guineas* Jane Marcus edition (Orlando: Harvest, 2006; first published 1938), p. 168.

1: Patriarchy Comes Out of Hiding

1 Hannah Arendt, *The Human Condition*, 2nd edn (Chicago: University of Chicago Press, 1998; first published 1958).
2 For Arendt's critique of representation, see Hannah Arendt, *On Revolution* (New York: Penguin, 2006; first published 1963), pp. 226–31.
3 See David A. J. Richards, *Women, Gays, and the Constitution: The Grounds for Feminism and Gay Rights in Culture and Law* (Chicago: University of Chicago Press, 1998), pp. 3, 155, 261, 354, 371, 458.
4 Carol Gilligan, "Moral Injury and the Ethic of Care: Reframing the Conversation about Differences," *Journal of Social Philosophy*, Vol. 45 No. 1 (Spring 2014), pp. 89–106.
5 Carol Gilligan and David A. J. Richards, *The Deepening Darkness: Patriarchy, Resistance, and Democracy's Future* (Cambridge: Cambridge University Press, 2008), p. 22.
6 Aeschylus, *The Oresteia* translated by Robert Fagles (New York: Penguin, 1977), p. 269.
7 See Thucydides, *History of the Peloponnesian War* translated by Rex Warner (New York: Penguin, 1972) on the murder of innocent Melians, rationalized as not requiring any moral justification, pp. 400–8 (the Melian Dialogue).
8 Ibid., p. 151.
9 Jill Abramson, "This May Shock You: Hillary Clinton is Fundamentally Honest," *The Guardian*, March 28, 2016, www.theguardian.com/commentisfree/2016/mar/28/hillary-clinton-honest-transparency-jill-abramson; see also Nicholas Kristof, "Is Hillary Clinton Dishonest?," *New York Times*, April 23, 2016, www.nytimes.com/2016/04/24/opinion/sunday/is-hillary-clinton-dishonest.html.
10 See, on this point, the essays in Diane Wachtell, ed., *Wolf Whistle Politics: The New Misogyny in America Today* (New York: The New Press, 2017).
11 Hannah Arendt, *The Origins of Totalitarianism* (Orlando: A Harvest Book, 1976; first published 1951) (Best Seller on Amazon.com).
12 George Orwell, *1984* (New York: Signet, 1950; first published 1949) (Best Seller on Amazon.com).
13 Arendt, *The Origins of Totalitarianism*, p. 474.
14 Virginia Woolf, *Three Guineas* Jane Marcus edition (Orlando: Harvest, 2006; first published 1938).
15 Ibid., p. 121.
16 Ibid., p. 119.
17 See, on this point, Woolf, *Three Guineas*, p. 122.
18 Ibid., p. 16.
19 See ibid., pp. 23–8.
20 Ibid., p. 99.
21 Ibid., p. 112.
22 Ibid., p. 123.
23 Ibid., p. 134.
24 Ibid., p. 170.
25 Virginia Woolf, *A Room of One's Own* (San Diego: Harvest, 1981; first published 1929), p. 35.
26 See, on this point, Woolf, *Three Guineas*, pp. 132, 135.
27 Ibid., p. 168.
28 Ibid., p. 153.
29 See Carol Gilligan, *The Birth of Pleasure: A New Map of Love* (New York: Vintage, 2003); Gilligan and Richards, *The Deepening Darkness*.

2: Infidelity and Silence

1 Aristophanes, *Lysistrata*, in Aristophanes, *Lysistrata and Other Plays* translated by Alan Sommerstein (London: Penguin, 2002), pp. 133–93.
2 Judy Y. Chu, *When Boys Become Boys: Development, Relationships, and Masculinity* (New York: New York University Press, 2014).
3 Niobe Way, *Deep Secrets: Boys' Friendships and the Crisis of Connection* (Cambridge: Harvard University Press, 2011).
4 See Carol Gilligan, Janie Victoria Ward, and Jill McLean Taylor, eds., *Mapping the Moral Domain: A Contribution of Women's Thinking to Psychological Theory and Education* (Cambridge: Harvard University Press, 1988); Carol Gilligan, Nona Plessner Lyons, and Trudy Hanmer, eds., *Making Connections: The Relational Worlds of Adolescent Girls at Emma Willard School* (Cambridge: Harvard University Press, 1990); Carol Gilligan, Annie G. Rogers, and Deborah Tolman, eds., *Women, Girls, and Psychotherapy: Reframing Resistance* (Binghamton: Haworth Press, 1991); Lyn Mikel Brown and Carol Gilligan, *Meeting at the Crossroads: Women's Psychology and Girls' Development* (Cambridge: Harvard University Press, 1992; paperback edition by Ballantine, New York, 1993); Jill McLean Taylor, Carol Gilligan, and Amy Sullivan, *Between Voice and Silence: Women and Girls, Race and Relationship* (Cambridge: Harvard University Press, 1995).
5 See Chu, *When Boys Become Boys*, pp. ix–xv.
6 Carol Gilligan, "Moral Injury and the Ethic of Care: Reframing the Conversation about Differences," *Journal of Social Philosophy*, Vol. 45 No. 1 (Spring 2014), pp. 89–106.
7 Donald Moss, *Thirteen Ways of Looking at a Man: Psychoanalysis and Masculinity* (London: Routledge, 2015).
8 See Jonathan Shay, *Achilles in Vietnam: Combat Trauma and the Undoing of Character* (New York: Scribner, 1994), pp. 20, 165–209.
9 Moss, *Thirteen Ways of Looking at a Man*.
10 Gilligan, "Moral Injury and the Ethic of Care", at pp. 97–8.
11 Ibid.
12 See Arundhati Roy, *The God of Small Things* (New York: Harper-Perennial, 1997).
13 See Ibid., p. 33.
14 See David A.J. Richards, *Why Love Leads to Justice: Love across the Boundaries* (New York: Cambridge University Press, 2016).
15 See Carol Gilligan, *In a Different Voice: Psychological Theory and Women's Development* (Cambridge: Harvard University Press, 1982).
16 *Roe* v. *Wade*, 410 U.S. 113 (1973) (Texas law forbidding abortions except to save the life of the mother held unconstitutional violation of the constitutional right to privacy).
17 See Barack Obama, *Dreams from My Father* (New York: Three Rivers Press, 2004; first published 1996), pp. 87–8.
18 See, for discussion and references on this point, Gilligan, *In a Different Voice*, at pp. 98–101.

3: Why Didn't We See It?

1 See Sarah Blaffer Hrdy, *Mothers and Others: The Evolutionary Origins of Mutual Understanding* (Cambridge: Harvard University Press, 2009).
2 Ibid., p. 287.
3 Carol Gilligan, *The Birth of Pleasure: A New Map of Love* (New York: Vintage, 2003).
4 David A. J Richards, *Disarming Manhood: Roots of Ethical Resistance* (Athens: Swallow Press/Ohio University Press, 2005).
5 Carol Gilligan, *Joining the Resistance* (Cambridge: Polity, 2011).
6 David A. J. Richards, *Why Love Leads to Justice: Love across the Boundaries* (New York: Cambridge University Press, 2016).

7 Moira Weigel, "Political Correctness: How the Right Invented a Phantom Enemy," in Diane Wachtell, ed., *Wolf Whistle Politics: The New Misogyny in America Today* (New York: The New Press, 2017), pp. 105–19, at p. 108.

8 Theodor Adorno, *The Jargon of Authenticity*, translated by Knut Tarnowski and Frederick Will (London: Routledge, 2003; first published 1973); for further documentation and exploration of Heidegger's fascism and even more appalling refusal to acknowledge mistake and remorse, see George Steiner, *Martin Heidegger* (Chicago: University of Chicago Press, 1989), pp. vii–xxxv, 118–26.

9 See Jason Stanley, *How Propaganda Works* (Princeton: Princeton University Press, 2015), pp. 11, 26. See also Jason Stanley, "Democracy and the Demagogue," *New York Times*, October 12, 2105, https://opinionator.blogs.nytimes.com/2015/10/12/democracy-and-the-demagogue/.

10 See Stanley, *How Propaganda Works*, pp. 123–4.

11 See Ian Haney Lopez, *Dog Whistle Politics: How Coded Racial Appeals Have Reinvented Racism and Wrecked the Middle Class* (New York: Oxford University Press, 2014).

12 May 13, 2009 interview of John Ehrlichman by G. Kerlikowske, heard in the documentary movie, *13th*, directed by Ava DuVernay (2016).

13 See Alex Rose, "The Frankfurt School Knew Trump Was Coming," *New Yorker*, December 5, 2016, at www.newyorker.com/culture/cultural-comment/the-frankfurt-school-knew-trump-was-coming. For the most brilliant and illuminating study, see Hannah Arendt, *The Origins of Totalitarianism* (Orlando: A Harvest Book, 1976; first published 1951).

14 See T. W. Adorno, Else Frenkel-Brunswick, Daniel J. Levinson, and R. Nevitt Sanford, *The Authoritarian Personality* (New York: Harper & Row, 1950), p. 60.

15 Jonathan Allen and Amie Parnes, *Shattered: Inside Hillary Clinton's Doomed Campaign* (New York: Crown, 2017).

16 See Victoria L. Brescoli and Eric Luis Uhlmann, "Can an Angry Woman Get Ahead: Status Conferral, Gender, and Expression of Emotion in the Workplace," *Psychological Science*, Vol. 19, No. 3 (March, 2008), pp. 268–75; Tyler G. Okimoto and Victoria L. Brescoli, "The Price of Power: Power Seeking and Backlash against Female Politicians," *Personality and Social Psychology Bulletin* Vol. 36, No. 7 (2010), pp. 923–36.

17 See Hillary Rodham Clinton, *What Happened* (New York: Simon & Schuster, 2017), pp. 209, 271–3.

18 David Remnick, "Still Here: Hillary Clinton Looks Back in Anger," *New Yorker*, September 25, 2017, pp. 58–67, at p. 67.

19 Susan Bordo, *The Destruction of Hillary Clinton* (Brooklyn: Melville House, 2017).

20 See Bordo, *The Destruction of Hillary Clinton*, pp. 133–49, 176–9.

21 See, on these points, Rebecca Traister, "Hillary Clinton is Furious. And Resigned and Funny. And Worried: The Surreal Post-election Life of the Woman Who Would Have Been President," *New York Magazine*, May 2, 2017, http://nymag.com/daily/intelligencer/2017/05/hillary-clinton-life-after-election.html.

22 See also David A. J. Richards, *Resisting Injustice and the Feminist Ethics of Care in the Age of Obama: "Suddenly,... All the Truth Was Coming Out"* (New York: Routledge, 2013).

23 David Remnick, *The Bridge: The Life and Rise of Barack Obama* (New York: Vintage, 2011).

24 See, on this point, Barack Obama, *Dreams from My Father* (New York: Three Rivers Press, 2004; first published 1996), pp. 428–9.

25 See, for a brilliant documentation of this phenomenon, Arlie Russell Hochschild, *Strangers in Their Own Land: Anger and Mourning on the American Right* (New York: The New Press, 2016).

26 Ibid., p. 56.

27 For an argument that such irrationalist appeal may also exist in American business culture, see Rakesh Khurana, *Searching for a Corporate Savior: The Irrational Quest for Charismatic CEOs* (Princeton: Princeton University Press, 2002).

28 See Lynn Nottage, *Sweat* (New York: Theatre Communications Group, 2017).

29 Nottage, *Sweat*, p. 109.

30 Michael Schulman, "The First Theatrical Landmark of the Trump Era: Lynn Nottage's play 'Sweat' Is a Tough Yet Empathetic Portrait of the America That Came Undone," *New Yorker*, March 27, 2017, www.newyorker.com/magazine/2017/03/27/the-first-theatrical-landmark-of-the-trump-era, pp. 1–11, at p. 1.

31 See "Black Lives Matter," *Wikipedia*, https://en.wikipedia/wiki/Black_Lives_Matter; see also Mary Beard, *Women & Power: A Manifesto* (New York: Liveright Publishing Corporation, 2017), p. 88 (photo of these women at Glamour Women of the World, 2016).

32 See, on this point, Carol Sanger, *About Abortion: Terminating Pregnancy in Twenty-first-century America* (Cambridge: Belknap Press of Harvard University Press, 2017), pp. 185–213.

33 See Wendy Davis, "Wolf Whistle Politics: Taking Back the Conversation to Advance Women's Rights," in Diane Wachtell, ed., *Wolf Whistle Politics: The New Misogyny in America Today* (New York: The New Press, 2017), pp. xvii–xxviii.

34 See Kristin Luker, *Abortion and the Politics of Motherhood* (Berkeley: University of California Press, 1985).

35 See, on this point, James Gilligan, *Violence: Reflections on a National Epidemic* (New York: Vintage, 1996).

36 See, on these points, the powerfully reasoned dissents of Justice Stevens in *District of Columbia* v. *Heller*, 128 S.Ct. 2783, 2822–47 (2008) and *McDonald* v. *City of Chicago*, 130 S.Ct. 3020, 3088–120 (2010).

37 For fuller critique of Scalia's originalism as rooted in patriarchy, see David A. J. Richards, *Fundamentalism in American Religion and Law: Obama's Challenge to Patriarchy's Threat to Democracy* (Cambridge: Cambridge University Press, 2010).

38 On this point, see Jeffrey Toobin, "Full-Court Press: The Man behind Trump's Supreme Court," *New Yorker*, April 17, 2017, pp. 24–8.

39 See, on this point, "Justice Gorsuch Delivers," Editorial, *New York Times*, Sunday, July 2, 2017, p. SR10.

40 For fuller critique of Scalia's originalism as rooted in patriarchy, see Richards, *Fundamentalism in American Religion and Law*.

41 Adam Liptak, "Let Me Finish, Please: Conservative Men Dominate the Debate," *New York Times National*, Tuesday, April 16, 2017, p. A13.

4: Why Now?

1 James Gilligan, *Violence: Reflections on a National Epidemic* (New York: Vintage, 1996).

2 Margaret Atwood, *The Handmaid's Tale* (New York: Anchor, 1998).

3 Quoted in Robert O. Paxton, *The Anatomy of Fascism* (New York: Vintage Books, 2004), p. 17.

4 See, for elaboration of this idea, James Gilligan, "Terrorism, Fundamentalism, and Nihilism," in Henry Parens and Stuart Twemlow, eds., *The Future of Prejudice: Applications of Psychoanalytic Understanding toward its Prevention* (New York: Rowman & Littlefield, 2006), pp. 37–62.

5 See Hannah Arendt, *The Origins of Totalitarianism* (Orlando: A Harvest Book, 1976; first published 1951).

6 See, on these points, ibid., pp. 341–88.

7 Arendt, *The Origins of Totalitarianism*, p. 474.

8 T. W. Adorno, Else Frenkel-Brunswick, Daniel J. Levinson, and R. Nevitt Sanford, *The Authoritarian Personality* (New York: Harper & Row, 1950).

9 See Erich Fromm, *Escape From Freedom* (New York: Henry Holt, 1965; first published 1941), pp. 161–3, 167–8.

10 Ibid., p. 164.

11 Ibid., p. 220.

12 Quoted at ibid., p. 220.

13 Ibid., p. 159.

14 See Adorno, et al., *The Authoritarian Personality*, p. 228. On homophobia, see ibid., p. 240.
15 Ibid., pp. 413–14
16 Ibid., pp. 428–9.
17 Ibid., p. 458.
18 Ibid., pp. 461–4, 479–82.
19 Ibid., pp. 464–5.
20 See Bob Altemeyer, *The Authoritarian Specter* (Cambridge: Harvard University Press, 1996), p. 6. For the relationship of Altemeyer's work to Adorno's, see ibid., pp. 45–7. See also Bob Altemeyer, *Right-Wing Authoritarianism* (Manitoba: The University of Manitoba Press, 1981); Bruce E. Hunsberger and Bob Altemeyer, *Atheists: A Groundbreaking Study of America's Nonbelievers* (Amherst: Prometheus Books, 2006).
21 See William James, "On a Certain Blindness in Human Beings," in William James, *Writings 1878–1899* (New York: The Library of America, 1992), pp. 841–60, at p. 841.
22 Virginia Woolf, *Mrs. Dalloway* (San Diego: Harvest Books, 1997; first published 1925). For further discussion, see Carol Gilligan and David A. J. Richards, *The Deepening Darkness: Patriarchy, Resistance, and Democracy's Future* (New York: Cambridge University Press, 2008), at pp. 213–14.
23 See, for further discussion, Gilligan and Richards, *The Deepening Darkness*, pp. 213–14.
24 See, on this point, Elisabeth Young-Bruehl, *Why Arendt Matters* (New Haven: Yale University Press, 2006).
25 See Joseph LeDoux, *The Emotional Brain: The Mysterious Underpinnings of Emotional Life* (New York: Touchstone, 1996).
26 See Antonio Damasio, *The Feeling of What Happens: Body and Emotion in the Making of Consciousness* (New York: Houghton Mifflin Harcourt, 1999).
27 See Sarah Blaffer Hrdy, *Mothers and Others: The Evolutionary Origins of Mutual Understanding* (Cambridge: Harvard University Press, 2009).
28 See Michael Tomasello, *Why We Cooperate* (Boston: Boston Review Books, 2009); Hrdy, *Mothers and Others*.
29 See, for cogent argument on this point, James Q. Whitman, *Hitler's American Model: The United States and the Making of Nazi Race Law* (Princeton: Princeton University Press, 2017).
30 See, for argument on this point, David A. J. Richards, *Foundations of American Constitutionalism* (New York: Oxford University Press, 1989), pp. 32–9.
31 See, for supporting historical and textual argument on these points, Richards, *Foundations of American Constitutionalism*; David A. J. Richards, *Fundamentalism in American Religion and Law: Obama's Challenge to Patriarchy's Threat to Democracy* (Cambridge: Cambridge University Press, 2010).
32 See Jan Barry, "When Veterans Protested the Vietnam War," *New York Times*, April 18, 2017, https:/nyti.ms/2oQGOc4, pp. 1–6.
33 See, on this point, David A. J. Richards, *Disarming Manhood: Roots of Ethical Resistance* (Athens: Swallow Press/Ohio University Press, 2005), p. 137.
34 See James Gilligan and Bandy Lee, "Report to the New York City Board of Correction," September 5, 2013. For the reports in the *New York Times* on the conditions at Rikers, including on the Gilligan and Lee report, see www.nytimes.com/topic/organization/rikers-island-prison-complex.
35 See Michelle Alexander, *The New Jim Crow: Mass Incarceration in the Age of Colorblindness* (New York: The New Press, 2010); see also the documentary movie, *13th*, directed by Ava DuVernay (2016).
36 See, on all these points, including the reactionary politics of the war on drugs, David A. J. Richards, *Resisting Injustice and the Feminist Ethics of Care in the Age of Obama: "Suddenly,... All the Truth Was Coming Out"* (New York: Routledge, 2013).
37 See, on this point, Manny Fernandez, "The Saturday Night in '89 When Trump Partied with Nixon," *New York Times*, December 19, 2016, pp. A10. A15.

38 Joshua Green, *Devil's Bargain: Steve Bannon, Donald Trump, and the Storming of the Presidency* (New York: Penguin, 2017), p. 44.

39 See PBS *Frontline*, "Bannon's War," aired on May 23, 2017. Bannon made documentaries celebrating both Ronald Reagan (*In the Face of Evil: Reagan's War in Word and Deed*, 2004) and Sarah Palin (*The Undefeated*, 2011). See also Green, *Devil's Bargain*.

40 See Green, *Devil's Bargain*, pp. 46–7, 132–5.

41 Peter Schweizer, *Clinton Cash: The Untold Story of How and Why Foreign Governments and Businesses Helped Make Bill and Hillary Rich* (New York: Harper, 2016). See Green, *Devil's Bargain*, pp. 151–7.

42 See Jane Mayer, "Trump's Money Man: How Robert Mercer, A Reclusive Hedge-Fund Tycoon, Exploited America's Populist Insurgency," *New Yorker*, March 27, 2017, pp. 34–45.

43 Green, *Devil's Bargain*, p. 50.

44 Ibid., pp. 50–1.

45 Ibid., p. 51.

46 Ibid., pp. 52–3.

47 See, on this point, ibid., pp. 49–52.

48 He was fascinated by such a book making such a cyclical historical claim: William Strauss and Neil Howe, *The Fourth Turning: An American Prophecy: What the Cycles of History Tell Us About America's Next Rendezvous with Destiny* (New York: Broadway Books, 1997). Indeed, Bannon made a documentary based on its thesis (*Generation Zero*, 2010).

49 Among the better scholarly studies of the Crusades are Steven Runciman, *A History of the Crusades, Volumes I, II, III* (Cambridge: Cambridge University Press, 1951), and Thomas Asbridge, *The Crusades: The Authoritative History of the War for the Holy Land* (New York: Harper Collins, 2010).

50 See Green, *Devil's Bargain*, pp. 46–7, 132–5, 151–2,

51 See Jonathan Allen and Amie Parnes, *Shattered: Inside Hillary Clinton's Doomed Campaign* (New York: Crown, 2017), pp. 338–54.

52 See PBS *Frontline*, "Bannon's War."

53 Green, *Devil's Bargain*, p. 52, quoting John Pudner on Steve Bannon.

54 Karl Marx, *The Eighteenth Brumaire of Louis Napoleon* (Seattle: Loki's Publishing, n.d.), p. 8.

55 See Carol Gilligan and Naomi Snider, "The Loss of Pleasure, or Why We are Still Talking about Oedipus," *Contemporary Psychoanalysis*, Vol. 53, No. 2 (2017), pp. 173–95.

56 Ibid., p. 21.

57 John Bowlby, *Attachment and Loss: Volume I, Attachment* (New York: Basic Books, 1969, 1982); John Bowlby, *Attachment and Loss: Volume II, Separation: Anxiety and Anger* (New York: Basic Books, 1973); John Bowlby, *Attachment and Loss: Volume III, Loss: Sadness and Depression* (New York: Basic Books, 1980)

58 Gilligan and Snider, "The Loss of Pleasure", p. 21.

59 See, for an illuminating recent discussion, Mary Beard, *Women & Power: A Manifesto* (New York: Liveright Publishing Corporation, 2017).

60 See, for pertinent discussion, Richards, *Disarming Manhood*, pp. 117–20.

61 See, on this point, Amanda Hess, "How a Fractious Women's Movement Came to Lead the Left," in Diane Wachtell, ed., *Wolf Whistle Politics: The New Misogyny in America Today* (New York: The New Press, 2017), pp. 139–54; LeRhonda Manigault-Bryant, "An Open Letter to White Liberal Feminists," in Diane Wachtell, ed., *Wolf Whistle Politics: The New Misogyny in America Today* (New York: The New Press, 2017), pp. 97–100.

62 See, on this point, Marjorie J. Spruill, *Divided We Stand: The Battle over Women's Rights That Polarized American Politics* (New York: Bloomsbury, 2017).

63 See Nathaniel Hawthorne, *The Scarlet Letter* (New York: Penguin, 1986; first published 1850), p. 141.

64 See Wendy Davis, "Wolf Whistle Politics: Taking Back the Conversation to Advance Women's Rights," in Diane Wachtell, ed., *Wolf Whistle Politics: The New Misogyny in*

America Today (New York: The New Press, 2017), pp. xvii–xxviii. On the politics underlying state limits on reproductive rights, see Carol Sanger, *About Abortion: Terminating
Pregnancy in Twenty-first-century America* (Cambridge: Belknap Press of Harvard University Press, 2017).
65 See ibid., p. xxiii, commenting on Rush Limbaugh's portrayal of Sandra Fluke.
66 See Jean Baker Miller, *Toward a New Psychology of Women*, 2nd edn (Boston: Beacon
Press, 1986; first published 1976), pp. 49–60.
67 Virginia Woolf, *Three Guineas* Jane Marcus edition (Orlando: Harvest, 2006; first published 1938), p. 159.
68 See "Women of Liberia Mass Action for Peace," *Wikipedia*, https://en.wikipedia.org/wiki/
Women_of_Liberia_Mass_Action_for_Peace. We are grateful to Chelsea Plyer, who spent
time working in Liberia, for bringing us valuable information about this movement.
69 See "Women Wage Peace," *Wikipedia*, https:/en.wikipedia.org/wiki/Women_Wage_Peace.
70 "Women of Liberia Mass Action for Peace," p. 1.
71 Ibid.
72 Ibid.
73 Ibid., p. 2. For an important documentary dealing with these events, see Gini Reticker,
Pray the Devil Back to Hell (2008). For discussion, see "Pray the Devil Back to Hell,"
Wikipedia, https:/en.wikipedia.org/wiki/Pray_the_Deveil_Back_to_Hell.
74 Alan Cowell, Laura Kasinof, and Adam Nossiter, "Nobel Peace Prize Awarded to Three
Activist Women," *New York Times*, October 7, 2011, www.nytimes.com/2011/10/08/world/
nobel-peace-prize-johnson-sirleaf-gbowee-karman.html?pagewanted=all, at p. 1.
75 Ibid., p. 1.
76 See "Women Wage Peace," *Wikipedia*, https:/en.wikipedia.org/wiki/Women_Wage_Peace,
p. 1.
77 See Rabbi Donna Kirschbaum, "Why Women and Why Now?", at http://womenwagepeace
.org.il/en/women-now-rabbi-donna-kirshbaum-member-women-wage-peace/, pp. 2–3.
78 Carol Gilligan, article in manuscript, to be published in Carol Gilligan and Naomi Snider,
Why Does Patriarchy Persist (Cambridge: Polity, in press)·
79 See Nir Hasson, "30,000 Israelis, Palestinians Take Part in Women Wage Peace Rally in
Jerusalem," *Israel News*, October 8, 2017, www.haaretz.com/Israel-news/1.816255.
80 Virginia Woolf, *Three Guineas*, p. 168.
81 Ibid. p. 170.

5 The Endgame of Patriarchy?

1 Jonathan Shay, *Achilles in Vietnam: Combat Trauma and the Undoing of Character* (New
York: Scribner, 1994), p. 4.
2 Samuel Beckett, *Endgame: A Play in One Act* (New York: Grove Press, 1958).
3 Ibid., pp. 80–1.
4 Beckett, *Endgame*, pp. 80–1.
5 Tatiana wrote us the following note explaining this speech: "In Hispanic communities,
when a girl turns fifteen – one's Quincinera – she becomes a woman. It is both a
transformation from child to adult and welcoming into society. With this transformation
come new expectations and new experiences such as being sexualized by your culture –
from catcalls on the streets to dating and soon after becoming a mother and a housewife.
Today, turning fifteen means striving to look a certain way (and often involves plastic
surgery – larger bosom and larger buttocks) in order for men to like you, society to accept
you, and for you to love yourself. The patriarchy stays strong by avoiding any sort of
initiation for boys until they turn eighteen and, even then, their transformation is not as
physical as a woman's is expected to be."
6 David D. Gilmore, *Manhood in the Making: Cultural Concepts of Masculinity* (New Haven:
Yale, 1990), p. 11.
7 Ibid., p. 16.

8 William Shakespeare, *King Lear*, in W. J. Craig, ed., *Shakespeare: Complete Works* (London: Oxford University Press, 1966), pp. 908–42, at p. 942.
9 Lynn Nottage, *Sweat* (New York: Theatre Communications Group, 2017), p. 112.

6 Maps of Resistance

1 See James Forman, Jr, *Locking Up Our Own: Crime and Punishment in Black America* (New York: Farrar, Straus and Giroux, 2017).
2 Ibid., p. 170.
3 On the history of anti-Semitism, see Carol Gilligan and David A. J. Richards, *The Deepening Darkness: Patriarchy, Resistance, and Democracy's Future* (New York: Cambridge University Press, 2008), pp. 129–37, 238–43.
4 See, for example, Brent Kendall, "Travel Ban Ruling Sets Stage for High Court," *The Wall Street Journal*, May 26, 2017, pp. A1, A5. For a more recent development in this legal saga, see Michael D. Shear and Adam Liptak, "Taking Up Case, Justices Let U.S. Start Travel Ban," *New York Times*, June 27, 2017, pp. A1, A12.
5 On the sanctuary movement, see Naomi Klein, *No Is Not Enough: Resisting Trump's Shock Politics and Winning the World We Need* (Chicago: Haymarket Books, 2017), p. 199.
6 See, for further argument about this development and its justification, David A. J. Richards, *Free Speech and the Politics of Identity* (Oxford: Oxford University Press, 1999).
7 See Erica Chenoweth and Jeremy Pressman, "This is What We Learned by Counting the Women's Marches," *Washington Post*, February 7, 2017, www.washingtonpost.com/news/monkey-cage/wp/2017/02/07/this-is-what-we-learned-by-counting-the-womens-marches/?utm_term=.710b0bfc9953; Klein, *No Is Not Enough*, p. 197.
8 See Robert Pear, "Draft Rule Makes It Far Easier to Deny Coverage for Birth Control," *New York Times*, Friday, July 2, 2017, A1, A15.
9 See Adam Liptak, "Let Me Finish, Please: Conservative Men Dominate the Debate," *New York Times National*, April 16, 2017, p. A13.
10 See, on these points, Klein, *No Is Not Enough*, pp. 145–6, 149–51.
11 See ibid., pp. 222–71. For Klein's magisterial study of the imperative to take climate control seriously, see Naomi Klein, *This Changes Everything: Capitalism vs. the Climate* (New York: Simon & Schuster, 2014). See also Naomi Klein, *The Shock Doctrine: The Rise of Disaster Capitalism* (New York: Picador, 2007); Naomi Klein, *No Logo: No Space No Choice No Jobs* (New York: Picador, 2009; first published 2000).
12 See, for argument that patriarchy has distorted both our sense of ethics and moral philosophy, reflected in the marginalization of an ethic of care, David A. J. Richards, *Resisting Injustice and the Feminist Ethics of Care in the Age of Obama: "Suddenly, . . . All the Truth Was Coming Out"* (New York: Routledge, 2013).

7: The Power and Invisibility of Gender

1 See Pankaj Mishra, *Age of Anger: A History of the Present* (New York: Farrar, Straus and Giroux, 2017); see also Pankaj Mishra, *From the Ruins of Empire: The Revolt Against the West and the Remaking of Asia* (New York: Picador, 2012).
2 See, on this point, Benjamin R. Barber, *Jihad vs. McWorld: Terrorism's Challenge to Democracy* (New York: Ballantine, 2001; first published 1995).
3 Charles King, "Civilization and Its Discontent: The Ruinous Cost of Angry Men at the Heart of Modern Political and Civic Engagement," *The Times Literary Supplement*, June 9, 2017, No. 5958, at p. 24 (reviewing Pankaj Mishra's *Age of Anger*).
4 Thucydides, *History of the Peloponnesian War* translated by Rex Warner (New York: Penguin, 1972), p. 49.
5 See, on this point, Graham Allison, *Destined for War* (New York: Houghton Mifflin Harcourt, 2017).

6 See, on this point, Lt Col Dave Grossman, *On Killing: The Psychological Cost of Learning to Kill in War and Society*, revised edition (New York: Back Bay Books, 2009; first published 1995).

7 See, on this point, ibid., pp. 251–99. See also John Shay, *Achilles in Vietnam: Combat Trauma and the Undoing of Character* (New York: Scribner, 1994). For a psychoanalytic study of military indoctrination, see Chaim F. Shatan, "Bogus Manhood, Bogus Honor: Surrender and Transfiguration in the United States Martin Corps," *Psychoanalytic Review*, Vol. 64, No. 4 (1977), pp. 585–610.

8 See Sebastian Junger, *War* (New York: Twelve, 2010), p. 239; see also Sebastian Junger, *Tribe: On Homecoming and Belonging* (New York: Twelve, 2016); Chris Hedges, *War Is a Force That Gives Us Meaning* (New York: Public Affairs, 2014; first published 2002).

9 See, for an illuminating general study of war and democracy, John Ferejohn and Frances McCall Rosenbluth, *Forged Through Fire: War, Peace, and the Democratic Bargain* (New York: Liveright, 2017).

10 163 U.S. 537 (1896).

11 See, on this point, Stephen Kinzer, *The True Flag: Theodore Roosevelt, Mark Twain, and the Birth of American Empire* (New York: Henry Holt and Company, 2017); Kristin L. Hoganson, *Fighting for American Manhood: How Gender Politics Provoked the Spanish-American and Philippine-American Wars* (New Haven: Yale University Press, 1998).

12 See, on this point, David W. Blight, *Race and Reunion: The Civil War in American History* (Cambridge: Belknap Press of Harvard University Press, 2001).

13 See, for example, Gail Bederman, *Manliness and Civilization* (Chicago: University of Chicago Press, 1995), pp. 170–215; Hoganson, *Fighting for American Manhood*; Kinzer, *The True Flag*; Kim Townsend, *Manhood at Harvard: William James and Others* (New York: W.W. Norton, 1996), pp. 256–86; Edward J. Renehan, Jr, *The Lion's Pride: Theodore Roosevelt and His Family in Peace and War* (New York: Oxford University Press, 1998).

14 Edmund Morris, *The Rise of Theodore Roosevelt* (New York: Random House, 1979), p. 144.

15 Ibid., pp. 229–34, 264–76.

16 Theodore Roosevelt, *The Winning of the West*, Volumes 1–4 Inclusive (London: American Cowboys Books, 2017). See Morris, *The Rise of Theodore Roosevelt*, pp. 474–8, 484.

17 Quoted at ibid., p. 425 (footnotes omitted).

18 Cited in Townsend, *Manhood at Harvard*, p. 244.

19 See, for fuller discussion, Renehan, Jr, *The Lion's Pride*.

20 On Twain's resistance, see Kinzer, *The True Flag*.

21 See, on this point, Robert D. Richardson, *William James: In the Maelstrom of American Modernism* (Boston: Houghton Mifflin, 2006), pp. 11–24.

22 See, on this point, Ron Bowers, *Mark Twain: A Life* (New York: Free Press, 2005), pp. 414–31, 580–98.

23 See, on this point, Michael Kazin, *War Against War: The American Fight for Peace 1914–1918* (New York: Simon & Schuster, 2017), p. 114.

24 Renehan, Jr, *The Lion's Pride*, p. 115.

25 Ibid.

26 See, on this point, PBS *American Experience*, "The Great War," aired on April 12, 2017.

27 See William James, "On a Certain Blindness in Human Beings," in William James, *Writings 1878–1899* (New York: The Library of America, 1992), pp. 841–60, at p. 841.

28 Jane Addams, *Newer Ideals of Peace* (Urbana: University of Illinois Press, 2007; first published 1906), p. 10.

29 Ibid., p. 17. See, for useful background, Jean Bethke Elshtain, *Jane Addams and the Dream of American Democracy* (New York: Basic Books, 2002).

30 See, on this point, David A. J. Richards, *Free Speech and the Politics of Identity* (Oxford: Oxford University Press, 1999).

31 See, on all these points, Kazin, *War Against War*.

32 John Maynard Keynes, *The Economic Consequences of the Peace* (available at ReadaClassic.com 2010; first published 1919).

33 See, on this point, David A. J Richards, *Disarming Manhood: Roots of Ethical Resistance* (Athens: Swallow Press/Ohio University Press, 2005), pp. 196–7, 199, 208–9.

34 Michael Holroyd, ed., *Lytton Strachey by Himself: A Self Portrait* (London: Heinemann, 1971), p. 136.

35 Michael Holroyd, *Lytton Strachey: The New Biography* (New York: W.W. Norton, 1994), p. 411.

36 Lytton Strachey, "Militarism and Theology," in Lytton Strachey, *Characters and Commentaries* (Westport: Greenwood Press, 1961; first published 1933), pp. 223–7, at p. 223.

37 Holroyd, *Lytton Strachey: The New Biography*, p. 362.

38 Robert Graves, *Good-Bye to All That* (New York: Anchor, 1998; first published 1929), p. 245.

39 Ibid., p. 245.

40 Quote at ibid., p. 260.

41 Ibid., p. 263.

42 See ibid., p. 264.

43 See ibid., p. 275. See, for fuller discussion of these events and Sassoon's later life, including his love affair with Stephen Tennant and his sudden marriage to a woman, and their estrangement, Max Egremont, *Siegfried Sassoon: A Life* (New York: Farrar, Straus and Giroux, 2005).

44 Pat Barker, *Regeneration* (New York: Plume, 1993).

45 Ibid., p. 149.

46 Ibid., p. 155.

47 See David Halberstam, *The Best and the Brightest* (New York: A Fawcett Book, 1992; first published 1969).

48 On this point, see ibid., pp. 80–2,

49 Ibid., p. 115.

50 Ibid., p. 118.

51 Ibid., p. 120.

52 Ibid., p. 463.

53 Ibid., p. 69.

54 Cited at ibid., p. 69.

55 See, on this point, ibid., pp. 40–63.

56 See, on this point, ibid., pp. 215–40.

57 See, on this point, ibid., pp. 162–81, 479–81.

58 See, on this point, ibid., pp. 538–62.

59 Ibid., p. 516.

60 Ibid., p. 468.

61 See, on MacBundy's irrationality, ibid., pp. 524–6.

62 See, on this point, ibid., pp. 284–5.

63 See, on this point, ibid., pp. 408–21.

64 See, on this point, ibid., pp. 513–36, 655–6.

65 Ibid., p. 512.

66 Ibid., p. 414. See, for other examples of Johnson's sexist and sometimes homophobic emoting, ibid., pp. 298, 373, 425, 499–500, 522.

67 Ibid., pp. 531 and 532.

68 See, on this point, ibid., pp. 305–6.

69 Ibid., p. 433.

70 Ibid., p. 656.

71 Robert A. Caro, *The Years of Lyndon Johnson: The Passage of Power* (New York: Vintage Books, 2012), p. 536.

72 Quoted at Halberstam, *The Best and the Brightest*, p. 309.

73 Ibid., p. 309.

74 Ibid., p. 655.

75 Tim O'Brien, *The Things They Carried* (Boston: Mariner, 2009; first published 1990), p. 49.

76 See ibid., pp. 54–8.
77 See, for fuller discussion, Richards, *Disarming Manhood*, pp. 43–91.
78 See, on this point, Richards, *Free Speech and the Politics of Identity*.
79 See, on this point, Richards, *Disarming Manhood*, p. 226,
80 See, on this point, Richardson, *William James*, pp. 380–5.
81 See, on this point, ibid., pp. 441–2.
82 William James, "The Moral Equivalent of War," in William James, *Writings 1902–1910* (New York: The Library of America, 1987), pp. 1281–93.
83 Ibid., p. 1290.
84 Ibid., p. 1289.
85 Addams, *Newer Ideals of Peace*, p. 10.
86 Ibid., p. 16.
87 Ibid., p. 38.
88 Ibid., p. 40.
89 Ibid.
90 Ibid., p. 11.
91 Ibid., p. 17.
92 See, on this point, ibid., pp. 33–5.
93 See, on this point, Allison, *Destined for War*.
94 Addams, *Newer Ideals of Peace*, p. 10.
95 Thucydides, *History of the Peloponnesian War*, p. 402.
96 King, "Civilization and Its Discontent," at p. 24.

8: Democracy's Future

1 See Nathaniel Hawthorne, *The Scarlet Letter* (New York: Penguin, 1986; first published 1850), pp. 15, 18, 20, 132, 190.
2 See, for further discussion and elaboration, David A. J. Richards, *Women, Gays, and the Constitution: The Grounds for Feminism and Gay Rights in Culture and Law* (Chicago: University of Chicago Press, 1998).
3 Hawthorne, *The Scarlet Letter*, p. 141.
4 See, for fuller discussion, Carol Gilligan, *The Birth of Pleasure: A New Map of Love* (New York: Vintage, 2003).
5 Hawthorne, *The Scarlet Letter*, p. 227.
6 See, on these points, David A. J. Richards, "Literature and Resisting Injustice: Melville and Hawthorne on Patriarchal Manhood and Homophobia," *Law and Literature*, Vol. 29, No. 1 (2017), pp. 109–22, DOI: 10.1080/1535685X.2016.1246917.
7 Carol Gilligan, "Moral Injury and the Ethic of Care: Reframing the Conversation about Differences," *Journal of Social Philosophy*, Vol. 45 No. 1 (Spring 2014), pp. 89–106, at p. 98.
8 Herman Melville, *Moby-Dick or, The Whale* (New York: Penguin, 2003; first published 1851), p. 30; see also pp. 28, 57–8, 60, 62–3, 66–8, 349.
9 See, for a powerful argument along these lines, Zevedei Barbu, *Problems of Historical Psychology* (New York: Grove Press, 1960), pp. 166–72.
10 See William Shakespeare, *Troilus and Cressida* in W. J. Craig, ed., *Shakespeare, Complete Works* (London: Oxford University Press, 1966), pp. 667–700, at p. 672, l. 85 (Ulysses).
11 See, on these points, Michael Walzer, *The Revolution of the Saints* (Cambridge: Harvard University Press, 1965); A. S. P. Woodhouse, ed., *Puritanism and Liberty* (London: Dent, 1938); Bernard Bailyn, *The Ideological Origins of the American Revolution* (Cambridge: Harvard University Press, 1967); Gordon S. Wood, *The Creation of the American Republic, 1776–1787* (New York: Norton, 1969); Douglass Adair, *Fame and the Founding Fathers* (New York: Norton, 1974); David A. J. Richards, *Toleration and the Constitution* (New York: Oxford University Press, 1986); David A. J. Richards, *Foundations of American Constitutionalism* (New York: Oxford University Press, 1989); David A. J. Richards, *Conscience and the Constitution* (Princeton: Princeton University Press, 1993).

12 See Hawthorne, *The Scarlet Letter*, pp. 15, 18, 20, 132, 190.
13 See, on these points, Walzer, *The Revolution of the Saints*; Woodhouse, *Puritanism and Liberty*; Bailyn, *The Ideological Origins of the American Revolution*; Wood, *The Creation of the American Republic*; Adair, *Fame and the Founding Fathers*; Richards, *Toleration and the Constitution*; Richards, *Foundations of American Constitutionalism*; Richards, *Conscience and the Constitution*.
14 Hawthorne, *The Scarlet Letter*, p. 141.
15 Ibid., pp. 7–43.
16 Ibid., pp. 139–46.
17 Ibid., p. 144.
18 Ibid., p. 143.
19 Ibid., p. 144.
20 Ibid.
21 Ibid.
22 Ibid.
23 Ibid., p. 225,
24 E. M. Forster, *Aspects of the Novel* (Orlando: A Harvest Book, 1955), p. 143.
25 See, on this point, Laurie Robertson-Lorant, *Melville: A Biography* (New York: Clarkson Potter, 1996), p. 140.
26 Melville, *Moby-Dick*, p. 178
27 Andrew Delbanco, *Melville: His World and Work* (New York: Alfred A. Knopf, 2005), pp. 162–6.
28 See, on this analogy, Delbanco, *Melville*, pp. 174–5.
29 Herman Melville, *Billy Budd, Sailor and Selected Tales* edited by Robert Milder (Oxford: Oxford University Press, 2009), p. 285.
30 Ibid., p. 285.
31 Ibid., p. 286.
32 See James Gilligan, *Violence: Reflections on a National Epidemic* (New York: Vintage, 1996).
33 Melville, *Billy Budd*, p. 358.
34 Ibid., p. 333.
35 See Richard H. Weisberg, *The Failure of the Word: The Protagonist as Lawyer in Modern Fiction* (New Haven: Yale University Press, 1984), pp. 147–59.
36 Melville, *Billy Budd*, pp. 340–5.
37 Ibid., p. 356.
38 Ibid., p. 342.
39 Ibid.
40 Ibid., p. 353.
41 Ibid., p. 346.
42 Ibid.
43 See, on this point, Hershel Parker, *Herman Melville: A Biography, Volume 2, 1851–1891* (Baltimore: The Johns Hopkins University Press, 2002), pp. 642–50.
44 See, on these points, Delbanco, *Melville*, pp. 180–1, 199–205, 200–2, 275–9; Robertson-Lorant, *Melville: A Biography*, pp. 295, 370–1, 503–4, 505–9, 509–17; Parker, *Herman Melville: A Biography Volume 2, 1851–1891*, pp. 628–35, 642–50.
45 See, for example, Elaine Showalter, *The Civil Wars of Julia Ward Howe: A Biography* (New York: Simon & Schuster, 2016).
46 The analysis that follows (about the collaboration of Britten and Forster) is drawn from David A. J. Richards, *Why Love Leads to Justice: Love across the Boundaries* (New York: Cambridge University Press, 2016), pp. 65–7.
47 Paul Kildea, *Benjamin Britten: A Life in the Twentieth Century* (London: Allen Lane, 2013), p. 324.
48 See ibid., p. 326.
49 Ibid., p. 327.

50 Ibid., p. 343.
51 Ibid.
52 Quoted at ibid., p. 346.
53 Ibid., p. 146.
54 Ibid., p. 347.
55 See E. M. Forster and Eric Crozier, *Libretto, Billy Budd*, conducted by Benjamin Britten, London c.d., at pp. 69–70.
56 Hershel Parker, *Herman Melville: A Biography, Volume 1, 1819–1851* (Baltimore: The Johns Hopkins University press, 1996), p. 760.
57 See Delbanco, *Melville*, pp. 126, 148.
58 See Herman Melville, "Hawthorne and His Mosses," in Harrison Hayford, ed., *Herman Melville* (New York: The Library of America, 1984), pp. 1154–71.
59 Ibid., p. 1167.
60 Ibid., p. 1165.
61 See Robert K. Martin, *Hero, Captain, and Stranger: Male Friendship, Social Critique, and Literary Form in the Sea Novels of Herman Melville* (Chapel Hill: The University of North Carolina Press, 1986). For a recent biographical study attributing Melville's inspiration to Sarah Morewood, see Michael Shelden, *Melville in Love: The Secret Life of Herman Melville and the Muse of Moby-Dick* (New York: Harper Collins, 2016). Leading biographers of Melville, including Herschel Parker, dismissed Shelden's thesis "as 'fantasy,' Sarah Morewood was 'a loose cannon,' Mr. Parker says. 'But there is absolutely no evidence that she had any sexual attraction to Melville or that he was attracted to her.'" Brenda Cronin, "Did Illicit Love Float 'Moby-Dick'?", *The Wall Street Journal*, May 27, 2016, at D3.
62 See, on these points, Brenda Wineapple, *Hawthorne: A Life* (New York: Random House, 2003), pp. 188–9, 199, 241, 322–3, 329–33, 349–50.
63 See Melville, *Billy Budd*, pp. 278–9.
64 See, on this point, Gregory Jay, "Douglass, Melville, and the Lynching of Billy Budd," in Robert S. Levine and Samuel Otter, eds., *Frederick Douglass and Herman Melville: Essays in Relation* (Chapel Hill: The University of North Carolina Press, 2008), pp. 369–95. See also Gregory Jay, "'Speak man!' Billy Budd in the Crucible of Reconstruction," *American Literary History*, Vol. 21, No. 3, (2009), pp. 492–517; Klaus Benesch, "Melville Black Jack: *Billy Budd* and the Politics of Race in 19th Century Maritime Life," in Joanne M. Braxton and Maria I. Dierich, eds., *Monuments of the Black Atlantic: Slavery and Memory* (Munster: Lit Verlag, 2004), pp. 67–75. See also Jon-Christian Suggs, "Something about the Boy: Law, Ironic Comedy, and the Ideology of Agape in *Billy Budd* " (unpublished paper, n.d.).
65 On how and why gay/lesbian loving relationships have led to creative ethical insights into injustice and resistance to injustice, see Richards, *Why Love Leads to Justice*.
66 Hawthorne, *The Scarlet Letter*, p. 177.
67 Ibid., p. 188.
68 August Wilson, *Jitney* (New York: Samuel French, 2002), pp. 29–30 (speech of Turnbo to Youngblood, explaining the relationship of father and son).
69 Wilson, *Jitney*, pp. 40–1.
70 Ibid., p. 41.
71 Ibid.
72 Ibid., pp. 42–3.
73 Ibid., p. 42.
74 Ibid., pp. 43–4.
75 See Daphne White, "Berkeley author George Lakoff says 'Don't underestimate Trump,'" *Berkeleyside*, May 2, 2017, www.berkeleyside.com/2017/05/02/berkeley-author-george-lakoff-says-dont-underestimate-trump, pp. 1–33.
76 See George Lakoff, *Moral Politics: How Liberals and Conservatives Think*, 3rd edition (Chicago: University of Chicago Press, 2016; first published 1996).
77 See George Lakoff, *Don't Think of an Elephant!: Know Your Values and Frame the Debate* (White Water Junction: Chelsea Green Publishing, 2014; first published, 2004); George

Lakoff, *Thinking Points: Communicating Our American Values and Vision* (New York: Farrar, Straus and Giroux, 2006).

78 Jean Baker Miller, *Toward a New Psychology of Women* (Boston: Beacon Press, 1986; first published 1976).

79 Dorothy Dinnerstein, *The Mermaid and the Minotaur* (New York: Harper & Row, 1976).

80 Nancy J. Chodorow, *The Reproduction of Mothering: Psychoanalysis and the Sociology of Gender* (Berkeley: University of California Press, 1999; first published 1978).

81 Christina Hoff Sommers, *The War Against Boys: How Misguided Feminism Is Harming Our Young Men* (New York: Simon & Schuster, 2000).

82 See Katha Pollitt, *Reasonable Creatures: Essays on Women and Feminism* (New York: Vintage, 1995), pp. 42–62,

83 Christopher Lasch, *Women and the Common Life: Love, Marriage, and Feminism* (New York: W.W. Norton, 1997), pp. 121–36.

84 See, for example, Lauren Schiller, "Gloria Steiner Explains Why Feminism Reached a Critical Turning Point in 2015," *Fortune*, http://fortune.com/2015/12/22/gloria-steinem-feminism-turning-point/.

85 Ariel Levy, "Lift and Separate: Why is Feminism Still So Divisive?," *New Yorker*, November 16, 2009, www.newyorker.com/magazine/2009/11/16/lift-and-separate, at pp. 2 and 3.

86 Ibid., p. 7.

87 Ibid., p. 9.

88 Ibid.

89 Carol Gilligan, *Joining the Resistance* (Cambridge: Polity, 2011), p. 49.

90 See Robert Ebert, *The Exterminating Angel*, RoberEbert.com, 11 May 1997.

91 Gavin Plumley, Program Note, Metropolitan Opera Playbill, October 30, 2017 performance, *The Exterminating Angel*, pp. 38B–38D, at 38D.

92 Tom Cairns (in collaboration with the composer), Libretto, *The Exterminating Angel: An Opera in Three Acts* (London: Faber Music, 2015), pp. 55–6.

9: Why Feminism and Why Now?

1 Jill Filipovic, "Trump's Man-Child Army," *New York Times*, November 5, 2017, SR 6. From *The New York Times*, issue published November 5 ©, 2017, *The New York Times*, https://www.nytimes.com/. All rights reserved. Used by permission and protected by the Copyright Laws of the United States. The printing, copying, redistribution, or retransmission of this Content without express written permission is prohibited.

2 Ibid.

3 Ibid.

4 We are grateful to Lucy Kissel for suggesting this way of putting our argument.

5 See David A. J. Richards, *Resisting Injustice and the Feminist Ethics of Care in the Age of Obama: "Suddenly,...All the Truth Was Coming Out"* (New York: Routledge, 2013), pp. 118–41.

6 Barack Obama, *Dreams from My Father* (New York: The Three Rivers Press, 2004), p. 68.

7 Ibid., p. 126.

8 Ibid., p. 127.

9 Ibid., p. 124.

10 Ibid., p. 48.

11 David Remnick, *The Bridge: The Life and Rise of Barack Obama* (New York: Vintage, 2011), p. 86.

12 See ibid., pp. 83–90.

13 Quotation of Alice Dewey, cited in ibid., p. 84.

14 Ibid., p. 86. Her dissertation has now been published. See S. Ann Dunham, *Surviving against the Odds: Village Industry in Indonesia* edited by Alice G. Dewey and Nancy I. Cooper (Durham: Duke University Press, 2009). For a recent illuminating biography of Obama's mother, see Janny Scott, *A Singular Woman: The Untold Story of Barack Obama's Mother* (New York: Riverhead Books, 2011).

15 Quoted from Mary Zurbuchen, who worked with Dunham at the Ford Foundation, cited in Remnick, *The Bridge*, p. 88.
16 Obama, *Dreams from My Father*, pp. 336–7.
17 Ibid., p. 348.
18 Ibid., p. 369.
19 Ibid., p. 407.
20 Ibid., p. 422.
21 See, on these points, ibid., pp. 386, 390, 402–7, 434,
22 See Remnick, *The Bridge*, pp. 63, 246–7.
23 Ibid., p. 246.
24 Obama, *Dreams from My Father*, pp. 220–1.
25 For evidence of Lolo's physical abuse of Obama's mother, see David Maraniss, *Barack Obama: The Story* (New York: Simon & Schuster, 2012), p. 243.
26 See Obama, *Dreams from My Father*, pp. 87–8.
27 Ibid., pp. 89–91.
28 Ibid., p. 429.
29 Ibid., p. 79.
30 Ibid., pp. 98–100.
31 Ibid., pp. 102–5.
32 Ibid., pp. 107–10.
33 On the fictionalization, see Maraniss, *Barack Obama: The Story*, pp. 371–3. Maraniss's biography also makes clear what Obama's autobiography does not, namely, that several of his sexual relationships, prior to his marriage, were with highly intelligent, white women. See ibid., pp. 420 ff. In fact, one of these women trenchantly observed to Obama that she felt separated from him by "the veil," ibid., p. 481, and sensitively urged upon him "an absolute conviction that his future lay down the road with a black woman," quoted at ibid., p. 497.
34 Obama, *Dreams from My Father*, p. 81.
35 On Obama's ethical universalism, see Maraniss, *Barack Obama: The Story*, p. 453.
36 Obama, *Dreams from My Father*, p. 134.
37 See Maraniss, *Barack Obama: The Story*, quoted at p. 375.
38 See Martin Luther King, Jr, *A Testament of Hope: The Essential Writings of Martin Luther King, Jr* edited by James M. Washington (San Francisco: Harper & Row, 1986), at p. 102.
39 See, for fuller discussion, David A. J Richards, *Disarming Manhood: Roots of Ethical Resistance* (Athens: Swallow Press/Ohio University Press, 2005), pp. 131–80.
40 Barack Obama, *The Audacity of Hope: Thoughts on Reclaiming the American Dream* (New York: Three Rivers Press, 2006), p. 66.
41 James Gilligan, *Preventing Violence* (New York: Thames & Hudson, 2001), p. 56.
42 See Michael Kimmel, *Guyland: The Perilous World Where Boys become Men* (New York: Harper, 2008). See also Michael Kimmel, *Angry White Men: American Masculinity at the End of an Era* (New York: Nation Books, 2013); Michael Kimmel, *Manhood in America: a Cultural History*, 3rd edn (New York: Oxford University Press, 2012).
43 Tony Porter, *Breaking Out of the "Man Box": The Next Generation of Manhood* (New York: Skyhorse Publishing, 2015).
44 Terrence Real, *I Don't Want to Talk About It: Overcoming the Secret Legacy of Male Depression* (New York: Scribner, 1997).
45 See Niobe Way, Jessica Cressen, Samuel Bodian, Justin Preston, Joseph Nelson, and Diane Hughes, "'It Might be Nice to Be a Girl...Then You Wouldn't Have to Be Emotionless:' Boys' Resistance to Norms of Masculinity During Adolescence," *Psychology of Men and Masculinity*, Vol. 15, No. 3 (2014), pp. 241–52; see also Niobe Way, Alisa Ali, Carol Gilligan, and Pedro Noguera, eds., *The Crisis of Connection: Roots, Consequences, and Solutions* (New York: New York University Press, in press).
46 Charles King, "Civilization and Its Discontent: The Ruinous Cost of Angry Men at the Heart of Modern Political and Civic Engagement," *The Times Literary Supplement*, June 9,

2017, No. 5958, at p. 24 (reviewing Pankaj Mishra's *Age of Anger*, moral politics themselves arise from the dominant patriarchal paradigm and thus works within and does not question).

47 James Gilligan, *Violence: Reflections on a National Epidemic* (New York: Vintage, 1997), pp. 229–39.

48 George Lakoff, *Don't Think of an Elephant!: Know Your Values and Frame the Debate* (White Water Junction: Chelsea Green Publishing, 2014; first published 2004), p. xi.

49 Ibid., p. xii.

50 See David A. J. Richards, *Why Love Leads to Justice: Love across the Boundaries* (New York: Cambridge University Press, 2016), pp. 224–9.

51 On these points, see Richards, *Why Love Leads to Justice*, pp. 189–208.

52 See "Never Again MSD", *Wikipedia*, https://en.wikipedia.org/wiki/Never_Again_MSD; Vivian Yee and Alan Blinder, "Thousands Walk Out of Class, Urging Action on Gun Control," *New York Times*, Thursday, March 15, 2018, A1, A19.

53 See, on this point, Robin Morgan, "The Not-So-Secret Ingredient," The Robin Morgan Blog, March 12, 2018 (commenting on the role of women among the teachers of West Virginia in the strike that secured higher wages).

54 See, on this point, James Gilligan, "Terrorism, Fundamentalism, and Nihilism," in Henry Parens and Stuart Twemlow, eds., *The Future of Prejudice: Applications of Psychoanalytic Understanding toward its Prevention* (New York: Rowman & Littlefield, 2006), pp. 37–62.

Bibliography

Abramson, Jill, "This May Shock You: Hillary Clinton is Fundamentally Honest," *The Guardian*, March 28, 2016, www.theguardian.com/commentisfree/2016/mar/28/hillary-clinton-honest-transparency-jill-abramson.

Adair, Douglass, *Fame and the Founding Fathers* (New York: Norton, 1974).

Addams, Jane, *Newer Ideals of Peace* (Urbana: University of Illinois Press, 2007; first published 1906).

Adorno, Theodor. *The Jargon of Authenticity*, translated by Knut Tarnowski and Frederic Will (London: Routledge, 2003; first published 1973).

Adorno, T. W., Else Frenkel-Brunswick, Daniel J. Levinson, and R. Nevitt Sanford. *The Authoritarian Personality* (New York: Harper & Row, 1950).

Aeschylus. *The Oresteia*, translated by Robert Fagles (New York: Penguin, 1977).

Alexander, Michelle, *The New Jim Crow: Mass Incarceration in the Age of Colorblindness* (New York: The New Press, 2010).

Allen, Jonathan and Amie Parnes, *Shattered: Inside Hillary Clinton's Doomed Campaign* (New York: Crown, 2017).

Allison, Graham, *Destined for War* (New York: Houghton Mifflin Harcourt, 2017).

Altemeyer, Bob, *Right-Wing Authoritarianism* (Manitoba: The University of Manitoba Press, 1981).

Altemeyer, Bob, *The Authoritarian Specter* (Cambridge: Harvard University Press, 1996).

Arendt, Hannah, *The Origins of Totalitarianism* (Orlando: A Harvest Book, 1976; first published 1951).

Arendt, Hannah, *The Human Condition*, 2nd edn (Chicago: University of Chicago Press, 1998; first published 1958).

Arendt, Hannah, *On Revolution* (New York: Penguin, 2006; first published 1963).

Aristophanes. *Lysistrata, in Aristophanes, Lysistrata and Other Plays*, translated by Alan Sommerstein (London: Penguin, 2002).

Asbridge, Thomas, *The Crusades: The Authoritative History of the War for the Holy Land* (New York: Harper Collins, 2010).

Atwood, Margaret, *The Handmaid's Tale* (New York: Anchor, 1998).

Bailyn, Bernard, *The Ideological Origins of the American Revolution* (Cambridge: Harvard University Press, 1967).

Baldwin, James, *Collected Essays* edited by Toni Morrison (New York: The Library of America, 1998).

Baldwin, James, *Early Novels and Stories* edited by Toni Morrison (New York: The Library of America, 1998).

Bannon, Steve, *In the Face of Evil: Reagan's War in Word and Deed*, 2004, documentary.

Bannon, Steve, *Generation Zero*, 2010, documentary.

Bannon, Steve, *The Undefeated*, 2011, documentary.

Barber, Benjamin R., *Jihad vs. McWorld: Terrorism's Challenge to Democracy* (New York: Ballantine, 2001; first published 1995).

Barbu, Zevedei, *Problems of Historical Psychology* (New York: Grove Press, 1960).

Barker, Pat, *Regeneration* (New York: Plume, 1993).

Barry, Jan, "When Veterans Protested the Vietnam War," *New York Times*, April 18, 2017, https:/nyti.ms/2oQGOc4, pp. 1–6.

Beard, Mary, *Women & Power: A Manifesto* (New York: Liveright Publishing Corporation, 2017).

Beckett, Samuel, *Endgame: A Play in One Act* (New York: Grove Press, 1958).

Bederman, Gail, *Manliness and Civilization* (Chicago: University of Chicago Press, 1995).

Benesch, Klaus, "Melville Black Jack: *Billy Budd* and the Politics of Race in 19th Century Maritime Life," in Joanne M. Braxton and Maria I. Dierich, eds., *Monuments of the Black Atlantic: Slavery and Memory* (Munster: Lit Verlag, 2004), pp. 67–75.

Blight, David W., *Race and Reunion: The Civil War in American History* (Cambridge: Belknap Press of Harvard University Press, 2001).

Bordo, Susan, *The Destruction of Hillary Clinton* (Brooklyn: Melville House, 2017).

Bowers, Ron, *Mark Twain: A Life* (New York: Free Press, 2005).

Bowlby, John, *Attachment and Loss: Volume I, Attachment* (New York: Basic Books, 1969; 1982).

Bowlby, John, *Attachment and Loss: Volume II, Separation: Anxiety and Anger* (New York: Basic Books, 1973).

Bowlby, John, *Attachment and Loss: Volume III, Loss: Sadness and Depression* (New York: Basic Books, 1980).

Brescoli, Victoria L. and Eric Luis Uhlmann, "Can an Angry Woman Get Ahead: Status Conferral, Gender, and Expression of Emotion in the Workplace," *Psychological Science*, Vol. 19, No. 3 (March, 2008), pp. 268–75.

"Black Lives Matter," *Wikipedia*, https://en.wikipedia.org/wiki/Black_Lives_Matter.

Brown, Lyn Mikel and Carol Gilligan, *Meeting at the Crossroads: Women's Psychology and Girls' Development* (Cambridge: Harvard University Press, 1992; paperback edition by Ballantine, New York, 1993).

Cairns, Tom (in collaboration with the composer), Libretto, *The Exterminating Angel: An Opera in Three Acts* (London: Faber Music, 2015).

Caro, Robert A., *The Years of Lyndon Johnson: The Passage of Power* (New York: Vintage Books, 2012).

Chenoweth, Erica and Jeremy Pressman, "This is What We Learned by Counting the Women's Marches," *Washington Post*, February 7, 2017, www.washingtonpost.com/news/monkey-cage/wp/2017/02/07/this-is-what-we-learned-by-counting-the-womens-marches/?utm_term=.710b0bfc9953.

Chodorow, Nancy J., *The Reproduction of Mothering: Psychoanalysis and the Sociology of Gender* (Berkeley: University of California Press, 1999; first published 1978).

Chu, Judy Y., *When Boys Become Boys: Development, Relationships, and Masculinity* (New York: New York University Press, 2014).

Cliff, Michelle, *The Land of Look Behind* (Ithaca: Firebrand Books, 1985).

Cliff, Michelle, *Free Enterprise: A Novel of Mary Ellen Pleasant* (New York: Dutton, 2004).

Clinton, Hillary Rodham, *What Happened* (New York: Simon & Schuster, 2017).

Cowell, Alan, Laura Kasinof, and Adam Nossiter, "Nobel Peace Prize Awarded to Three Activist Women," *New York Times*, October 7, 2011, www.nytimes.com/2011/10/08/world/nobel-peace-prize-johnson-sirleaf-gbowee-karman.html?pagewanted=all.

Cronin, Brenda, "Did Illicit Love Float 'Moby-Dick'?", *The Wall Street Journal*, May 27, 2016, at D3.

Damasio, Antonio, *The Feeling of What Happens: Body and Emotion in the Making of Consciousness* (New York: Houghton Mifflin Harcourt, 1999).

Damasio, Antonio R., *Descartes' Error: Emotion, Reason, and the Human Brain* (Orlando: Harcourt, Inc., 2003).

Davis, Wendy, "Wolf Whistle Politics: Taking Back the Conversation to Advance Women's Rights," in Diane Wachtell, ed., *Wolf Whistle Politics: The New Misogyny in America Today* (New York: The New Press, 2017), pp. xvii–xxviii.

Delbanco, Andrew, *Melville: His World and Work* (New York: Alfred A. Knopf, 2005).

Dinnerstein, Dorothy, *The Mermaid and the Minotaur* (New York: Harper & Row, 1976)

District of Columbia v. Heller, 128 S.Ct. 2783, 2822–2847 (2008), Justice Stevens.

Du Bois, W. E. B., *Black Reconstruction in America, 1860–1880* (New York: Atheneum, 1969; first published 1935).

Du Bois, W. E. B., *The Souls of Black Folk*, in Nathan Higgins, ed., *W. E. B. Du Bois: Writings* (New York: Library of America, 1986; first published 1903).

Dunham, S. Ann, *Surviving against the Odds: Village Industry in Indonesia* edited by Alice G. Dewey and Nancy I. Cooper (Durham: Duke University Press, 2009).

DuVernay, Ava, 13th, 2016, documentary.

Ebert, Robert, *The Exterminating Angel*, RoberEbert.com, 11 May 1997.

Egremont, Max, *Siegfried Sassoon: A Life* (New York: Farrar, Straus and Giroux, 2005).

Elshtain, Jean Bethke, *Jane Addams and the Dream of American Democracy* (New York: Basic Books, 2002).

Ferejohn, John and Frances McCall Rosenbluth, *Forged Through Fire: War, Peace, and the Democratic Bargain* (New York: Liveright, 2017).

Fernandez, Manny, "The Saturday Night in '89 When Trump Partied with Nixon," *New York Times*, December 19, 2016, pp. A10, A15.

Filipovic, Jill, "Trump's Man-Child Army," *New York Times*, November 5, 2017, SR 6.

Forman, Jr, James, *Locking Up Our Own: Crime and Punishment in Black America* (New York: Farrar, Straus and Giroux, 2017).

Forster, E. M., *Aspects of the Novel* (Orlando: A Harvest Book, 1955).

Forster, E. M. and Eric Crozier, *Libretto, Billy Budd*, conducted by Benjamin Britten, London c.d.

Fromm, Erich, *Escape from Freedom* (New York: Henry Holt, 1965; first published 1941).

Gilligan, Carol, *In a Different Voice: Psychological Theory and Women's Development* (Cambridge: Harvard University Press, 1982).

Gilligan, Carol, *The Birth of Pleasure: A New Map of Love* (New York: Vintage, 2003).

Gilligan, Carol, *Joining the Resistance* (Cambridge: Polity, 2011).

Gilligan, Carol, "Moral Injury and the Ethic of Care: Reframing the Conversation about Differences," *Journal of Social Philosophy*, Vol. 45 No. 1 (Spring 2014), pp. 89–106.

Gilligan, Carol and Naomi Snider, "The Loss of Pleasure, or Why We are Still Talking about Oedipus," *Contemporary Psychoanalysis*, Vol. 53, No. 2 (2017), pp. 173–95.

Gilligan, Carol and David A. J. Richards, *The Deepening Darkness: Patriarchy, Resistance, and Democracy's Future* (New York: Cambridge University Press, 2008).

Gilligan, Carol and Naomi Snider, *Why Does Patriarchy Persist?* (Cambridge: Polity, in press).

Gilligan, Carol, Janie Victoria Ward, and Jill McLean Taylor, eds., *Mapping the Moral Domain: A Contribution of Women's Thinking to Psychological Theory and Education* (Cambridge: Harvard University Press, 1988).

Gilligan, Carol, Nona Plessner Lyons, and Trudy Hanmer, eds., *Making Connections: The Relational Worlds of Adolescent Girls at Emma Willard School* (Cambridge: Harvard University Press, 1990).

Gilligan, Carol, Annie G. Rogers, and Deborah Tolman, eds., *Women, Girls, and Psychotherapy: Reframing Resistance* (Binghamton: Haworth Press, 1991).

Gilligan, James, *Violence: Reflections on a National Epidemic* (New York: Vintage, 1996).

Gilligan, James, *Preventing Violence* (New York: Thames & Hudson, 2001).

Gilligan, James, "Terrorism, Fundamentalism, and Nihilism: Analyzing the Dilemmas of Modernity," in Henri Parens and Stuart Twemlow, eds., *The Future of Prejudice: Applications of Psychoanalytic Understanding toward its Prevention* (New York: Rowman & Littlefield, Inc., 2006), pp. 37–62.

Gilligan, James and Bandy Lee, "Report to the New York City Board of Correction," September 5, 2013.

Gilmore, David D., *Manhood in the Making: Cultural Concepts of Masculinity* (New Haven: Yale, 1990).

Graves, Robert, *Good-Bye to All That* (New York: Anchor, 1998; first published 1929).

Green, Joshua, *Devil's Bargain: Steve Bannon, Donald Trump, and the Storming of the Presidency* (New York: Penguin, 2017).

Grossman, Lt Col, Dave, *On Killing: The Psychological Cost of Learning to Kill in War and Society*, revised edition (New York: Back Bay Books, 2009; first published 1995).

Halberstam, David, *The Best and the Brightest* (New York: A Fawcett Book, 1992; first published 1969).

Hasson, Nir, "30,000 Israelis, Palestinians Take Part in Women Wage Peace Rally in Jerusalem," *Israel News*, October 8, 2017, www.haaretz.com/Israel-news/1.816255.

Hawthorne, Nathaniel, *The Scarlet Letter* (New York: Penguin, 1986; first published 1850).

Hedges, Chris, *War Is a Force That Gives Us Meaning* (New York: Public Affairs, 2014; first published 2002).

Hess, Amanda, "How a Fractious Women's Movement Came to Lead the Left," in Diane Wachtell, ed., *Wolf Whistle Politics: The New Misogyny in America Today* (New York: The New Press, 2017), pp. 139–54.

Hochschild, Arlie Russell, *Strangers in Their Own Land: Anger and Mourning on the American Right* (New York: The New Press, 2016).

Hoganson, Kristin L., *Fighting for American Manhood: How Gender Politics Provoked the Spanish-American and Philippine-American Wars* (New Haven: Yale University Press, 1998).

Holroyd, Michael, ed., *Lytton Strachey by Himself: A Self Portrait* (London: Heinemann, 1971).

Holroyd, Michael, *Lytton Strachey: The New Biography* (New York: W.W. Norton, 1994).

Hrdy, Sarah Blaffer, *Mothers and Others: The Evolutionary Origins of Mutual Understanding* (Cambridge: Harvard University Press, 2009).

Hunsberger, Bruce E. and Bob Altemeyer, *Atheists: A Groundbreaking Study of America's Nonbelievers* (Amherst: Prometheus Books, 2006).

Jacobs, Harriet A., *Incidents in the Life of a Slave Girl* edited by Jean Fagan Yellin (Cambridge: Harvard University Press, 1987; first published 1861).

James, William, "The Moral Equivalent of War," *in William James, Writings 1902–1910* (New York: The Library of America, 1987), pp. 1281–93.

James, William, "On a Certain Blindness in Human Beings," *in William James, Writings 1878–1899* (New York: The Library of America, 1992), pp. 841–60.

Jay, Gregory, "Douglass, Melville, and the Lynching of Billy Budd," in Robert S. Levine and Samuel Otter, eds., *Frederick Douglass and Herman Melville: Essays in Relation* (Chapel Hill: The University of North Carolina Press, 2008), pp. 369–95.

Jay, Gregory, "'Speak man!' Billy Budd in the Crucible of Reconstruction," *American Literary History*, Vol. 21, No. 3 (2009), pp. 492–517.

Junger, Sebastian, *War* (New York: Twelve, 2010).

Junger, Sebastian, *Tribe: On Homecoming and Belonging* (New York: Twelve, 2016).

"Justice Gorsuch Delivers," Editorial, *New York Times*, July 2, 2017, p. SR10.

Kazin, Michael, *War Against War: The American Fight for Peace 1914–1918* (New York: Simon & Schuster, 2017).

Kendall, Brent, "Travel Ban Ruling Sets Stage for High Court," *The Wall Street Journal*, May 26, 2017, pp. A1, A5.

Keynes, John Maynard, *The Economic Consequences of the Peace* (available at ReadaClassic.com 2010; first published 1919).

Khurana, Rakesh, *Searching for a Corporate Savior: The Irrational Quest for Charismatic CEOs* (Princeton: Princeton University Press, 2002).

Kildea, Paul, *Benjamin Britten: A Life in the Twentieth Century* (London: Allen Lane, 2013).

Kimmel, Michael, *Guyland: The Perilous World Where Boys become Men* (New York: Harper, 2008).

Kimmel, Michael, *Manhood in America: A Cultural History*, 3rd edn (New York: Oxford University Press, 2012).

Kimmel, Michael, *Angry White Men: American Masculinity at the End of an Era* (New York: Nation Books, 2013).

King, Charles, "Civilization and Its Discontent: The Ruinous Cost of Angry Men at the Heart of Modern Political and Civic Engagement," *The Times Literary Supplement*, June 9, 2017, No. 5958, at p. 24 (reviewing Pankaj Mishra's *Age of Anger*).

King, Jr, Martin Luther, *A Testament of Hope: The Essential Writings of Martin Luther King, Jr* edited by James M. Washington (San Francisco: Harper & Row, 1986).

Kinzer, Stephen, *The True Flag: Theodore Roosevelt, Mark Twain, and the Birth of American Empire* (New York: Henry Holt and Company, 2017).

Kirschbaum, Rabbi Donna, "Why Women and Why Now?", Women Wage Peace, http://womenwagepeace.org.il/en/women-now-rabbi-donna-kirshbaum-member-women-wage-peace/.

Klein, Naomi, *The Shock Doctrine: The Rise of Disaster Capitalism* (New York: Picador, 2007).

Klein, Naomi, *No Logo: No Space No Choice No Jobs* (New York: Picador, 2009; first published 2000).

Klein, Naomi, *This Changes Everything: Capitalism vs. the Climate* (New York: Simon & Schuster, 2014).

Klein, Naomi, *No Is Not Enough: Resisting Trump's Shock Politics and Winning the World We Need* (Chicago: Haymarket Books, 2017).

Kristof, Nicholas, "Is Hillary Clinton Dishonest?," *New York Times*, April 23, 2016 www.nytimes.com/2016/04/24/opinion/sunday/is-hillary-clinton-dishonest.html.

Krugman, Paul, "How Republics End," *New York Times*, December 19, 2018, p. A21.

Lakoff, George, *Thinking Points: Communicating Our American Values and Vision* (New York: Farrar, Straus and Giroux, 2006).

Lakoff, George, *Don't Think of an Elephant!: Know Your Values and Frame the Debate* (White Water Junction: Chelsea Green Publishing, 2014; first published 2004).

Lakoff, George, *Moral Politics: How Liberals and Conservatives Think*, 3rd edn (Chicago: University of Chicago Press, 2016; first published 1996).

Lasch, Christopher, *Women and the Common Life: Love, Marriage, and Feminism* (New York: W.W. Norton, 1997).

LeDoux, Joseph, *The Emotional Brain: The Mysterious Underpinnings of Emotional Life* (New York: Touchstone, 1996).

Levy, Ariel, "Lift and Separate: Why is Feminism Still So Divisive?," *New Yorker*, November 16, 2009, www.newyorker.com/magazine/2009/11/16/lift-and-separate.

Lewis, Robin Coste, *Voyage of the Sable Venus* (New York: Knopf, 2016).

Liptak, Adam, "Let Me Finish, Please: Conservative Men Dominate the Debate," *New York Times National*, April 16, 2017, p. A13.

Lopez, Ian Haney, *Dog Whistle Politics: How Coded Racial Appeals Have Reinvented Racism and Wrecked the Middle Class* (New York: Oxford University Press, 2014).

Lorde, Audre, *Sister Outsider* (New York: Ten Speed Press, 2007).

Luker, Kristin, *Abortion and the Politics of Motherhood* (Berkeley: University of California Press, 1985).

Manigault-Bryant, LeRhonda, "An Open Letter to White Liberal Feminists," in Diane Wachtell, ed., *Wolf Whistle Politics: The New Misogyny in America Today* (New York: The New Press, 2017), pp. 97–100.

Maraniss, David, *Barack Obama: The Story* (New York: Simon & Schuster, 2012).

Martin, Robert K., *Hero, Captain, and Stranger: Male Friendship, Social Critique, and Literary Form in the Sea Novels of Herman Melville* (Chapel Hill: The University of North Carolina Press, 1986).

Marx, Karl, *The Eighteenth Brumaire of Louis Napoleon* (Seattle: Loki's Publishing, n.d.).

Mayer, Jane, "Trump's Money Man: How Robert Mercer, a Reclusive Hedge-fund Tycoon, Exploited America's Populist Insurgency," *New Yorker*, March 27, 2017, pp. 34–45.

McDonald v. City of Chicago, 130 S.Ct. 3020, 3088–3120 (2010), Justice Stevens.

Melville, Herman, "Hawthorne and His Mosses," in Harrison Hayford, ed., *Herman Melville* (New York: The Library of America, 1984), pp. 1154–71.

Melville, Herman, *Moby-Dick or, The Whale* (New York: Penguin, 2003; first published 1851).

Melville, Herman, *Billy Budd, Sailor and Selected Tales* edited by Robert Milder (Oxford: Oxford University Press, 2009).

Miller, Jean Baker *Toward a New Psychology of Women*, 2nd edn (Boston: Beacon Press, 1986; first published 1976).

Mishra, Pankaj, *Age of Anger: A History of the Present* (New York: Farrar, Straus and Giroux, 2017).

Mishra, Pankaj, *From the Ruins of Empire: The Revolt Against the West and the Remaking of Asia* (New York: Picador, 2012).

Morgan, Robin, "The Not-So-Secret Ingredient," The Robin Morgan Blog, March 12, 2018.

Morris, Edmund, *The Rise of Theodore Roosevelt* (New York: Random House, 1979).

Morrison, Toni, *Beloved* (New York: Knopf, 1987).

Morrison, Toni, *Playing in the Dark: Whiteness and the Literary Imagination* (Cambridge: Harvard University Press, 1992).

Morrison, Toni, *The Bluest Eye* (New York: Vintage, 2007).

Morrison, Toni, *The Origin of Others*, Foreword by Ta-Nehisi Coates (Cambridge: Harvard University Press, 2017).

Moss, Donald, *Thirteen Ways of Looking at a Man: Psychoanalysis and Masculinity* (London: Routledge, 2015).

"Never Again MSD," *Wikipedia*, https://en.wikipedia.org/wiki/Never_Again_MSD.

New York Times, reports on the conditions at Rikers, including on the Gilligan and Lee report, www.nytimes.com/topic/organization/rikers-island-prison-complex.

Nottage, Lynn, *Sweat* (New York: Theatre Communications Group, 2017).

Obama, Barack, *Dreams from My Father* (New York: Three Rivers Press, 2004; first published 1996).

Obama, Barack, *The Audacity of Hope: Thoughts on Reclaiming the American Dream* (New York: Three Rivers Press, 2006).

O'Brien, Tim, *The Things They Carried* (Boston: Mariner, 2009; first published 1990).

Okimoto, Tyler G. and Victoria L. Brescoli, "The Price of Power: Power Seeking and Backlash against Female Politicians," *Personality and Social Psychology Bulletin*, Vol. 36, No. 7 (2010), pp. 923–36.

Orwell, George, *1984* (New York: Signet, 1950; first published 1949).

Parker, Hershel, *Herman Melville: A Biography, Volume 1, 1819–1851* (Baltimore: The Johns Hopkins University Press, 1996).

Parker, Hershel, *Herman Melville: A Biography, Volume 2, 1851–1891* (Baltimore: The Johns Hopkins University Press, 2002).

Paxton, Robert O., *The Anatomy of Fascism* (New York: Vintage Books, 2004).

PBS *American Experience*, "The Great War," aired on April 12, 2017.

PBS *Frontline*, "Bannon's War," aired on May 23, 2017.

Pear, Robert, "Draft Rule Makes It Far Easier to Deny Coverage for Birth Control," *New York Times*, July 2, 2017, pp. A1, A15.

Plessy v. *Ferguson*, 163 U.S. 537 (1896).

Plumley, Gavin, Program Note, Metropolitan Opera Playbill, October 30, 2017 performance, *The Exterminating Angel*, pp. 38B–38D.

Pollitt, Katha, *Reasonable Creatures: Essays on Women and Feminism* (New York: Vintage, 1995).

Porter, Tony, *Breaking Out of the "Man Box": The Next Generation of Manhood* (New York: Skyhorse Publishing, 2015).

"Pray the Devil Back to Hell," *Wikipedia*, https:/en.wikipedia.org/wiki/Pray_the_Devil_Back_to_Hell.

Rand, Ayn, *The Fountainhead* (New York: Penguin, 1993; first published 1943).

Real, Terrence, *I Don't Want to Talk About It: Overcoming the Secret Legacy of Male Depression* (New York: Scribner, 1997).

Remnick, David, *The Bridge: The Life and Rise of Barack Obama* (New York: Vintage, 2011).

Remnick, David, "Still Here: Hillary Clinton Looks Back in Anger," *New Yorker*, September 25, 2017, pp. 58–67.

Renehan, Jr, Edward J., *The Lion's Pride: Theodore Roosevelt and His Family in Peace and War* (New York: Oxford University Press, 1998).

Reticker, Gini, *Pray the Devil Back to Hell*, 2008, documentary.

Richards, David A. J., *Toleration and the Constitution* (New York: Oxford University Press, 1986).

Richards, David A. J., *Foundations of American Constitutionalism* (New York: Oxford University Press, 1989).

Richards, David A. J., *Conscience and the Constitution* (Princeton: Princeton University Press, 1993).

Richards, David A. J., *Women, Gays, and the Constitution: The Grounds for Feminism and Gay Rights in Culture and Law* (Chicago: University of Chicago Press, 1998).

Richards, David A. J., *Free Speech and the Politics of Identity* (Oxford: Oxford University Press, 1999).

Richards, David A. J., *Disarming Manhood: Roots of Ethical Resistance* (Athens: Swallow Press/Ohio University Press, 2005).

Richards, David A. J., *Fundamentalism in American Religion and Law: Obama's Challenge to Patriarchy's Threat to Democracy* (Cambridge: Cambridge University Press, 2010).

Richards, David A. J., *Resisting Injustice and the Feminist Ethics of Care in the Age of Obama: "Suddenly, . . . All the Truth Was Coming Out"* (New York: Routledge, 2013).

Richards, David A. J., *The Rise of Gay Rights and the Fall of the British Empire* (New York: Cambridge University Press, 2013).

Richards, David A. J., *Why Love Leads to Justice: Love across the Boundaries* (New York: Cambridge University Press, 2016).

Richards, David A. J., "Literature and Resisting Injustice: Melville and Hawthorne on Patriarchal Manhood and Homophobia," *Law and Literature*, Vol. 29, No. 1 (2017), pp. 109–22, DOI: 10.1080/1535685X.2016.1246917.

Richardson, Robert D., *William James: In the Maelstrom of American Modernism* (Boston: Houghton Mifflin, 2006).

Robertson-Lorant, Laurie, *Melville: A Biography* (New York: Clarkson Potter, 1996).

Roe v. Wade, 410 U.S. 113 (1973).

Roosevelt, Theodore, *The Winning of the West, Volumes 1–4 Inclusive* (London: American Cowboys Books, 2017).

Rose, Alex, "The Frankfurt School Knew Trump Was Coming," *New Yorker*, December 5, 2016, www.newyorker.com/culture/cultural-comment/the-frankfurt-school-knew-trump-was-coming.

Roy, Arundhati, *The God of Small Things* (New York: Harper-Perennial, 1997).

Runciman, Steven, *A History of the Crusades, Volumes I, II, and III* (Cambridge: Cambridge University Press, 1951).

Sanger, Carol, *About Abortion: Terminating Pregnancy in Twenty-first-century America* (Cambridge: Belknap Press of Harvard University Press, 2017).

Schiller, Lauren, "Gloria Steiner Explains Why Feminism Reached a Critical Turning Point in 2015," *Fortune*, December 22, 2015, http://fortune.com/2015/12/22/gloria-steinem-feminism-turning-point/.

Schulman, Michael, "The First Theatrical Landmark of the Trump Era: Lynn Nottage's Play 'Sweat' Is a Tough Yet Empathetic Portrait of the America That Came Undone," *New Yorker*, March 27, 2017, www.newyorker.com/magazine/2017/03/27/the-first-theatrical-landmark-of-the-trump-era, pp. 1–11.

Schweizer, Peter, *Clinton Cash: The Untold Story of How and Why Foreign Governments and Businesses Helped Make Bill and Hillary Rich* (New York: Harper, 2016).

Scott, Janny, *A Singular Woman: The Untold Story of Barack Obama's Mother* (New York: Riverhead Books, 2011).

Shakespeare, William, *King Lear*, in W. J. Craig, ed., *Shakespeare: Complete Works* (London: Oxford University Press, 1966), pp. 908–42.

Shakespeare, William, *Troilus and Cressida* in W. J. Craig, ed., *Shakespeare, Complete Works* (London: Oxford University Press, 1966), pp. 667–700.

Shatan, Chaim F., "Bogus Manhood, Bogus Honor: Surrender and Transfiguration in the United States Martin Corps," *Psychoanalytic Review*, Vol. 64, No. 4 (1977), pp. 585–610.

Shay, Jonathan, *Achilles in Vietnam: Combat Trauma and the Undoing of Character* (New York: Scribner, 1994).

Shear, Michael D. and Adam Liptak, "Taking Up Case, Justices Let U.S. Start Travel Ban," *New York Times*, June 27, 2017, pp. A1, A12.

Shelden, Michael, *Melville in Love: The Secret Life of Herman Melville and the Muse of Moby-Dick* (New York: Harper Collins, 2016).

Showalter, Elaine, *The Civil Wars of Julia Ward Howe: A Biography* (New York: Simon & Schuster, 2016).

Sommers, Christina Hoff, *The War Against Boys: How Misguided Feminism Is Harming Our Young Men* (New York: Simon & Schuster, 2000).

Spruill, Marjorie J., *Divided We Stand: The Battle over Women's Rights That Polarized American Politics* (New York: Bloomsbury, 2017).

Stanley, Jason, "Democracy and the Demagogue," *New York Times*, October 12, 2015, https://opinionator.blogs.nytimes.com/2015/10/12/democracy-and-the-demagogue/.

Stanley, Jason, *How Propaganda Works* (Princeton: Princeton University Press, 2015).

Steiner, George, *Martin Heidegger* (Chicago: University of Chicago Press, 1989).

Stewart, Jeffrey, ed., *Narrative of Sojourner Truth* (New York: Oxford University Press, 1991; first published 1850).

Strachey, Lytton, "Militarism and Theology," in Lytton Strachey, *Characters and Commentaries* (Westport: Greenwood Press, 1961; first published 1933), pp. 223–7.

Strauss, William and Neil Howe, *The Fourth Turning: An American Prophecy: What the Cycles of History Tell Us about America's Next Rendezvous with Destiny* (New York: Broadway Books, 1997).

Suggs, Jon-Christian, "Something about the Boy: Law, Ironic Comedy, and the Ideology of Agape in Billy Budd" (unpublished paper, n.d.).

Taylor, Jill McLean, Carol Gilligan, and Amy Sullivan, *Between Voice and Silence: Women and Girls, Race and Relationship* (Cambridge: Harvard University Press, 1995).

Thucydides. *History of the Peloponnesian War*, translated by Rex Warner (New York: Penguin, 1972).

Tomasello, Michael, *Why We Cooperate* (Boston: Boston Review Books, 2009).

Toobin, Jeffrey, "Full-Court Press: The Man behind Trump's Supreme Court," *New Yorker*, April 17, 2017, pp. 24–8.

Townsend, Kim, *Manhood at Harvard: William James and Others* (New York: W.W. Norton, 1996).

Traister, Rebecca, "Hillary Clinton is Furious. And Resigned and Funny. And Worried: The Surreal Post-election Life of the Woman Who Would Have Been President," *New York Magazine*, May 2, 2017, http://nymag.com/daily/intelligencer/2017/05/hillary-clinton-life-after-election.html.

Vivian, Yee and Alan Blinder, "Thousands Walk Out of Class, Urging Action on Gun Control," *New York Times*, Thursday, March 15, 2018, A1, A19.

Wachtell, Diane, ed., *Wolf Whistle Politics: The New Misogyny in America Today* (New York: The New Press, 2017).

Walzer, Michael, *The Revolution of the Saints* (Cambridge: Harvard University Press, 1965).

Way, Niobe, *Deep Secrets: Boys' Friendships and the Crisis of Connection* (Cambridge: Harvard University Press, 2011).

Way, Niobe, Jessica Cressen, Samuel Bodian, Justin Preston, Joseph Nelson, and Diane Hughes, "'It Might be Nice to Be a Girl…Then You Wouldn't Have to Be Emotionless:' Boys' Resistance to Norms of Masculinity During Adolescence," *Psychology of Men and Masculinity*, Vol. 15, No. 3 (2014), pp. 241–52.

Way, Niobe, Alisha Ali, Carol Gilligan, and Pedro Noguera, eds., *The Crisis of Connection: Roots, Consequences, and Solutions* (New York: New York University Press, in press).

Weigel, Moira, "Political Correctness: How the Right Invented a Phantom Enemy," in Diane Wachtell, ed., *Wolf Whistle Politics: The New Misogyny in America Today* (New York: The New Press, 2017).

Wells-Barnett, Ida B., *Selected Works of Ida B. Wells-Barnett* edited by Trudier Harris (New York: Oxford University Press, 1991).

Weisberg, Richard H., *The Failure of the Word: The Protagonist as Lawyer in Modern Fiction* (New Haven: Yale University Press, 1984).

White, Daphne, "Berkeley author George Lakoff says 'Don't underestimate Trump,'" *Berkeleyside*, May 2, 2017, www.berkeleyside.com/2017/05/02/berkeley-author-george-lakoff-says-dont-underestimate-trump, pp. 1–33.

Whitman, James Q., *Hitler's American Model: The United States and the Making of Nazi Race Law* (Princeton: Princeton University Press, 2017).

Wilson, August, *Jitney* (New York: Samuel French, 2002).

Wineapple, Brenda, *Hawthorne: A Life* (New York: Random House, 2003).

"Women of Liberia Mass Action for Peace," *Wikipedia*, https://en.wikipedia.org/wiki/Women_of_Liberia_Mass_Action_for_Peace.

"Women Wage Peace," *Wikipedia*, https://en.wikipedia.org/wiki/Women_Wage_Peace.

Wood, Gordon S., *The Creation of the American Republic, 1776–1787* (New York: Norton, 1969).

Woodhouse, A. S. P., ed., *Puritanism and Liberty* (London: Dent, 1938).

Woolf, Virginia, *A Room of One's Own* (San Diego: Harvest, 1981; first published 1929).

Woolf, Virginia, *Mrs. Dalloway* (San Diego: Harvest Books, 1997; first published 1925).

Woolf, Virginia, *Three Guineas*, Jane Marcus edition (Orlando: Harvest, 2006; first published 1938).

Wright, Richard, Black Boy, in Arnold Rampersad, ed., *Richard Wright: Later Works* (New York: The Library of America, 1991), pp. 5–365.

Young-Bruehl, Elisabeth, *Why Arendt Matters* (New Haven: Yale University Press, 2006).

Index

1984, 13, 15

Abraham binding of Isaac, 86, 101, 106
Abramson, Jill, 13
Access Hollywood tapes. *See* pussygate
Adam (student), 19–23, 28, 45, 65, 73, 91,
    125–6
Adams, Henry, 82
Addams, Jane, 83, 92–4
    on immigrants, 93–4
Ades, Thomas, 114
Adorno, T. W., 39, 51–2
    on "jargon of authenticity," 38–9
Aeschylus, 10
Age of Anger, 80, 94, 125
Albert Herring, 102
Alexander, Michelle, 55
Altemeyer, Bob, 52
America First, 7, 38, 56, 58, 82–3, 94
"Angel in the House," 65
Anna Karenina, 33, 96
anti-establishment of religion, 78
anti-Semitism, 39, 78, 114
    analogy with Muslims, 57, 78
anti-Vietnam War resistance, 92
Arendt, Hannah, 6–7, 13, 51, 53–4, 128
    on representation, 9
Athenian democracy, 10–11
    imperialist state, 11
    Melians, 94
    patriarchy within, 80–1
Attwater, Lee, 39
Atwood, Margaret, 50
authenticity, 38–9
authoritarian personality, 52, 58

Baldwin, James, 3
Ball, George, 89

Bannon, Stephen K., 51, 56–9, 78
    Catholicism, 56
    Islam, 57–8
    Trump, 58–9
Barker, Pat, 86
Beckett, Samuel, 71–2
Benedict, Ruth, 127
Bernie Sanders supporters, 43
Best and The Brightest, The, 88–9
betrayal, 19–22, 27, 29–31, 42, 70, 86, 128–9
    of relationship, 20
Billy Budd, 96, 100–4
Birth of Pleasure, The, 37, 95
black community, 4
    debate over manhood, 106–10
Black Lives Matter, 36, 45, 69, 77, 124
Bordo, Susan, 41
Bowlby, John, 61–2, 65
Bowles, Chester, 88
Bridge, The, 42, 118
British Empire in India, 87
Britten, Benjamin, 102–4
Bundy, McGeorge, 89
Bunuel, Luis, 113
Bush, George W., 1, 50, 110, 117
Butler, Josephine, 13

Calhoun, John, 100
Call to Peace, 69
Camille (student), 31
Caro, Robert A., 91
China, 81, 94
Chodorow, Nancy, 111
Christianity, 85, 121–2
    M. L. King Jr.'s interpretation, 121–2
Chu, Judy, 18–19
Churchill, Winston, 13, 83, 87
Civil Rights Act of 1964, 55

Civil Rights movement, 55, 92, 109, 117, 121
Claude (student), 72–3
Cliff, Michelle, 4
Clinton, Hillary R., 4–5, 12, 34–5, 47–8, 58–60, 64, 118–26
  campaign, 110
  criticism of, 17, 28, 39–43, 110
Clinton, William J., 12, 48, 58
Comey, James, 41
coming out, 26
communalization of trauma, 20, 70
complicity (with patriarchy), 17–19, 60
confessions, 18–19
contraception, 1, 79
cooperation, 3
criminal justice system, 93
Crozier, Eric, 102
Crusades, 57
Cullops, Patrisse, 45

Damasio, Antonio, 3, 53, 125
Davis, Wendy, 46, 64–5
Deep Secrets, 18–19
Deepening Darkness, The, 1, 15, 50, 63
democracy, 1, 6–7, 10
  equal voice, 9
  rule of law and great principles of liberty, equality and justice, 35
  vs. patriarchy, 6, 8
democratic framework or lens, 5, 41, 60
Descartes's Error, 3
Destruction of Hillary Clinton, The, 41
Dinnerstein, Dorothy, 111
Disarming Manhood, 37
discrimination, racial and religious, 78
divide and conquer, 63–5, 112
Don't Think of an Elephant, 125
dream (Mattie's dream), 28–30, 33
Dreams from My Father, 31, 118, 120–1
Du Bois, W. E. B., 3
Dunham, Ann S., 118–20

Ehrlichman, John, 39, 55
Eisenhower, Dwight D., 87–8
Eliana (student), 74
empathy, 3, 122
Endgame, 71–2
endgame of patriarchy, 71, 74
English Civil War, 97
Equal Protection Clause, 78, 122
ethic of care, 12, 42, 50, 79, 124–5, 127
ethical intelligence, 1, 3, 9, 90

evolution, 3, 35
Exterminating Angel, The, 113–14

faction, James Madison on, 54
fake news, 12
fascism, 13, 39, 50, 83, 114, 126–7
  America, 54
  patriarchy, 13, 15, 53
  rise of, 50–1, 83
fascist politics, 7, 51
Federalist Society, 47
feminine goodness, 3, 6, 62
femininity, 3, 18, 20, 127
  silence, 27–33
feminism, 6, 8, 79, 111–16, 124–9
  distortion of, 110
  divisiveness, 64, 112
  ethic of care, 12, 55, 127
  for men and women, 6, 12, 94, 111–13, 127–9
  gender binary, 124
  movement to free democracy from patriarchy, 6, 8, 12, 111, 113–14
  Obama advocating, 118–20, 124
  political viewpoints, 111
  second wave feminism, 42, 55, 79, 111–13, 118–19
  view through the prism of patriarchy, 110–13
Filipovic, Jill, 115–16
First Amendment, US Constitution, 78
force of truth, 117, 122
Forman, James Jr., 77
Forster, E. M., 99, 102–4
Foucault, M. 126
Four Mothers movement, 67
framework shift from democracy to patriarchy, 4–6, 34–7, 48, 60, 115, 126
fraternity initiations, 25–6
Free Enterprise: A Novel of Mary Ellen Pleasant, 4
free exercise of religion, 78
free speech, 122
Fromm, Erich, 51–2
F-scale, 52

Gandhi, M. 122
Garland, Merrick, 45, 47
Garza, Alicia, 45
gay marriage, 122
gay men, 26, 37, 83
gay rights, 7, 23, 47, 55, 117, 122
Gaza War 2014, 67

Gbowee, Leymah, 67
gender, 2–5, 43, 48, 52–3, 60, 65, 80, 82, 94,
    111, 113, 117–18, 122, 124–7, *See also*
    gender binary and hierarchy; patriarchal
    lens
  2016 election, 40–4
  as linchpin of oppression, 4
  codes, 47, 50, 61, 70, 74
  equality, 116
  full spectrum of, 127
  Hitler and gender, 52
  in relation to race and class, 5, 9, 40
  initiation, 62
  manhood and womanhood, 65, 83
  militarism, 82–93
  resistance to discussion about, 17, 39
gender binary, 2, 6, 12, 37, 43, 46, 59–60,
    63–4, 79, 84, 92–4, 101, 103, 110–11,
    115, 122–3, 125–7, *See also* patriarchy
  authoritariansm, 52
  boys acceptance of, 61
  feminism, 124
  "Guyland," 123
  Hillary Clinton, 47
  induction into, 61
  manhood, 75, 89
  queer and transgender, 117, 125
gender binary and hierarchy, 2–3, 5, 7–12,
    35, 59–61, 63, 111, 124, 126
  as building blocks of patriarchy, 2
  as psychological fault line, 7
  internalization of, 53
gender gap, political, 4
gender norms, 124
German fascism, 50
Gilligan, Carol, 10, 19–21, 37, 42, 60–3, 68,
    70, 95, 112–13, 125
Gilligan, James, 6–7, 49–50, 100, 123, 125
  "male-role belief system," 123
Gilligan-Snider thesis, 60–6
Gilmore, David, 75
Ginsberg, Ruth Bader, 47
Glorious Revolution, 97
God of Small Things, The, 22
Gorsuch, Neil, 47
Graves, Robert, 85–6
gun rights, 46
"Guyland," 123

Halberstam, David, 86–9, 91
Halevi, Yehuda, 114
Handmaid's Tale, The, 50
Harvard Project on Women's Psychology
    and Girls' Development, 18, 27, 61, 111

#MeToo, 69, 125, 127
#NeverAgain movement, 127
"Hawthorne and His Moses," 104
Hawthorne, Nathaniel, 64, 94–9
Heidegger, 51
hierarchy, 59
  definition, 10
  purpose of, 3
Hitler, Adolf, 5, 15, 39, 50–2, 59, 90
  undoing the shame of Versailles, 5, 50, 83,
    100
Ho Chi Minh, 87
Hochschild, Arlie, 44
homophobia, 25, 52, 55, 100, 102, 104
homosexuality, repressed, 100, 102
Hrdy, Sarah Blaffer, 35
human capacities, 3
Human Condition, The, 9
human sciences, 2, 8
Hutchinson, Ann, 98
"hyphenated Americans," 83, 93

I Don't Want to Talk About It, 123
immigrants, 70, 93–4
imperialism, 63, 81–3, 87, 92, 100
In a Different Voice, 28, 79, 125
initiation, 15–16, 18–27, 29, 53, 61–2
  later initiation of girls, 62, 81–2
intersectionality, 33
Iraq War, 122
Isaac story, 86, 101, 106
Islam
  Bannon's view of, 57–8
  Crusades, 57
Israel/Palestine, 67–9
  Women Wage Peace rally, 68

Jackie (student), 31–3
Jacobs, Harriet, 4
James, Henry, 82
James, William, 52, 82, 92–3
Jasmin (student), 30–1
Jitney, 106–10
Johnson, Lyndon B., 89–91
Joining the Resistance, 37, 112–13
Junger, Sebastian, 81

Kant, Immanuel, 50
Karman, Tawakhol, 67
Kennedy, John F., 88
Keynes, John Maynard, 83
killing, psychology of, 81
Kimmel, Michael, 123
King Lear, 76

King, Charles, 80, 94, 125
King, Martin Luther Jr., 92, 109, 117, 121–2
    on, 118
Kirschbaum, Donna, 67
Klein, Naomi, 79
Krugman, Paul, 2

Lakoff, George, 110–11, 117–26
Land of Look Behind, The, 4
Lebanon, South, 67
LeDoux, Joseph, 53
Levy, Ariel, 112
Lewis, Robin Coste, 4
Lewis, Wyndham, 85
liberalism, 88
Liberia, 66–7
listening, 70
Long Day's Journey Into Night, 101
Lopez, Ian Haney, 39
Lorde, Audre, 4
"Loss of Pleasure, or Why We are still
    Talking About Oedipus?, The," 60
love, 2–3, 12, 16, 37–8, 62, 105, 121, 126, 128
    patriarchy destroys love, 102
    power to uproot patriarchy, 37, 120–1
Love Laws, 22–3, 121
    breaking and resisting, 118
    Obama's mother's resistance to, 120,
        122
lynchings in US, 92, 105
Lysistrata, 17

machismo
    Halberstam on, 89
Madison, James, 54
Make America Great Again slogan, 5, 7, 37,
    49, 56
Malcolm X, 109
manhood, 26–7, 88–91, 107, 116–17, 120,
    122–3
    in terms of gender binary, 92
    shame and honor, 15, 44, 49, 89, 91–2,
        107–10
    shaming of manhood, 6, 45, 50, 58, 63, 81,
        89, 92
    violence, 27, 92
Manhood in the Making: Cultural Concepts of
    Masculinity, 75
Martin, Robert, 105
Marx, K. 59
masculinity, 3, 5–6, 18–20, 27, 36, 61, 75,
    127
    American, 117
    betrayal, 19–22, 27

breakdown within patriarchal
    masculinity, 116
independent man, 65
masculine honor, 3
patriarchy, 107
toxic, 75
mass incarceration, 55, 77, 122
Matt (student), 72
Mattie (student), 28–30, 33, 72
Maurice, 102
McCarthy, Joseph R., 87
McConnell, Mitch, 45, 47, 122
McNamara, Robert, 89
Mean Team (Judy Chu), 18
Melville, Herman, 94–6, 99–102
Mercer, Rebecca, 56
"Militarism and Theology," 84
military training, 81
Miller, Jean Baker, 111
Mishra, Pankaj, 80, 94
misogyny, 25, 58–9, 73, 78, 116–17
Moby Dick, 51, 94–6, 99–100
Moore, Roy, 121–6
moral frameworks, 125–6
    vs. policy, 110–11
moral injury, 10, 19–20, 70, 127, 129
"Moral Injury and the Ethic of Care
    Reframing the Conversation about
    Differences," 96
Moral Politics, 110, 125
moral slavery, 9, 12, 14, 127, 129
Morrison, Toni, 4
Moss, Donald, 19, 21–4
Mrs. Dalloway, 52–3
Muslim travel ban, 78, 94
Mussolini, Benito, 15, 50

neuroscience, 3, 9, 15, 53
New Jim Crow, The, 55
Niebuhr, 122
nihilism, moral, 58, 126
Nixon's War on Crime, 39
nonviolence, 109, 119
Nottage, Lynn, 44–5, 76

O'Brien, Tim, 91–2
O'Neill, Eugene, 101
Obama, Barack H., 1, 4, 31, 34, 38, 40, 43,
    48–9, 55, 59–60, 78, 110, 115–22, 124
    autobiography, 118–21
    critique of patriarchy, 118–21
    relationship to mother, 118–21
    Reverend Wright speech, 4
Obama, Michelle, 43, 111, 121–2

Obamacare, 42, 122
Occupy Wall Street, 77
Oresteia, The, 10–11, 23, 80
originalism, 47, 54
Origins of Totalitarianism, The, 13, 15
Orwell, George, 7, 13, 15
Osama Bin Laden, 50
"Outsiders' Society" (V. Woolf), 14

Palin, Sarah, 113
paradigm shift, 111, 115, 125, *See also*
    framework shift, from democracy to
    patriarchy
Parker, Hershel, 104
patriarchal lens, 5–7, 9, 34, 36, 60, 110–13,
    115, 123, 126
patriarchy, 1–2, 9–10, 31, 33, 35–6, 48, 54, 60,
    95, 99–101
  as a strand in American politics, 110
  as harmful to men as well as women, 12,
    43, 111
  aspects of, 2
  caring as feminine, 79
  codes of white patriarchy, 3
  construction of manhood, 7
  culture seeming like nature, 22, 35
  damages created by, 63, 104
  definition, 10
  democracy vs., 1, 4–5, 8, 10, 37, 80–1, 115
  distorted view of feminism, 110–13
  false authority, 53
  false claims, 53
  fascism, patriarchy and fascism, 7, 13, 15,
    127
  fragility of, 7
  framework shift from democracy to
    patriarchy, 4–6, 34–7, 48, 60, 115, 126
  gender binary and hierarchy, 2–6, 9, 43, 47
  gender initiation timing, 61–2, 64
  gendered stereotypes, 83
  harm, 12, 43, 65, 104, 111, 123, 125
  harms to men, 12, 43, 80–94, 96–7, 103–6,
    123–5
  history, 10
  initiation, 53, 61
  patriarchal voice, 124
  persistance of, 62
  psychology and politics of, 100, 103
  race, 45, 77
  racism, 3
  resistance to, 55, 120
  Roman Empire, 63–4
  shame culture, 7, 122
Peabody, Elizabeth, 95

Pears, Peter, 102–3
"Peasant Blacksmithing in Indonesia:
    Surviving and Thriving Against All
    Odds," 119
Peloponnesian War, 11, 81
Pelosi, Nancy, 48
Philippine-American Wars, 82
Plessy v. *Ferguson*, 81
policy vs. moral framework, 110–11
political correctness, 5, 36, 38
political psychology, 13, 44, 51, 56, 59, 85,
    100, 127
Porter, Tony, 123
presidential election (2016), 3, 6, 12–13, 17,
    38–40, 56, *See also* framework shift from
    democracy to patriarchy
  confessions, 16
  gender, 40–4
  manhood, 75, 122
  race, 30
  resistance, 63
  student reactions, 19
propaganda, 51
prophetic novels, 95
  E. M. Forster, 99–100
Puritan resistance to absolutism, 97
pussygate, 2, 4, 12, 32, 58

race, 17, 27, 29–30, 49, 65, 121
racism, 3–4, 31, 37, 44, 78, 82, 117, 123, 127
  dividing white and black women, 64
rape, 31
Real, Terry, 123
Regeneration, 86
relational abilities, 3
  humans as relational beings, 3
relationships, 61–2
  loss of relationship, 62–3
Remnick, David, 41–2, 118–19
repressed homosexuality, 96, 100, 102
Republican Party, 55
resistance, 1, 3, 8, 13–14, 37–8, 54–5, 60–1,
    74, 78, 85–6, 91–2, 117–18, 120–1, 123–6,
    128
  ban on Muslim immigrants, 78
  black, 78
  feminist, 118
  resistance movements of the 1960s and
    1970s, 7, 54–5
  undercutting the resistance, 63
Resisting Injustice seminar, ix, 15, 17–18, 42,
    71
Rich (student), 73–4
Richards, David, 9, 37, 104, 126–7

Rikers Island jail (New York), 55
Rivers, W. H. R., 86
Roe v. *Wade*, 28, 45–6
Roman Empire, 2, 63–4
Roosevelt, Franklin, 87
Roosevelt, Theodore, 82, 92–3
Roy, Arundhati, 22
Rusk, Dean, 91
Russell, Bertrand, 83–4
Russian interference, 41

sanctuary movements, 78
Sanders, Bernie, 77
Sassoon, Siegfried, 83, 85–6
satyagraha, 109
Scalia, Anthony, 46–7, 79
Scarlet Letter, The, 64, 94–9
    as a resistance novel, 95
Second Amendment, 46
Sessions, Jeff, 56, 77
Shakespeare, 75–6, 96
shame, 6, 44–5, 49–51, 58, 75
shame culture, 7, 15, 65
Shattered, 40
Shay, Jonathan, 20, 70
silencing of girls and women, 16, 28–33, 63
Sirleaf, Ellen Johnson, 67
Sister Outsider, 4
Snider, Naomi, 60–3
Spanish-American War, 81–2
splitting of human capacities, 3, 7, 9
    mind and body, 3, 53
    reason and emotion, 3, 6, 53, 124
    self and relationship, 6
Stalin, Josef, 51, 59
Stanley, Jason, 39
Steinem, Gloria, 112
Steve (student), 24–6
Strachey, Lytton, 83–5
Supreme Court, 46–7
Sweat, 44–5, 76

Tatiana (student), 73
Taylor, Charles, 66
Taylor, Maxwell, 89
Theodore Roosevelt, 82
Thirteen Ways of Looking at a Man, 19, 21
Three Guineas, 7, 13–15, 66
Thucydides, 11, 81
Tolstoy, Leo, 33, 91–2
Tomasello, Michael, 54
Tometi, Opal, 45
Tonkin Gulf Resolution, 89
totalitarianism, 13–14

Toward a New Psychology of Women, 65
transgender, 7, 17, 37, 40, 49
trauma, 3, 8, 15, 20, 53, 75
Trump, Donald J., 2, 4–6, 12, 27, 32, 34–49,
    51, 54–6, 65–6, 79, 81, 92, 111, 115–17,
    124–5
    appeal, 59–60
    Bannon, 58–9
    compared to Obama, 117–19
    criminal justice system, 77
    democracy, 35
    election, 7, 19
    misogyny, 59
    patriarchy, 59, 63, 78
    resistance to, 126
    shamed manhood, 44
    social inferiority, 59
Truth, Sojourner, 80
Twain, Mark, 82

US Bill of Rights of 1791, 78, 97
US Constitution of 1787, 97

Vietnam War, 78, 86–92
    combat veterans, 70
    resistance to, 92
violence, 6, 27, 49, 102, 122–3
    shame and violence, 6–7, 58
Violence: Reflections on a National Epidemic,
    6, 49
voice, 2–3, 15, 30, 36–7, 79, 121–2
Voting Rights Act of 1965, 55
Voyage of the Sable Venus, 4

war on drugs, 55, 77, 122
Warren, Elizabeth, 48, 77
Way, Niobe, 18–19, 62, 123–4
Weigel, Moira, 38
Weinstein, Harvey, 116
Weisberg, Richard, 100
Wells, Ida B., 4
Westmoreland, William, 89
What Happened, 41
When Boys Become Boys, 18–19
white women, 4, 30, 32, 37, 43, 49–50, 59,
    64–5, 126
Why Love Leads to Justice, 38, 126
"Why Women and Why Now?," 67
Wilson, August, 106–11
Wilson, Woodrow, 82–3, 93
Winning of the West, The, 82
Wolf Whistle Politics, 46, 64–5
Women of Liberia Mass Action for Peace,
    66–7

Women Wage Peace (Israel-Palestine),
    67–9
women's march, 40, 69, 78
Woolf, Virginia, 7, 13–15, 52–3, 66

World War I, 81, 83
    injustice of, 81
Wright, Reverend, 4
Wright, Richard, 3